高等学校应用型特色规划教材 经管系列

国际商务谈判理论与实战
(双语版)

马 俊 毕劲芳 马欣玥 编 著

清华大学出版社
北 京

内 容 简 介

本书涵盖国际商务谈判理念、理论、谈判者素质、策略、技巧、礼仪、实战问题及解析等，以谈判理念为纲，重点诠释中外谈判理念的形成、发展与应用，将谈判的常用策略、技巧进行梳理归纳，以精练简洁的方式呈现，便于阅读掌握，作为实用工具运用于谈判实践，"国际商务谈判实战问题及解析"列举国际商务谈判，尤其是外贸谈判多个实战问题，相应解析，帮助读者增长谈判经验，提高谈判能力。中英双语编写，方便读者对照学习参考。

本书可作为高校国际商务、商务英语、国际经济与贸易、国际关系等专业的教材，还可供强调案例分析、模拟训练等手段方法的国际商务硕士培养使用，也可供外经贸企业、跨国公司、三资企业、政府涉外机构谈判人员参考。

本书封面贴有清华大学出版社防伪标签，无标签者不得销售。
版权所有，侵权必究。举报：010-62782989，beiqinquan@tup.tsinghua.edu.cn。

图书在版编目(CIP)数据

国际商务谈判理论与实战：双语版/马俊，毕劲芳，马欣玥编著. —北京：清华大学出版社，2021.4（2025.1重印）

高等学校应用型特色规划教材　经管系列

ISBN 978-7-302-57660-0

Ⅰ.①国… Ⅱ.①马… ②毕… ③马… Ⅲ.①国际商务—商务谈判—高等学校—教材 Ⅳ.①F740.41

中国版本图书馆 CIP 数据核字(2021)第 039800 号

责任编辑：温　洁
封面设计：杨玉兰
责任校对：王明明
责任印制：刘海龙

出版发行：清华大学出版社
网　　址：https://www.tup.com.cn，https://www.wqxuetang.com
地　　址：北京清华大学学研大厦 A 座　　邮　编：100084
社 总 机：010-83470000　　邮　购：010-62786544
投稿与读者服务：010-62776969，c-service@tup.tsinghua.edu.cn
质量反馈：010-62772015，zhiliang@tup.tsinghua.edu.cn
课件下载：https://www.tup.com.cn，010-62791865

印 装 者：北京同文印刷有限责任公司
经　　销：全国新华书店
开　　本：185mm×230mm　　印　张：11.75　　字　数：280 千字
版　　次：2021 年 4 月第 1 版　　印　次：2025 年 1 月第 6 次印刷
定　　价：35.00 元

产品编号：086951-01

出版说明

  应用型人才是指能够将专业知识和技能应用于所从事的专业岗位的一种专门人才。应用型人才的本质特征是具有专业基本知识和基本技能，即具有明确的职业性、实用性、实践性和高层次性。进一步加强应用型人才的培养，是"十三五"时期我国经济转型升级、迫切需要教育为社会培养输送各类人才和高素质劳动者的主要任务，也是协调高等教育规模速度与培养各类人才服务国家和区域经济社会发展的重要途径。

  教育部要求今后需要有相当数量的高校致力于培养应用型人才，以满足市场对应用型人才需求量的不断增加。为了培养高素质应用型人才，必须建立完善的教学计划和高水平的课程体系。在教育部有关精神的指导下，我们组织全国高校的专家教授，努力探求更为合理有效的应用型人才培养方案，并结合当前高等教育的实际情况，编写了这套《高等学校应用型特色规划教材》丛书。

  为使教材的编写真正切合应用型人才的培养目标，我社编辑在全国范围内走访了大量高等学校，拜访了众多院校主管教学的领导，以及教学一线的系主任和教师，掌握了各地区各学校所设专业的培养目标和办学特色，并广泛、深入地与用人单位进行交流，明确了用人单位的真正需求。这些工作为本套丛书的准确定位、合理选材、突出特色奠定了坚实的基础。

◆ 教材定位

- ➢ 以就业为导向。在应用型人才培养过程中，充分考虑市场需求，因此本套丛书充分体现"就业导向"的基本思路。
- ➢ 符合本学科的课程设置要求。以高等教育的培养目标为依据，注重教材的科学性、实用性和通用性。
- ➢ 定位明确。准确定位教材在人才培养过程中的地位和作用，正确处理教材的读者层次关系，面向就业，突出应用。
- ➢ 合理选材、编排得当。妥善处理传统内容与现代内容的关系，大力补充新知识、新技术、新工艺和新成果。根据本学科的教学基本要求和教学大纲的要求，制定编写大纲(编写原则、编写特色、编写内容、编写体例等)，突出重点、难点。
- ➢ 建设"立体化"的精品教材体系。提倡教材与电子教案、学习指导、习题解答、课程设计、毕业设计等辅助教学资料配套出版。

❖ 丛书特色

- ➢ 围绕应用讲理论，突出实践教学环节及特点，包含丰富的案例，并对案例作详细解析，强调实用性和可操作性。
- ➢ 涉及最新的理论成果和实务案例，充分反映岗位要求，真正体现以就业为导向的培养目标。
- ➢ 国际化与中国特色相结合，符合高等教育日趋国际化的发展趋势，部分教材采用双语形式。
- ➢ 在结构的布局、内容重点的选取、案例习题的设计等方面符合教改目标和教学大纲的要求，把教师的备课、授课、辅导答疑等教学环节有机地结合起来。

❖ 读者定位

本系列教材主要面向普通高等院校和高等职业技术院校，适合应用型、复合型及技术技能型人才培养的高等院校的教学需要。

❖ 关于作者

丛书编委特聘请执教多年且有较高学术造诣和实践经验的教授参与各册教材的编写，其中有相当一部分教材的主要执笔者是精品课程的负责人，本丛书凝聚了他们多年的教学经验和心血。

❖ 互动交流

本丛书的编写及出版过程，贯穿了清华大学出版社一贯严谨、务实、科学的作风。伴随我国教育改革的不断深入，要编写出满足新形势下教学需求的教材，还需要我们不断地努力、探索和实践。我们真诚希望使用本丛书的教师、学生和其他读者提出宝贵的意见和建议，使之更臻成熟。

清华大学出版社

前　　言

已出版的多数《国际商务谈判》教材，普遍重视国际商务谈判策略技巧的介绍，有关策略技巧的篇幅较多，有的书中策略技巧部分在全书中占比高达 60%～70%，而忽略了对国际商务谈判理念的介绍诠释，有的书甚至根本不提及谈判理念。"小胜靠智，大胜靠德"，树立正确的国际商务谈判理念，不仅有利于准确理解和灵活运用策略技巧，还有助于促进谈判者素质、能力的提高，提升谈判效率，发展、维系、推进外经贸关系和商务联系。

本书的特色

(1) 以谈判理念为纲，重点诠释中外谈判理念的形成、发展与应用。

(2) 已出版的多数《国际商务谈判》教材，从编写语言来看，要么全中文，要么纯英语，对中国读者而言，有的国际商务谈判理论，即便是以全中文介绍，也不易理解，何况全英语，所以本书的另外一个特色是，以中英双语编写，方便读者对照学习参考，而且有关国际商务谈判的理论部分，以简明扼要的方式做介绍。

(3) 本书专门撰写一章"国际商务谈判实战问题及解析"，列举国际商务谈判，尤其是外贸谈判多个实战问题，并做相应的解析，帮助读者增长谈判经验，提高谈判能力。

(4) 本书简明实用，最明显体现在将国际商务谈判的常用策略、技巧进行梳理归纳，以精练简洁的方式呈现给读者，便于阅读掌握，作为实用工具运用于谈判实践。

昆明学院马俊主持本书编写，负责构思方案、框架等工作。全书共 9 章，马俊负责第 3、4、6、7、9 章的编写，毕劲芳负责第 1、2、5、8 章的编写，马欣玥负责全书中英文的对照复核。

本书可作为高校国际商务、商务英语、国际经济与贸易、国际贸易、国际关系等专业的国际商务谈判、外经贸谈判课程的教材，也可供外经贸企业、跨国公司、三资企业、政府涉外机构谈判人员参考。

国际商务硕士(Master of International Business，MIB)教育作为专业学位硕士研究生(专硕)培养项目，注重实践，强调应用，本书契合国际商务硕士培养思路，不仅提供相关理论知识，还提供丰富的国际商务谈判实战问题和准确到位的分析，可供国际商务硕士教学使用。

本书在编写过程中，参阅了大量学者专家的著述，参考了不少国际商务谈判实践者的宝贵经验，在此表示诚挚的感谢！由于作者理论和经验不足、水平有限，书中难免有不妥和不尽如人意之处，敬请广大业界、学界专家和读者批评指正！

编　者

目 录

Chapter 1　Overview of International Business Negotiation 1
第 1 章　国际商务谈判概述 1

    Section 1　Concept and Characteristics of Negotiation 1
    第 1 节　谈判的概念和特点 1

    Section 2　Concept and Characteristics of Business Negotiation 4
    第 2 节　商务谈判的概念和特点 4

    Section 3　Concept and Characteristics of International Business Negotiation 6
    第 3 节　国际商务谈判的概念和特点 6

    Terminology　本章术语 10
    Exercises　本章练习 11
    Answers for Reference　参考答案 11

Chapter 2　Types of International Business Negotiation 13
第 2 章　国际商务谈判的主要类型 13

    Section 1　According to Contents of Negotiation 13
    第 1 节　按谈判的内容划分 13

    Section 2　According to the Attitude of Both Parties 20
    第 2 节　按谈判双方的态度划分 20

    Section 3　According to the Number and Importance of Negotiation Matters 22
    第 3 节　按谈判事项的个数和重要性的不同划分 22

    Terminology　本章术语 23
    Exercises　本章练习 24
    Answers for Reference　参考答案 24

Chapter 3　Theories of International Business Negotiation 26
第 3 章　国际商务谈判理论 26

    Section 1　Theory of Hierarchy of Needs 26

第 1 节　需求层次理论 26
Section 2　Game Theory 36
第 2 节　博弈论 36
Section 3　Theory of Harvard Principled Negotiation 49
第 3 节　哈佛原则谈判理论 49
Terminology　本章术语 56
Exercises　本章练习 56
Answers for Reference　参考答案 57

Chapter 4　International Business Negotiation Concept 61

第 4 章　国际商务谈判理念 61

Section 1　Chinese Negotiators' Idea — "Negotiation is an Art of Compromise between the Two Sides" 61
第 1 节　中国谈判者的"谈判是双方相互妥协的艺术"理念 61
Section 2　Concept of "Win-Win Negotiation" in Western Academic Circle and Business Word 69
第 2 节　西方学界业界的"谈判双赢"理念 69
Terminology　本章术语 72
Exercises　本章练习 72
Answers for Reference　参考答案 73

Chapter 5　Quality of International Business Negotiators 74

第 5 章　国际商务谈判者素质 74

Section 1　Political and Moral Qualities of International Business Negotiators 75
第 1 节　国际商务谈判者的政治素质和品德素质 75
Section 2　Cultural Quality of International Business Negotiators 76
第 2 节　国际商务谈判者的文化素质 76
Section 3　Physical Quality of International Business Negotiators 80
第 3 节　国际商务谈判者的身体素质 80
Section 4　Psychological Quality of International Business Negotiators 83
第 4 节　国际商务谈判者的心理素质 83
Section 5　Professional Quality of International Business Negotiators 90
第 5 节　国际商务谈判者的专业素质 90
Terminology　本章术语 93

Exercises 本章练习 93
Answers for Reference 参考答案 94

Chapter 6　International Business Negotiation Strategy 95
第6章　国际商务谈判策略 95

Section 1　Preparation Strategy 95
第1节　准备阶段策略 95

Section 2　Strategy in Opening Stage 102
第2节　开局阶段策略 102

Section 3　Strategy in Quotation Stage 104
第3节　报价阶段策略 104

Section 4　Strategy in Negotiation Stage 107
第4节　磋商阶段策略 107

Section 5　Strategy in Transaction Stage 111
第5节　成交阶段策略 111

Terminology 本章术语 113
Exercises 本章练习 113
Answers for Reference 参考答案 114

Chapter 7　International Business Negotiation Skills 119
第7章　国际商务谈判技巧 119

Section 1　Listening Skills 119
第1节　听的技巧 119

Section 2　Narration Skills 122
第2节　叙的技巧 122

Section 3　Asking Skills 125
第3节　问的技巧 125

Section 4　Answering Skills 130
第4节　答的技巧 130

Section 5　Watching Skills 132
第5节　看的技巧 132

Section 6　Debating Skills 137
第6节　辩的技巧 137

Section 7　Persuasion Skills 138

第 7 节　说服的技巧 138

Terminology　本章术语 140

Exercises　本章练习 141

Answers for Reference　参考答案 141

Chapter 8　Etiquette of International Business Negotiation 144

第 8 章　国际商务谈判礼仪 144

Section 1　Dress Etiquette 144

第 1 节　服饰礼仪 144

Section 2　Meeting Etiquette 146

第 2 节　会见礼仪 146

Section 3　Banquet Etiquette 150

第 3 节　宴会礼仪 150

Terminology　本章术语 152

Exercises　本章练习 153

Answers for Reference　参考答案 153

Chapter 9　Practical Questions, Issues and Analyses on International Business Negotiation 154

第 9 章　国际商务谈判实战问题及解析 154

参考文献 175

Chapter 1　Overview of International Business Negotiation

第 1 章　国际商务谈判概述

Section 1　Concept and Characteristics of Negotiation

第 1 节　谈判的概念和特点

1. Concept of negotiation　谈判的概念

Negotiation refers to the behavior process in which participants exchange information and negotiate agreements with each other based on certain needs, aiming to coordinate mutual relations and win or maintain their own interests.

In *The Art of Negotiating*, Nierenberg, president of the American Negotiation Association and a famous lawyer, has a very clear view: the definition of negotiation is the simplest, but the scope of negotiation is the most extensive, every desire to meet and every need to meet are at least the potential cause of inducing people to start the negotiation process. As long as people exchange views in order to change their relationship, as long as people negotiate an agreement in order to reach an agreement, they are negotiating.

Negotiation is a process in which both parties of interest negotiate on issues of common concerns or interests, coordinate and adjust their respective economic, political or other interests, and seek compromise, so that both parties feel that they have reached an agreement and reached a balance under favorable conditions. The purpose of negotiation is to coordinate conflicts of interest and realize common interests.

As an important means to coordinate the relations among all parties, negotiation is widely used in politics, economy, diplomacy, military, science and technology and other fields.

谈判，指参与各方基于某种需要彼此进行信息交流、磋商协议，旨在协调相互关系，赢得或维护各自利益的行为过程。

美国谈判协会会长、著名律师尼尔伦伯格在《谈判的艺术》一书中观点非常明确：谈判的定义最为简单，而涉及的范围却最为广泛，每一个要求满足的愿望和每一次要求满足的需要，至少都是诱发人们展开谈判过程的潜因。只要人们为了改变相互关系而交换观点，只要人们为了取得一致而磋商协议，他们就是在进行谈判。

谈判是一个过程，在这个过程中利益双方就共同关心或感兴趣的问题进行磋商，协调和调整各自的经济、政治或其他利益，谋求妥协，从而使双方都感到是在有利的条件下达成协议、促成均衡。

谈判的目的是协调利害冲突，实现共同利益。

谈判作为协调各方关系的重要手段，广泛应用于政治、经济、外交、军事、科技等各个领域。

2. Characteristics of negotiation 谈判的特点

(1) Every negotiation involves two or more parties.
每次谈判都有两个或两个以上的当事方参加。

Even though you can role-play another person to negotiate with yourself, the counterpart that you role-play is bound to represent interests different from yours. In effect there are at least two or more key participants in a negotiation. The number of the major parties in a negotiation, from the debate of the United Nations with more than 200 members to a talk about marriage arrangements, may be as many as over a hundred, but absolutely never fewer than two.

即使你可以扮演另一个人来和自己谈判，你扮演的对手必然代表不同于你的利益。实际上谈判中至少有两个或更多的关键参与者。从联合国与 200 多个会员国的辩论到谈论婚姻安排，谈判的主要当事方可能多达 100 多个，但绝对不会少于两个。

(2) The objective of a negotiation must be definite.
谈判的目的必须明确。

Different from everyday talk, the purpose of a negotiation is to persuade someone else into accepting one's own ideas and to maintain or achieve mutual interests. At the same time, the other side participates in the negotiation with the similar purpose of maintaining his or her self-interest and advocating his or her ideas and persuade the counterpart to accept his or hers. Rambling negotiation without a clear purpose is nothing but a waste of time, leading to nowhere. In essence, it is not negotiation.

与日常谈话不同的是，谈判的目的是说服别人接受自己的想法，并保持或实现双方的利益，另一方以维护自身利益、倡导自己的观点、说服对方接受自己的观点为目的来参加谈判。没有明确目标的、漫无目的的谈判只能是浪费时间，毫无结果。实质上，这不是谈判。

(3) Negotiation involves the exchange of ideas, communication, persuasion, compromise and such like.

谈判包括思想交流、沟通、说服、妥协等。

During negotiation, the interaction among all participants facilitates information sharing and mutual understanding. Meanwhile, negotiation turns to be a process of persuading and being persuaded. Its major task is to attempt persuading the opposing party into accepting one's idea, self-retained interests and satisfied behavior.

在谈判过程中，所有参与者之间的互动有利于信息共享和相互理解。同时，谈判也变成了一个说服和被说服的过程。其主要任务是试图说服对方接受自己的想法、利益和行为。

(4) Principally, negotiation is conducted on an equal basis.

原则上，谈判是在平等的基础上进行的。

Regardless of whether it is a high level negotiation or a low level negotiation, both sides are independent and equal in dignity and legal status. Neither side is the subordinate to the other side or supposed to force the other side into giving in. Only under the prerequisite of independent dignity and equal status all sides of negotiations are likely to sit down to serious talks and give a complete and accurate amount of one's ideas. For instance, when a person applies for a position or talks about a pay raise with the boss, he or she is conversing with the boss independently and equally. There are no rules that the minority should submit to the majority and the lower level should be subordinate to the higher level.

无论是高级别谈判还是低级别谈判，双方都是独立的，在尊严和法律地位上是平等的。任何一方都不是另一方的下属，也不应该强迫另一方让步。只有在独立尊严和平等地位的前提下，谈判各方才有可能坐下来认真谈判，完整准确地表达自己的想法。例如，当一个人申请一个职位或跟老板谈判要求加薪时，他或她是在与老板独立平等地交谈。没有规定少数服从多数，下级服从上级。

(5) Principally, a consensus is built on the basis of mutual concession.

原则上，共识是建立在相互让步的基础上的。

In negotiation, the self-interests of all sides do not necessarily increase or decrease on a same percentage. Nevertheless, only one side makes concession or gain complete victory, it is not a genuine negotiation. The arrangement established in a negotiation, in which one side totally lost its self-interest, is hard implemented.

在谈判中，各方的自身利益不一定在同一比例上增加或减少。然而，只有一方作出让步或取得完全胜利，这不是真正的谈判。在谈判中达成的一方完全丧失自身利益的安排是很难执行的。

Section 2　Concept and Characteristics of Business Negotiation

第2节　商务谈判的概念和特点

1. Concept of business negotiation　商务谈判的概念

Business negotiation is mainly concentrated in the economic field. It is the behavior process of all parties involved to coordinate and improve each other's economic relations and meet the needs of trade, around the trading conditions of the subject matter, through information exchange and negotiation agreement, to achieve the trading purpose. It is one of the most common activities in the circulation field under the market economy.

The fields involved in business negotiation include commodity trading, investment, labor export and input, technology transfer, project contracting, etc.

商务谈判主要集中在经济领域，是参与各方为了协调、改善彼此的经济关系，满足贸易的需求，围绕标的物的交易条件，彼此通过信息交流、磋商协议，达到交易目的的行为过程，是市场经济条件下流通领域最普遍的活动之一。

商务谈判涉及的领域具体包括商品买卖、投资、劳务输出输入、技术转让、工程承包等。

2. Characteristics of business negotiation　商务谈判的特点

(1) The objective of business negotiation is to obtain financial interests.
商务谈判的目的是获得经济利益。

It is the financial interests that all parties concerned hope to gain to satisfy their needs through negotiation that enables them to negotiate over a matter of common concern. In business negotiation what the negotiators care are the cost and efficiency involved. The success of the business negotiation is judged by the satisfying financial interests gained from the negotiation, therefore, financial interests serve the purpose of the negotiation. In other words, a business negotiation without any financial interests and benefits is of no value.

正是有关各方希望通过谈判获得满足其需要的经济利益,使他们能够就共同关心的问题进行谈判。在商务谈判中,谈判双方关心的是谈判的成本和效率。商务谈判的成功与否取决于谈判所获得的满意的经济利益,因此,经济利益服务于谈判的目的,即没有任何经济利益和好处的商务谈判是没有价值的。

(2) The core of business negotiation is price.
   商务谈判的核心是价格。

Now that the purpose of negotiation is to gain financial interests, the measure used to show how much interest each negotiator can get is the price. And all other terms, including the product quality, quantity, delivery, payment and so on are closely tied to it and could be measured by it. Price is indicative of the profits from the sale with small margin but quick turnover, promptness, security and so on that makes it focus and major issue of business negotiation.

既然谈判的目的是为了获得经济利益,那么用来显示谈判双方能获得多少利益的方法就是价格。而所有其他条款,包括产品质量、数量、交货期、付款等,都与之紧密相连,可以用它来衡量。价格是销售利润的指示性指标,利薄,但交易速度快、及时性强、安全性高等的价格是商务谈判的重要追求和主要问题。

(3) Items of the contract should keep stricktly accurate and rigorous.
   合同条款应严格准确。

A business negotiation comes to a conclusion when two sides sign an agreement or a contract. The items and conditions related in the contract represent the rights and obligations of each side. These terms and conditions are expected to be worded with great accuracy, caution, and prudence, which are the prerequisite for the guarantee of each side's interests. A negotiator who has reached a favorable settlement may walk into the trap of a tricky written contract by the other side, especially when they are not careful enough in drafting the contract failing to ensure the completeness, vigorousness, correctness or accuracy equitability and legitimacy of the contract. Once such a "mishap" occurs, the interests nearly in their hands may get devalued or they may be totally divested of these interests, unfortunately, the negotiation may turn out to be fruitless and their efforts produce nothing in the end. Such cases are rather common in practice,therefore, in business negotiation, negotiators should take the written contract seriously, as well as the oral commitment with more emphasis on the accuracy and rigorousness so as to avoid being deceived or losing money but without any evidence to defend themselves.

当双方签订协议或合同时，商务谈判即告结束。合同中有关的条款和条件，代表双方的权利和义务。这些条款和条件的措辞应该非常准确、小心和谨慎，这是保证双方利益的先决条件。一个达成了有利的解决方案谈判者仍有可能会落入对方狡猾的书面合同的陷阱，特别是当他们在起草合同时不够谨慎，不能保证合同的完整性、活力、正确性或准确性、公平性和合法性，一旦发生这种"事故"，他们几乎到手的利益可能会贬值或被完全剥夺，很不幸，谈判可能没有好结果，他们努力的结果最后是什么都没有。这种情况在实践中相当普遍，因此，在商务谈判中，谈判者应认真对待书面合同，且更加注重准确性和严谨性的口头承诺，以避免在没有任何证据的情况下被欺骗或赔钱。

(4) The principle is equality and mutual benefit.
原则是平等互利。

The basis of any business negotiation must be equality. It is the only way to mutual benefit. In a negotiation, if one side takes the upper hand, the arrangement established is most unlikely to be followed. Only equality and mutual benefit can lead to "win-win" or "multi-win".

任何商务谈判的基础都必须是平等。只有这样才能互惠互利。在谈判中，如果一方占上风，所达成的安排就不可能被遵守，只有平等互利才能实现"双赢"或"多赢"。

Section 3　Concept and Characteristics of International Business Negotiation

第3节　国际商务谈判的概念和特点

1. Concept of international business negotiation　国际商务谈判的概念

International business negotiation refers to the process in which the parties of business activities in different countries or regions negotiate with each other on various conditions of the transaction through information exchange in order to reach a certain transaction.

International business negotiation is an important part of international business activities, the main content of international business theory, and the extension and development of domestic business negotiation. International business negotiation is a common way in foreign economic and trade activities. It is an essential means to solve the conflicts of interests among commercial institutions of different countries and realize the common interests.

国际商务谈判是指在国际商务活动中处于不同国家或地区的商务活动当事人为了达成

某笔交易，彼此通过信息交流，就交易的各项要件进行协商的行为过程。

国际商务谈判是国际商务活动的重要组成部分，是国际商务理论的主要内容，是国内商务谈判的延伸和发展。国际商务谈判是一种在对外经贸活动中普遍存在的，解决不同国家的商业机构之间的利害冲突、实现共同利益的一种必不可少的手段。

2. Characteristics of international business negotiation　国际商务谈判的特点

In addition to the characteristics of negotiation and business negotiation, international business negotiation has its special features, which are mainly reflected in the following aspects.

国际商务谈判除了具备谈判和商务谈判的特点之外，还有其特殊之处，主要体现在以下几方面。

(1) The influencing factors are complex and diverse.
影响因素复杂多样。

① Political, diplomatic and legal factors　政治、外交、法律因素

International business negotiation is not only a negotiation, but also a political and diplomatic one with strong policy nature. The business relationship between the two sides is a part of the economic relationship between one country and other countries or regions, which often involves the political and diplomatic relationship between one country and other countries or regions. In international business negotiations, the state's guiding principles and policies on foreign economic and trade as well as a series of laws, regulations and rules must be implemented.

International business negotiation deals with the business relations between enterprises in different countries or regions. In terms of law application, it cannot be completely based on the economic law of the country or region where either party is located, but relevant parties must be guided by international economic law and act according to international practices.

国际商务谈判既是商洽也是政治和外交，具有较强的政策性。谈判双方之间的商务关系是一国同别国或地区之间的经济关系的一部分，常常涉及一国同别国或地区之间的政治关系和外交关系。国际商务谈判必须贯彻执行国家有关对外经济贸易的方针政策和一系列法规和规章制度。

国际商务谈判商讨的是不同国家或地区的企业之间的商务关系。在法律适用方面，不能完全以任何一方所在国家或地区的经济法为依据，而必须以国际经济法为准则，按国际惯例行事。

② Language barrier 语言障碍

In face to face communication or in written correspondence one of the first obstacles encountered in international business negotiation is language barrier unless your counterpart also speaks your mother tongue and writes in your native language. English is the most commonly used language in international trade and business activities while most international trade practices and terms are expressed in English, generally, negotiators should be equipped themselves with at least English communicative competence. If the other parties are not from the English speaking countries, other languages such as French, Spanish, Russian, and Arabic may also be used in negotiation. People with multilingual skills are viewed as a master key to international business negotiation. However, such talents are rare. A person who often participates in international business negotiation must at least command one foreign language, as above mentioned, generally it is English. In very formal and important international business negotiations, all parties occasionally have their own special interpreters and most often hire temporary ones who know the language of the counterparts well, say, immigrants and international students. This can produce an effective communication and reduce the cost of negotiation.

在面对面交流或书面通信中，国际商务谈判中遇到的首要障碍之一是语言障碍，除非对方也会说你的母语并用你的母语写作。英语是国际贸易和商务活动中最常用的语言，而大多数国际贸易惯例和术语都是用英语表达的，通常谈判者至少须具备英语语言能力。如果对方来自非英语国家，谈判中也可能会使用其他语言，如法语、西班牙语、俄语和阿拉伯语。掌握多种语言技能的人被视为国际商务谈判的关键，然而，这样的人才并不多见。经常参加国际商务谈判的人必须至少掌握一门外语，如上所述，一般是英语。在非常正式和重要的国际商务谈判中，各方有时也会配备自己专门的翻译，而且大多数情况下都会雇用临时翻译，例如移民和留学生，他们对对方的语言非常熟悉，这样可以进行有效的沟通，降低谈判成本。

③ Cultural difference 文化差异

The differences in culture, customs, religion and belief among countries are greater than those among different ideas within a country. These differences manifest themselves more obviously in international business negotiation. If negotiators fail to understand these differences due to different cultural backgrounds, they are more likely to encounter unnecessary misunderstandings, which may even endanger the normal negotiation. For example, when an Indian businessman is shaking his head to show his satisfaction with the features of the product you have just presented, you may be quite puzzled that he is not identified with your quality product; or after you quote a high price to the other side, the Swiss negotiator, waiting in your usual way for bargaining over it, but your counterparts may not be used to this kind of bargaining, they may think that perhaps you lack common knowledge of the prices on the international market, or perhaps you do not have a real interest in this transaction, as a result they will leave you alone. Besides, the diverse religious beliefs and social ideologies also have a great impact on the international business negotiation.

An experienced business person must know how to overcome the cultural barriers, try to find out common interests to get along and deal with these differences with tolerance. If necessary, you may even cater to and compliment the opposing cultures so as to reduce the conflicts or barriers produced by cultural differences, or turn these differences into an accelerator for negotiation.

国家间的文化、习俗、宗教和信仰的差异大于一个国家内部不同思想的差异。这些差异在国际商务谈判中表现得更为明显。如果谈判者由于不同的文化背景而不能理解这些差异，就更容易遇到不必要的误解，甚至危及正常的谈判。例如，当一个印度商人摇着头对你刚才介绍的产品的特性表示满意时，你可能会很困惑，因为他不认同你的优质产品；或者在你向对方——瑞士谈判代表报高价后，以你通常的方式等待着讨价还价，但是你的谈判对手可能不习惯这种讨价还价，他们可能会认为，也许你对国际市场上的价格缺乏常识，或者你对这笔交易没有真正的兴趣，因此他们不再理会你。还有，多元化的宗教信仰和社会意识形态也对国际商务谈判产生了重大影响。

一个有经验的商人必须知道如何消除文化障碍，努力找出共同的兴趣爱好，以宽容的态度来处理这些差异。如果有必要，你甚至可以迎合和赞美对立的文化，以减少文化差异所产生的冲突或障碍，或将这些差异转变为谈判的加速器。

(2) Wide coverage and wide content.

涉及面宽、内容广泛。

For example, international trade negotiations involve international transport and insurance, import and export inspection and quarantine, customs clearance, pricing and currency payment. International transport company, insurance company, institution of inspection and quarantine, customs, foreign exchange control and other institutions, as well as their businesses, services and management measures, are involved, but they will not be involved in ordinary domestic business negotiations.

以国际货物买卖谈判为例，国际商务谈判会涉及国际货物运输和保险、商品进出口检验检疫、货物进出口海关通关、计价和支付货币等内容，国际运输、保险、检验检疫、海关、外汇管理等机构及其业务、服务、管理措施等都会牵涉进来，而普通的国内商务谈判，不会涉及这些。

(3) More difficult and costly.

难度更大、成本更高。

International business negotiations involve more elements and tend to be more complex than domestic ones. As a consequence of above mentioned features including languages, social conventions, values, legal environment, political and diplomatic factors and so on, international business negotiation is more difficult to conduct.

Additionally, the expenditures on travel, conferences, study tours and entertainments are also higher. For example, to close a deal of cargo trade worth a huge amount of money, you need to visit your counterpart's country and check the goods and so on. Occasionally you have to go there for rounds of negotiations and investigations to ensure that the other party has a satisfying credit rating, reliable technical standards, good resources, and efficient implement of the contract. In a sense, international business negotiation is an overall competition of knowledge, skills, perseverance and wealth.

国际商务谈判比国内商务谈判涉及的因素多，而且往往比国内商务谈判复杂。由于语言、社会习俗、价值观、法律环境、政治外交因素等上面提及的特点，国际商务谈判更难进行。

此外，旅行、会议、考察和娱乐的支出也较高。例如，要完成一笔价值巨大的货物贸易，你需要访问对方的国家并检验货物等。有时你不得不去那里进行一轮又一轮的谈判和调查，以确保对方有令人满意的信用评级、可靠的技术标准、良好的资源和有效的合同执行能力。从某种意义上说，国际商务谈判是知识、技能、毅力和财富的全面竞争。

Terminology　本章术语

1. negotiation 谈判
2. business negotiation 商务谈判
3. international business negotiation 国际商务谈判

Exercises　本章练习

1. What are characteristics of negotiation?
   谈判的特点有哪些？
2. What are characteristics of business negotiation?
   商务谈判的特点有哪些？
3. What are characteristics of international business negotiation?
   国际商务谈判的特点有哪些？

Answers for Reference　参考答案

1. Characteristics of negotiation　谈判的特点

(1) Every negotiation involves two or more parties.
   每次谈判都有两个或两个以上的当事方参加。

(2) The objective of a negotiation must be definite.
   谈判的目的必须明确。

(3) Negotiation involves the exchange of ideas, communication, persuasion, compromise and such like.
   谈判包括思想交流、沟通、说服、妥协等。

(4) Principally, negotiation is conducted on an equal basis.
   原则上，谈判是在平等的基础上进行的。

(5) Principally, a consensus is built on the basis of mutual concession.
   原则上，共识是建立在相互让步的基础上的。

2. Characteristics of business negotiation　商务谈判的特点

(1) The objective of business negotiation is to obtain financial interests.
   商务谈判的目的是获得经济利益。

(2) The core of business negotiation is price.
   商务谈判的核心是价格。

(3) Items of the contract should keep strictly accurate and rigorous.
   合同条款应严格准确。

(4) The principle is equality and mutual benefit.
原则是平等互利。

3. Characteristics of international business negotiation
国际商务谈判的特点

(1) The influencing factors are complex and diverse.
影响因素复杂多样。

(2) Wide coverage and wide content.
涉及面宽、内容广泛。

(3) More difficult and costly.
难度更大、成本更高。

Chapter 2　Types of International Business Negotiation

第 2 章　国际商务谈判的主要类型

Section 1　According to Contents of Negotiation

第 1 节　按谈判的内容划分

The contents of foreign economic activities of enterprises are various, so there are different types of foreign-related business negotiations, mainly including negotiation of goods sales, labor cooperation, technology transfer, investment, project contracting, etc.

企业涉外经济活动的内容多种多样，因此涉外商务谈判有不同的类型，主要有货物买卖谈判、劳务合作谈判、技术转让谈判、投资谈判、工程承包谈判等。

1. Negotiation of international sales of goods　国际货物买卖谈判

The meaning of international sales of goods: the transaction of tangible goods across the border.

国际货物买卖的含义：跨越国境的有形商品的交易。

The main contents of the negotiation on international sales of goods:

The subject matter of the contract, commodity quality, quantity, packaging, inspection, price, payment for goods, delivery conditions, cargo transport insurance, force majeure clause, claim, disputes handling and arbitration clause, etc.

国际货物买卖谈判的主要内容：

合同标的、商品品质、数量、包装、检验、价格、货款支付、交货条件、货物运输保险、不可抗力条款、索赔、异议处置和仲裁条款等。

The characteristics of negotiation of international sales of goods: negotiation of international sales of goods is the basic form of international business negotiation. Compared with other international business negotiations, negotiation of international sales of goods has two characteristics: one is relatively low difficulty, the other is comparatively comprehensive terms and conditions.

国际货物买卖谈判的特点：国际货物买卖谈判是国际商务谈判的基本形态，与其他国际商务谈判相比，国际货物买卖谈判有两个特点：一是难度相对较低，二是条款比较全面。

2. International labor cooperation negotiation　国际劳务合作谈判

The meaning of international labor cooperation: international labor cooperation, also known as labor service or labor force export, refers to activities in which various types of technical and ordinary labor services of one country are sent to another country to provide productive or service-type labor services for government agencies, enterprises or individuals of another country and receive due remuneration. In fact, it is a combination and allocation of labor factors in the world. According to the General Agreement on Trade in Services (GATS) of WTO, the narrow sense of international labor cooperation mainly refers to the provision of labor services by personnel dispatched to foreign countries and the collection of wages or agreed service fees from foreign employers; and the collection of fees from foreign employers for services (such as undertaking topographic mapping, resource exploration, project feasibility study, technical guidance and training personnel, equipment maintenance, etc.). That is, "presence of natural persons" in the four ways of providing international services defined in the General Agreement on Trade in Services (GATS), "cross-border supply", "consumption abroad", "commercial presence" and "presence of natural persons".

国际劳务合作的含义：国际劳务合作也称劳务或劳动力输出，指一国的各类技术和普通劳务到另一国为另一国的政府机构、企业或个人提供各种生产性或服务性劳动服务，并获取应得报酬的活动，它实际上是一种劳动力要素在国家间的重新组合与配置。根据世界贸易组织的《服务贸易总协定》(GATS)，狭义的国际劳务合作主要是指，对外派出人员提供劳务，向外国雇主收取工资或议定的服务费用；以服务(比如承担地形地貌测绘、资源勘探、项目可行性研究、技术指导和培训人员、维修设备等)向境外雇主收取费用。即世界贸易组织的《服务贸易总协定》(GATS)所定义的提供国际服务四种方式"跨境交付""境外消费""商业存在"和"自然人流动"中的"自然人流动"。

Types of international labor service cooperation: according to the content of labor cooperation, it can be divided into general labor service output (i.e. providing simple labor service, usually combined with international project contracting), special labor service output (i.e. providing some specific industries and professional labor to meet specific needs, such as exporting nurses, chefs, engineers and other professionals), technical service output (i.e. dispatching experts and technical personnel abroad to carry out technical project cooperation with labor importing countries, or carry out technical diagnosis and technical guidance for them), technical personnel training (that is, the labor exporting countries provide technical training for technical personnel and operators in the country where the project is located in terms of technological process and operation essentials, etc., and also help the country where the project is located in terms of equipment installation, testing and debugging, maintenance and other services).

国际劳务合作的种类：按劳务合作的内容可划分为一般劳务输出(即提供简单的劳动力服务，通常与国际工程承包结合在一起)、特种劳务输出(即提供某些特定行业和满足特定需要的专业劳务，比如输出护士、厨师、工程师等专业人员)、技术服务输出(即派遣专家和技术人员到国外与劳务输入国开展技术项目合作，或对其进行技术诊断和技术指导)、技术人员培训(即劳务输出国为工程所在国的技术人员和操作人员提供工艺流程和操作要领等方面的技术培训，也包括帮助工程所在国进行设备的安装、调试和维修等服务)。

The ways of international labor export are as follows: export labor service through foreign project contracting, export labor service through technology and equipment, export labor service through foreign direct investment, employ senior labor service by the government or relevant organizations, recruit by recruitment agencies or employers, and export labor service according to labor contract.

国际劳务输出的方式：通过对外工程承包输出劳务、通过技术和设备的出口输出劳务、通过对外直接投资进行劳务输出、政府或有关机构聘请高级劳务、通过招工机构或雇主招募、根据劳务合同输出劳务。

Contract terms of international labor negotiation: generally including dispatched personnel, obligations and responsibilities of the employer, obligations and responsibilities of the dispatched personnel, cost composition (basic wage, allowance, working time and remuneration, overtime, idling, travel, etc.), industrial injury, disease and death, leave, work interruption, payment method, working conditions, work outside the contract, local laws and regulations, safety regulations, replacement and dismissal of personnel, sanctions, performance security, transfer, confidentiality, dispute resolution.

国际劳务谈判的合同条款：一般包括派遣的人员、业主的义务和责任、派遣人的义务和责任、费用构成(基本工资、津贴、工作时间和报酬、加班、窝工、旅费等)、工伤疾病和死亡、休假、工作中断、支付办法、工作条件、合同之外的工作、当地法律规章、安全条例、人员的更换和解雇、制裁、履约担保、转让、保密、争议的解决。

3. International technology transfer negotiation　国际技术转让谈判

The meaning of international technology transfer: the economic and technological activities in which the technology transferor transfers the technology beyond the border of the country to the transferee.

国际技术转让的含义：技术出让方将技术越出国境转让给受让方的经济技术活动。

Objects of international technology transfer: patents, trademarks, know-how, etc.

国际技术转让的标的：专利、商标、专有技术等。

Commercial (for-profit) international technology transfer: international technology trade (including international technology licensing trade, international technology consultation and service, etc.) or international economic cooperation (cooperative production, joint venture, compensation trade, international project contracting, etc.).

商业性(营利性)国际技术转让的途径：国际技术贸易(包括国际技术许可贸易、国际技术咨询与服务等方式)或国际经济合作(合作生产、合资经营、补偿贸易、国际工程承包等方式)。

Basic terms of commercial (for-profit) international technology transfer negotiation contract: definition terms; authorization terms; payment terms; confidentiality terms; other terms (such as quality control terms, technology improvement terms, contract validity terms, applicable law terms).

商业性(营利性)国际技术转让谈判的合同基本条款：定义条款；授权条款；支付条款；保密条款；其他条款(比如，质量控制条款、技术改进条款、合同有效期条款、适用法律条款)。

4. International investment negotiation　国际投资谈判

International investment mainly refers to the international movement of international capital elements, which includes international direct investment and international indirect investment (it refers to the transnational investment behavior that investors do not directly participate in the investment construction and the production as well as the operation process of their assets, but invest capital in the form of purchasing international securities or providing international loans to obtain interests, dividends and trading differences, mainly in international financial sector, also known as international financial investment, including international securities investment and international credit investment). We are here to discuss international direct investment.

国际投资主要指国际资本要素在国际上的移动,包括国际直接投资和国际间接投资(指投资者不直接参与投资建设及其资产的生产经营过程,而是通过购买国际有价证券或提供国际贷款等形式投放资本,以获取利息、股息和买卖差价收益的跨国投资行为,主要在国际金融领域展开,因此也称国际金融投资,包括国际证券投资和国际信贷投资)。我们在此主要讨论国际直接投资。

The meaning of international direct investment: a state's natural persons, legal persons or other economic organizations independently or jointly contribute to create new enterprises or increase capital to expand the original enterprises or acquire existing enterprises in the territory of other countries, participate in the operation and management of enterprises, and have an effective voice in the operation and management of enterprises.

国际直接投资的含义:一国的自然人、法人或其他经济组织单独或共同出资在其他国家的境内创立新企业或增加资本扩展原有企业或收购现有企业,参与企业的经营管理,对企业的经营管理具有有效的发言权的投资行为。

Methods of international direct investment: including the creation of overseas enterprises (also known as greenfield investment, mainly through the establishment of wholly foreign-owned enterprises or international joint ventures or international cooperation enterprises in the host country) and cross-border merger and acquisition.

国际直接投资的方式:包括创建境外企业[也称绿地投资(greenfield investment),主要通过在东道国创办国际独资企业或国际合资企业或国际合作企业来实现]和跨国并购(merger and acquisition)。

The process and content of international direct investment negotiation and enterprise establishment are complex. The following is just a basic introduction to the negotiation of international joint venture establishment.

国际直接投资谈判及企业设立的过程和内容较复杂,下面仅以国际合资企业设立谈判为例,作基本介绍。

Basic process and content of establishing an international joint venture:
设立国际合资企业的基本流程和内容:

Setting up a joint venture is a long and complicated process that involves four stages, preliminary investigation, pre-negotiation, negotiation and implementation.

合资企业的设立是一个漫长而复杂的过程,包括初步调查、前期谈判、谈判和实施四个阶段。

Preliminary investigation is an exploratory stage, and also the initial approach to get to know the market. Exploratory stage is mainly a phase for collecting information before acting.

初步调查,是个探索的阶段,它也是了解市场的初步途径。探索阶段主要是在行动前收集信息的阶段。

Pre-negotiation phase includes making the first contact with the company that could be a partner assessing the compatibility of the two parties' objects, ascertaining if they have common views on market strategy, conducting the feasibility study and signing a letter of intent.

前期谈判阶段,包括与可能成为合作伙伴的公司进行第一次接触,评估双方目标的兼容性,确定双方对市场战略是否有共同看法,进行可行性研究,并签署意向书。

Negotiation. When the feasibility study has been approved by the authorities, the full negotiation takes place. At this stage, the partners concerned discuss everything necessary to set up and operate the future joint venture, such as the rights and obligations of each party as well as the respective contribution of capital technology, expertise and other resources. The negotiation also addresses issues concerning the management of the joint venture, decision-making structure, policy for personnel management and the conditions for its termination. At this stage, parties also explore such issues as domestic and export pricing of the future products for sale. This phase is rather difficult involving a large number of negotiators, lasting a long time and is subject to multiple unexpected events.

谈判。当可行性研究获得当局批准后,进行全面谈判。在这一阶段,有关合作伙伴讨论建立和运营未来合资企业所需的一切,如各方的权利和义务以及各自的资本技术贡献、专业知识和其他资源。谈判还涉及合资企业的管理、决策结构、人事管理政策和终止条件等问题,在该阶段,双方还探讨未来销售产品的国内和出口定价等问题。这一阶段相当困难,谈判人员众多,持续时间长,容易发生多项意料之外的事件。

Implementation. The last stage of the whole process concerns the implementation of the agreement. It would be logical to think the negotiation is over, but this is usually not the case. At this stage, surprises crop up on a daily basis, for instance, the working conditions or supplies of raw materials may undergo dramatic, unforeseeable external changes. As a matter of fact, numerous negotiations may take place.

执行。整个过程的最后一个阶段涉及协议的执行,认为执行阶段谈判结束是合乎逻辑的,但通常情况并非如此。在这一阶段,每天都会出现意外,例如,工作条件或原材料供应可能会发生戏剧性的、不可预见的外部变化,事实上,在执行阶段也可能会发生许多谈判。

5. International project contracting negotiation 国际工程承包谈判

The meaning of international project contracting: it refers to a commercial activity mode in which a contractor of a country uses his own funds, technology, labor, equipment, materials, management license, etc. to carry out project construction or handle other economic affairs for the project owner through international bidding, negotiation or other negotiation channels, and charges fees according to the agreed contract conditions in advance.

国际工程承包的含义:指一国的承包商通过国际上的招标、议标或其他协商途径,用自己的资金、技术、劳务、设备、材料、管理许可证等为工程发包人实施项目建设或办理其他经济事务,并按事先商定的合同条件收取费用的一种商业活动方式。

The specific contents of international project contracting include engineering design, technology transfer, supply and installation of mechanical equipment, supply of raw materials and energy, construction, capital, acceptance, personnel training, technical guidance and operation management.

国际工程承包的具体内容:大致包括工程设计、技术转让、机械设备的供应与安装、原材料和能源的供应、施工、资金、验收、人员培训、技术指导、经营管理。

The main methods of international project contracting: general contracting, subcontracting partly, subcontracting wholly/contract transferring, joint contracting and cooperative contracting.

国际工程承包的主要方式:总包、分包、转包、联合承包、合作承包。

Transaction mode of international project contracting: the transaction mode of international project contracting is mainly completed by international bidding.

国际工程承包的成交方式:国际工程承包的成交主要采用国际招标投标的方式完成。

Types of international project contract: according to the price composition and determination method, it is divided into total price contract, unit price contract, cost plus remuneration contract; according to the contracted business, it is divided into engineering consulting contract, construction contract, engineering service contract, equipment supply contract and equipment supply and installation contract, turnkey contract, turn of product contract, BOT contract, etc.

国际工程承包合同的种类:按价格构成和确定方法划分为总价合同、单价合同、成本加酬金合同;按承包的业务划分为工程咨询合同、施工合同、工程服务合同、设备供应合同及设备供应与安装合同、交钥匙合同、交产品合同、BOT 合同等。

Main terms of contract for international engineering contract negotiation: the most widely used contract form at present is the "Civil Engineering (International) Construction Contract Terms" formulated by the International Federation of Consulting Engineers (Fédération Internationale Des lngénieurs Conseils, FIDIC). Its basic terms are: contract scope, project period, contractor's obligations and breach of contract, owner's responsibility and breach of contract, engineer and his representative, price and payment, guarantee, insurance, project change, dispute resolution, delay, transfer and subcontract partly, acceptance, project handover and force majeure.

国际工程承包谈判的合同主要条款：目前最广泛使用的合同格式是由国际顾问工程师联合会(FIDIC)拟定的《土木建筑工程(国际)施工合同条款》。其基本条款为，合同范围、工程期限、承包商的义务与违约、业主的责任与违约、工程师及其代表、价格与支付、担保条款、保险条款、工程变更条款、争议解决条款、误期条款、转让与分包、验收条款、工程移交、不可抗力条款。

Section 2 According to the Attitude of Both Parties

第2节 按谈判双方的态度划分

1. Soft negotiation   软式谈判

Soft negotiation is also called relationship-type negotiation or compromising negotiation. Such negotiation does not treat others as enemies, but as friends, stresses not getting the upper hand, but establishing and maintaining good relations. Soft negotiators hope to avoid conflict and are always ready to make concessions to reach an agreement. Their aim is to reach an agreement instead of a victory.

软式谈判也称作关系型谈判或让步型谈判。这种谈判不把对方当作敌人而当作朋友，强调的不是要占上风，而是要建立和维持良好的关系。软式谈判者希望避免冲突，总是做好让步达成协议的准备，他们的目标是达成协议，而非取得所谓的胜利。

2. Hard negotiation   硬式谈判

Hard negotiation is also called positioned negotiation. Such negotiation regards the other parties as rivals, emphasizing the firmness of position in negotiations, and stressing in tit for tat. Hard negotiators treat negotiation as a contest of wills, and think only consistency with the will of their own sides the victory of the negotiation. Under this case, both parties distrust and accuse each other, the negotiations could easily fall into a deadlock and consequently can not reach an agreement.

硬式谈判也称作立场型谈判。这种谈判中一方将谈判的对方视作敌手，强调立场强硬和以牙还牙。硬式谈判者将谈判视为一场意志的较量，认为只有与己方意愿一致才是谈判的胜利。在这种情况下，谈判双方互不信任、互相指责，谈判很容易就陷入僵局，结果是无法达成协议。

3. Collaborative principled negotiation 合作原则型谈判

Collaborative principled negotiation is also called Harvard principled negotiation and negotiation on merits.

合作原则型谈判也称作哈佛原则型谈判和价值型谈判。

This type of negotiation requires both sides of the negotiation to treat each other as a cooperative colleague rather than an enemy, that is to say, they should pay attention to the interpersonal relationship with each other first, but collaborative principled negotiation is not the same as compromising negotiation emphasizing just only the relationship between the two sides and ignoring the acquisition of interests, it requires both sides of the negotiation to respect the basic needs of each other and seek common gound on interests of both sides, envisage various plans that will enable both sides to gain. When the interests of both sides conflict, they insist on making decisions according to fair standards, rather than through the contest of willpower. Compared with positioned negotiation, collaborative principled negotiation pays attention to the reconciliation of the interests of both sides, rather than the positions of both sides. In doing so, alternative positions that are consistent with both of their own interests can be found.

这种谈判类型要求谈判双方首先将对方作为与自己并肩合作的同事对待，而不是作为敌人来对待，也就是说首先要注意与对方的人际关系，但是合作原则型谈判并不像让步型谈判那样只强调双方的关系而忽视利益的获取，它要求谈判双方尊重对方的基本需要，寻求双方利益上的共同点，设想各种使双方各有所获的方案。当双方的利益发生冲突时，则坚持根据公平的标准来作决定，而不是通过双方意志力的较量一决胜负。与立场型谈判相比，合作原则型谈判注意调和双方的利益，而不是双方的立场。这样做常常可以找到既符合自己的利益，又符合对方利益的替代性立场。

The advocates of collaborative principled negotiation believe that there are some common interests and conflicting interests behind the opposing positions of both sides. We often think that all the interests of the other party are in conflict with our own interests because the other party's position is opposite to ours, however, in fact, in many negotiations, after you analyze in depth the hidden or representative interests behind the opposing positions of both parties, you will find that the common interests of both parties are more than the conflicting interests, if the two parties can recognize and value the common interests, it will be easier to mediate the conflicting interests.

合作原则型谈判的倡导者认为，在谈判双方对立立场的背后，存在着某种共同性利益和冲突性利益。我们常常因对方的立场与我们的立场相对立，而认为对方的全部利益与我方的利益都是冲突的，但是，事实上在许多谈判中，在深入地分析双方对立立场背后隐含的或代表的利益后，你就会发现双方共同性的利益要多于冲突性利益，如果双方能认识到并看重共同性利益，调解冲突性利益也就比较容易了。

Collaborative principled negotiation emphasizes the value gained through negotiation. This value includes not only economic value, but also interpersonal value, therefore, collaborative principled negotiation is a kind of rational and human negotiation, which is highly praised by negotiation researchers and actual negotiators all over the world.

合作原则型谈判强调通过谈判所取得的价值。这种价值既包括经济上的价值，也包括人际关系的价值，因而合作原则型谈判是一种既理性又富有人情味的谈判，为世界各国的谈判研究人员和实际谈判人员所推崇。

Section 3　According to the Number and Importance of Negotiation Matters

第3节　按谈判事项的个数和重要性的不同划分

According to the number and importance of negotiation matters, negotiation can be divided into integrated negotiation and distributive negotiation.

根据谈判事项的个数和重要性的不同，谈判分为整合式谈判和分配式谈判。

1. Distributive negotiation　分配式谈判

In distributive negotiation, each party can only allocate fixed value for a single event.

The key of distributive negotiation is to ask for resources, declare value and maximize their own interests. In most cases, the parties to the negotiation are often persistent in making a 50% to 50% compromise on a single matter and are not aware of the potential common interests.

在分配式谈判中,各方只能就单一事件分配固定价值。

分配式谈判的关键是索取资源,声明价值,使自己的利益最大化。大多数情况下,谈判各方当事人往往执着于就单个事项进行50%对50%的妥协,意识不到潜在的共同利益。

2. Integrative negotiation 整合式谈判

In the integrated negotiation, the total amount of allocable resources is variable, and there are more than one negotiation item. Negotiators can package and exchange the items according to their importance and priority, make concessions to each other, and create common value to achieve a win-win situation.

The key of integrated negotiation is to find out the consistence and compatability of the interests of both parties, create value and reach an integrated agreement, which requires one party to make concessions on some matters in exchange for the other party's return on other matters.

在整合式谈判中,可分配资源总额可变,谈判事项不止一个。谈判者可以根据事项对自己的重要性和优先权不同将其打包交换,互相作出让步,创造共同价值以达到双赢的局面。

整合式谈判的关键是发现谈判双方利益的一致性和相容性,创造价值达成整合式协议,要求谈判一方在某些事项上作出让步,以换取对方在其他事项上的回报。

Terminology　本章术语

1. negotiation of goods sales　货物买卖谈判
2. negotiation of labor cooperation　劳务合作谈判
3. negotiation of technology transfer　技术转让谈判
4. negotiation of investment　投资谈判
5. negotiation of project contracting　工程承包谈判
6. soft negotiation　软式谈判
7. hard negotiation　硬式谈判
8. collaborative principled negotiation　合作原则型谈判
9. distributive negotiation　分配式谈判
10. integrated negotiation　整合式谈判

Exercises　本章练习

1. Why collaborative principled negotiation is highly praised by negotiation researchers and actual negotiators all over the world?

　　为什么合作原则型谈判为世界各国的谈判研究人员和实际谈判人员所推崇？

2. What are the characteristics of negotiation of international sales of goods, compared with other international business negotiations?

　　与其他国际商务谈判相比，国际货物买卖谈判有什么特点？

Answers for Reference　参考答案

1. This type of negotiation requires both sides of the negotiation to treat each other as a cooperative colleague rather than an enemy, that is to say, they should pay attention to the interpersonal relationship with each other first, but collaborative principled negotiation is not the same as compromising negotiation emphasizing just only the relationship between the two sides and ignoring the acquisition of interests, it requires both sides of the negotiation to respect the basic needs of each other and seek common gound on interests of both sides, envisage various plans that will enable both sides to gain. When the interests of both sides conflict, they insist on making decisions according to fair standards, rather than through the contest of willpower. Compared with positioned negotiation, collaborative principled negotiation pays attention to the reconciliation of the interests of both sides, rather than the positions of both sides. In doing so, alternative positions that are consistent with both of their own interests can be found.

　　Collaborative principled negotiation emphasizes the value gained through negotiation. This value includes not only economic value, but also interpersonal value, therefore, collaborative principled negotiation is a kind of rational and human negotiation, which is highly praised by negotiation researchers and actual negotiators all over the world.

　　这种谈判类型要求谈判双方首先将对方作为与自己并肩合作的同事对待，而不是作为敌人来对待，也就是说首先要注意与对方的人际关系，但是合作原则型谈判并不像让步型谈判那样只强调双方的关系而忽视利益的获取，它要求谈判双方尊重对方的基本需要，寻求双方利益上的共同点，设想各种使双方各有所获的方案。当双方的利益发生冲突时，则坚持根据公平的标准来作决定，而不是通过双方意志力的较量一决胜负。与立场型谈判相比，合作原则型谈判注意调和双方的利益，而不是双方的立场。这样做常常可以找到既符合自己的利益，又符合对方利益的替代性立场。

合作原则型谈判强调通过谈判所取得的价值。这种价值既包括经济上的价值，也包括人际关系的价值，因而合作原则型谈判是一种既理性又富有人情味的谈判，为世界各国的谈判研究人员和实际谈判人员所推崇。

2. The characteristics of negotiation of international sales of goods: negotiation of international sales of goods is the basic form of international business negotiation, compared with other international business negotiations, negotiation of international sales of goods has two characteristics: one is relatively low difficulty, the other is comparatively comprehensive terms and conditions.

国际货物买卖谈判的特点：国际货物买卖谈判是国际商务谈判的基本形态，与其他国际商务谈判相比，国际货物买卖谈判有两个特点：一是难度相对较低，二是条款比较全面。

Chapter 3   Theories of International Business Negotiation

第 3 章   国际商务谈判理论

Section 1   Theory of Hierarchy of Needs

第 1 节   需求层次理论

**1. Research history and researchers of theory of hierarchy of needs
需求层次理论的研究史和研究者**

The hierarchy of needs theory was proposed by a psychologist called Abraham Maslow. In the paper *A Theory of Human Motivation* published in *Psychological Review* in 1943, he divided human needs into 5 levels: physiological needs, safety needs, love and belonging(social) needs, respect needs, self-actualization needs. In his 1954 book *Motivation and Personality*, behind the needs for respect, he added the needs for knowledge and aesthetic, and further divided human needs into 7 levels. 1968 In his book *Toward a Psychology of Being*, he elaborated on the needs of people at all levels. Theory of hierarchy of needs has been widely spread, which is of great significance to the research and application of management science and behavior science.

需求层次理论由心理学家亚伯拉罕·马斯洛提出。他于 1943 年发表在《心理评论》(*Psychological Review*)上的论文《人类动机理论》(*A Theory of Human Motivation*)中把人的需要分为 5 个层次：生理的需要、安全的需要、爱和归属(社交)的需要、尊重的需要、自我实现的需要。他在 1954 年的著作《激励与个性》(*Motivation and Personality*)中，在尊重的需要后面，增加了求知的需要和审美的需要，进而把人的需要分为 7 个层次。他在 1968 年的著作《走向存在的心理学》(*Toward a Psychology of Being*)中，又详细阐述了人的各个层次的需要。需求层次理论被广泛传播，对管理科学、行为科学的研究和应用有重要的借鉴意义。

2. Contents of theory of hierarchy of needs　　需求层次理论的内容

In the seven-level version of Maslow's hierarchy of needs, physiological needs, saefty needs, love and belonging (social) needs, respect needs, knowledge needs, aesthetic needs, and self-actualization needs, are arranged from low to high according to the importance in a pyramid shape. The bottom of the pyramid is the lowest level of needs, and the top of the pyramid is the highest level of needs. Before the low level needs are met, the high level needs cannot be inspiring.

在7个层次马斯洛的需求理论中，生理的需要、安全的需要、爱与归属(社交)的需要、尊重的需要、求知的需要、审美的需要和自我实现的需要，按各自的重要性依次从低到高排列，呈金字塔状。金字塔底部是最低层次的需要，金字塔顶部是最高层次的需要，在低层次的需要得到满足之前，高层次的需要不能起到激励人的作用。

Physiological needs　　生理的需要

Physiological needs include the needs for food, water, air and housing, which are at the lowest level. People always try their best to meet these needs before turning to higher level needs. A man is not interested in anything else when he is hungry. His main motivation is to get food. Even today, there are many people who can't meet these basic physiological needs.

生理的需要包括对食物、水、空气及住房等的需要，这类需要的层级最低。人们在转向较高层级的需要之前，总是尽力满足这类需要。一个人在饥饿时不会对其他任何事物感兴趣，他的主要动力是得到食物。即使在今天，还有许多人不能满足这些基本的生理上的需要。

Safety needs　　安全的需要

Safety needs include the need for personal safety, life stability and freedom from pain, threat or disease. Like physiological needs, the only thing people care about before safety needs are met is safety needs. For many people, safety needs to be reflected in safety and stability of the job as well as medical insurance, unemployment insurance and retirement benefits. People, who are primarily motivated by these safety needs, when evaluating their careers, see them as basic guarantee that they can not lose. If managers think that safety needs are the most important for personnel, they will focus on the use of such needs in management, emphasize rules and regulations, occupational security, welfare treatment, and protect personnel from unemployment.

If people have a strong need for safety, managers should not be unconventional when dealing with problems, and should avoid or oppose risks, and people will follow the rules and regulations to complete the work.

安全需要包括对人身安全、生活稳定以及免遭痛苦、威胁或疾病等的需要。和生理上的需要一样,在安全需要没有得到满足之前,人们唯一关心的就是这种需要。对许多人而言,安全需要表现为工作安全而稳定以及有医疗保险、失业保险及退休福利等,主要受安全需要激励的人,在评估职业时,把这些看作不能失去的基本保障。如果管理者认为对人员来说安全需要最重要,他们就在管理上着重利用这种需要,强调规章制度、职业保障、福利待遇,并保护人员不致失业。如果人员对安全需要非常强烈时,管理者在处理问题时就不应标新立异,并应该避免或反对冒险,而人员将循规蹈矩地完成工作。

Love and belonging (social) needs   爱与归属(社交)的需要

Social needs include the need for friendship, love and affiliation. When the physiological needs and safety needs are met, social needs will be highlighted, and then have an incentive effect. In Maslow's need level, this level is quite different from the first two levels. If these needs are not met, it will affect people's spirit, leading to high absenteeism, low productivity, dissatisfaction with work and depression. Managers must be aware that when social needs become the main source of motivation, jobs are regarded as opportunities to find and establish warm and harmonious interpersonal relationships, and jobs that can provide opportunities for social interaction among colleagues will be valued. When managers feel that their subordinates are striving to meet such needs, they usually adopt the attitude of support and approval, emphasize that they can be accepted by the people they work with, carry out business activities such as organized sports competitions and group gatherings, and request them to comply with the norms of collective behavior.

社交需要包括对友谊、爱情以及隶属关系的需要。当生理上的需要和安全需要得到满足后,社交需要就会突显出来,进而产生激励作用。在马斯洛需求层次中,这一层级是与前两层级截然不同的另一层级。这些需要如果得不到满足,就会影响人的精神,导致高缺勤率、低生产率、对工作不满及情绪低落。管理者必须意识到,当社交需要成为主要的激励源时,工作被视为寻找和建立温馨和谐的人际关系的机会,能够提供同事间社交往来机会的职业会受到重视。管理者感到下属努力追求满足这类需要时,通常会采取支持与赞许的态度,十分强调能为共事的人所接受,开展有组织的体育比赛和集体聚会等业务活动,并且要求他们遵从集体行为规范。

Respect needs/Esteem needs 尊重的需要

The needs for respect include not only personal feelings of achievement or self-worth, but also the recognition and respect of others for themselves. People with respect needs expect others to accept them according to their actual image and think that they are capable and competent for the job. They are concerned with achievement, reputation, status and promotion opportunities. It's because people recognize their talents. When they get these, they not only win people's respect, but also have confidence in their hearts because they are satisfied with their own values. Failure to meet such needs will depress them. If other people's honor is not based on their true learning, but on their vanity, it will also pose a threat to their psychology. When motivating people with respect needs, managers should adopt the way of public reward and praise, and the arrangement of work should especially emphasize the arduousness of the work and the superb skills needed for success. The methods such as awarding medal of honor, publishing articles of praise in the company's journals, and publishing the honor list of excellent employees can improve people's pride in their work.

尊重的需要既包括对成就或自我价值的个人感觉，也包括他人对自己的认可与尊重。有尊重需要的人希望别人按照他们的实际形象来接受他们，并认为他们有能力，能胜任工作。他们关心的是成就、名声、地位和晋升机会。这是由于别人认识到他们的才能而得到的。当他们得到这些时，不仅赢得了人们的尊重，同时其内心因对自己的价值感到满足而充满自信。不能满足这类需要，就会使他们感到沮丧。如果别人给予的荣誉不是根据其真才实学，而是徒有虚名，也会对他们的心理构成威胁。管理者在激励有尊重需要的人员时，应采取公开奖励和表扬的方式，布置工作要特别强调工作的艰巨性以及成功所需要的高超技巧等。颁发荣誉奖章、在公司的刊物上发表表扬文章、公布优秀员工光荣榜等方法都可以提高人员对自己工作的自豪感。

Knowledge needs 求知的需要

People have the needs to know, understand and explore things, and the understanding of the environment is the result of curiosity. Curiosity could be regarded as one of these needs.

人有知道、了解和探索事物的需要，对环境的认识则是好奇心作用的结果，好奇心可视为这类需要之一。

Aesthetic needs 审美的需要

People have the needs to pursue symmetry, tidiness and beauty, and get satisfaction through the transformation from ugliness to beauty. Maslow found that in a strictly biological sense, people need beauty, just as their diet needs calcium, which helps them become healthier.

人都有追求匀称、整齐和美丽的需要，并且通过从丑向美转化而得到满足。马斯洛发现，从严格的生物学意义上来说，人需要美，正如人的饮食需要钙一样，美有助于人变得更健康。

Self-actualization needs　自我实现的需要

The goal of self-actualization is self realization, or the realization of potential. Those who reach the realm of self realization accept themselves and others. The ability to solve problems is enhanced, the consciousness is improved, the ability to deal with affairs independently is improved, and they require to be alone without being disturbed. In order to meet this need to give full play to his ability, he should have met other needs partly at some time. Of course, people who realize themselves may pay too much attention to the satisfaction of the needs at the highest level, so that they consciously or unconsciously give up meeting the needs at the lower level. People with dominant self-actualization needs are motivated to use the most creative and constructive skills in his work. Managers who value this need will realize that no matter what kind of work can be innovated, creativity is not unique to managers, but everyone expects to have. In order to make the work meaningful, managers who emphasize self realization will consider the use of strategies to adapt to complex situations when designing work, assign special tasks to people with unique skills to display their talents, or leave room for people when designing work procedures and making implementation plans. Maslow used the autobiographies and manuscripts of 21 successful people to study the needs of human beings at this level. However, this research method is seriously limited by the author's own temperament and prejudice, and lacks objective data support. Therefore, Maslow's conclusion at the level of self realization needs should not be unconditionally accepted by the scientific community.

自我实现需要的目标是自我实现，或是发挥潜能。达到自我实现境界的人，接受自己，也接受他人。解决问题能力增强，自觉性提高，善于独立处事，要求不受打扰地独处。要满足这种尽量发挥自己才能的需要，他应该已在某个时刻部分地满足了其他的需要。当然，自我实现的人可能过分关注这种最高层级的需要的满足，以至于自觉或不自觉地放弃满足较低层级的需要。自我实现需要占支配地位的人，会受到激励在工作中运用最富创造性和建设性的技巧。重视这种需要的管理者会认识到，无论哪种工作都可以进行创新，创造性并非管理者独有，而是每个人都期望拥有的。为了使工作有意义，强调自我实现的管理者，会在设计工作时考虑运用适应复杂情况的策略，会给身怀绝技的人委派特别任务以施展才华，或者在设计工作程序和制订执行计划时为人员群体留有余地。马斯洛在研究这一层级的人类需要时，采用了21位成功人士的自传和文稿，通过研究这些文字作品来得到作者本人的需要特征。但是这种研究方式严重受限于作者本人的性情和偏见，缺乏客观的数据支持，因此马斯洛在自我实现需要这一层级结论不应该被科学界无条件地接受。

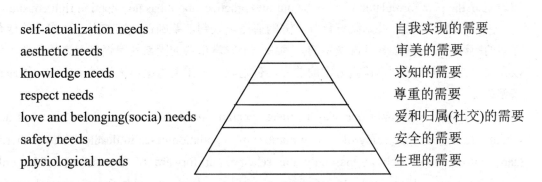

self-actualization needs	自我实现的需要
aesthetic needs	审美的需要
knowledge needs	求知的需要
respect needs	尊重的需要
love and belonging(socia) needs	爱和归属(社交)的需要
safety needs	安全的需要
physiological needs	生理的需要

3. Application of theory of hierarchy of needs in negotiation
   需求层次理论在谈判中的应用

(1) The theory of hierarchy of needs provides a theoretical basis for finding out the motivation of the negotiation opponent, because needs may transform into motivations to promote people to engage in certain behaviors, including negotiation activities. Mastering the theory helps negotiators to know themselves and the other, find out the needs behind the other party's participation in the negotiation, analyze how to choose different methods to adapt, resist or change the motivation of the other party, understand the corresponding motivation and effect of each need, so as to choose the best negotiation method.

(1) 需求层次理论为摸清谈判对手的动机提供了理论基础，因为需要可转化为动机，推动人们去从事某种行为，包括从事谈判活动。掌握需求层次理论，有助于使谈判者知己知彼，找出对方参与谈判背后的需要，分析如何选择不同的方法去适应、抵制或者改变对方的动机，了解每一种需要的相应动力和作用，以便选择最佳的谈判方法。

(2) The theory of hierarchy of needs provides a theoretical basis for the formulation of a variety of negotiation schemes, which can help negotiators to formulate a variety of negotiation schemes.

(2) 需求层次理论为多种谈判方案的制订提供了理论基础，可以帮助谈判人员制订多种谈判方案。

① It is the premise of making a negotiation plan to make clear the needs of each party. Before negotiation, a negotiation plan should be made. The successful negotiation plan is determined by many factors, and one of the most important factors is the needs of both parties. Therefore, to make clear the needs of both parties is the premise of making a negotiation plan, otherwise, the plan formulated will not be put into practice, and it has no intention righteousness.

① 搞清各自的需要是制订谈判方案的前提。谈判前要制订谈判方案,而成功的谈判方案的制订是由多种因素共同决定的,其中一个非常重要的因素就是谈判双方的需要,所以弄清双方的需要是制订谈判方案的前提,否则制订出来的方案将无法付诸实施,因而也毫无意义。

② There is not only one way to meet a certain need, but also a variety of ways and schemes to choose. The study of a large number of negotiation cases in deadlock shows that in many cases, people believe that only the scheme put forward by themselves is the only acceptable one, which leads to negotiation stalling, deadlock and finally breakdown of negotiation. In fact, as the saying goes, all roads lead to Rome, and there are many plans to meet the needs of both sides, which may only be different in the degree of profit. Smart negotiators can always imagine a variety of alternative ways and plans to meet the needs of both sides before the negotiation, so as to apply them at any time in the negotiation and gradually guide the negotiation to success.

② 满足某种需要不是只有一种途径,而是有多种途径和多种方案可供选择。对大量陷入僵局的谈判案例的研究表明,在很多情况下,由于人们认定只有自己提出的方案才是唯一可接受的,从而导致谈判搁浅、形成僵局,并最终使谈判破裂。其实正如俗话所说的那样,条条大路通罗马,满足双方需要的方案有很多,可能只是在获利的程度上有所不同。聪明的谈判者总能在谈判前设想出满足双方需要的可供选择的多种途径与方案,以便在谈判中随时加以应用,逐步引导谈判走向成功。

(3) The theory of hierarchy of needs provides a theoretical basis for the use of negotiation strategies and skills.

(3) 需求层次理论为谈判谋略和技巧的运用提供了理论依据。

① Physiological needs and negotiation 生理的需要与谈判

Negotiation is a kind of high-level intellectual labor that consumes a lot of physical and mental energy, but also bears great psychological pressure. If the physiological needs of the negotiators are not guaranteed, it will affect the energy and emotions of the negotiators, and affect the realization of the scheduled negotiation goals. Physiological needs are mainly manifested in negotiators' needs for clothing, food, housing/living and transportation. The demand for clothes is to dress neatly and appropriately, to conform to their own image and temperament, to get the recognition of the other party, and to increase their own negotiation momentum. The demand for food is rich nutrition in line with their own taste and eating habits, in line with the requirements of safety and health. The demand for living refers to a quiet, comfortable and convenient living environment in line with their own status and living habits, which is conducive to eliminating fatigue, restoring physical energy, and maintaining a friendly psychology. The demand for transportation refers to the convenience of transportation and communication, so as to get in touch with and contact with superior departments at any time and improve negotiation efficiency.

In the negotiation, the reception party should not only make a thorough arrangement for himself, but also consider providing the other party with good conditions for food, clothing, housing and transportation, so as to reduce the tension, suspicion and huge psychological pressure caused by the other party's participation in the negotiation and create a good negotiation atmosphere.

谈判是一种消耗大量体力和脑力的高级智力劳动，同时要承受极大的心理压力，如果谈判人员的生理需要得不到保证，就会影响到谈判人员的精力与情绪，影响预定谈判目标的实现。生理需要在谈判中主要表现为谈判者对衣食住行的需求。对衣着的需求是穿着整洁得体，符合自己形象和气质，得到对方的认同，增强自己的谈判气势。对食的需求是营养丰富，符合自己的口味和饮食习惯，合乎安全卫生的要求。对住的需求是指符合自己的身份地位和居住习惯，有一个安静舒适和方便的居住环境，这样有利于消除疲劳，恢复体力精力，也有利于保持友善的心理。对行的需求，是指有交通通信的便利条件，以便随时和上级部门取得接触和联系，提高谈判效率。

谈判中的接待一方除了为谈判本身做周密的部署外，还要考虑为谈判的对方提供良好的衣食住行条件，这样可减轻对方参与谈判而带来的紧张、怀疑和巨大心理压力，创造一种良好的谈判氛围。

② Safety needs and negotiation 安全的需要与谈判

The need of safety mainly lies in personal safety and status safety. Personal safety is mainly aimed at the negotiators of the visiting party, because they don't know the social conditions, customs, public security, traffic and other conditions of the visiting place, the visitors usually lack a sense of safety. The receiving party should take care of it in all aspects as much as possible, such as the special person is responsible for the pick-up, accompanying the visit and shopping, etc. Status security is mainly manifested in that both sides of the negotiation may take reaching an agreement as their own task, or even mistakenly think that it is better to reach a less ideal negotiation agreement than to reach no agreement and get nothing. This is the crux of compromise and repeated concessions in the negotiation. For this issue, negotiators and their superiors should have a correct understanding of the equality and mutual benefit of negotiation, and can not simply assess the performance of negotiators by whether they reach an agreement.

安全的需要主要表现在人身安全和地位安全。人身安全主要针对来访一方的谈判者，由于对访问地的社会民情、风俗习惯、治安、交通等状况不了解，来访者通常会缺乏安全感。接待一方应尽可能地在各方面予以照顾，比如，专人负责接送、陪同参观游览和购物等。地位安全主要表现在谈判双方都可能会把达成协议作为自己的任务，甚至错误地认为达成一个不太理想的谈判协议，总比达不成协议而一无所获的结果要好，这是谈判中委曲求全以及一再退让的症结所在。对于这个问题，谈判者及其上级应对谈判的平等互利，有一个正确的认识，不能简单地以是否达成协议作为标准来考核谈判人员的业绩。

③ Love and belonging needs and negotiation 爱和归属的需要与谈判

Negotiators all hope that friendly relations can be established between the two sides and friendship can be obtained from each other. In addition, they also hope that the negotiation team of their own side can strengthen communication and cooperation to jointly strive for the success of the negotiation. Therefore, the reception party should hold a friendly and cooperative attitude and take advantage of all opportunities, including language, expression, banquet, entertainment, gift giving, etc. to develop friendship with the other side. Once the two sides have established good interpersonal relationship, it is easier to communicate and understand each other. At the same time, the person in charge of the negotiation team should maintain the unity and cooperation within the team, fully listen to the opinions of each member, try to adopt its reasonable part, and make a reasonable explanation for the opinions that can not be adopted. However, all members at the negotiation table should be consistent in caliber, unite in fighting, and not show any differences and opinions, so as to avoid giving the other party a chance.

谈判者都希望，双方之间能建立友好关系，得到对方的友谊，另外也希望自己一方的谈判班子内部加强沟通和协作，共同争取谈判的成功，因此接待一方，应当持有一种友好合作的心态，利用一切机会，包括语言、表情、宴请、娱乐、赠送礼品等发展与对方的友谊。一旦双方建立了良好的人际关系，彼此之间就更容易沟通和了解。同时，谈判班子的负责人应当保持班子内部的团结和协作，充分听取每个成员的意见，尽量采纳其合理部分，并对不能采纳的意见作出合理解释。但在谈判桌上全体成员应口径一致，团结作战，不能把任何分歧和意见显示出来，以免给对方可乘之机。

④ Respect/esteem needs and negotiation 尊重的需要与谈判

Every negotiator wants to be respected by his counterpart. In order to be respected by his counterpart, he must first respect his counterpart. Therefore, in the negotiation process, the negotiator should show respect for his counterpart everywhere. First of all, you should respect the other party's personality, use language with civility and politeness instead of insulting, attacking and abusing. Secondly, the identity and status of the opponent should be respected. In the negotiation, the identity and status of the two sides should be equal, even if there is a gap, it should not be too big. Otherwise, when people with lower identity and status negotiate with people with higher identity and status, the latter will think that he is not respected, which affects the negotiation, or even causes the negotiation to break down. Thirdly, you should respect the knowledge and ability of the other party. Sometimes, in the negotiation, the other party will intentionally or unintentionally disturb the negotiation order or deliberately confuse some clear and simple concepts. At this time, you should not belittle, mock or ridicule the other party's shallow knowledge, but just clarify the problem from the front.

每个谈判者都希望得到谈判对手的尊重，要想得到对手的尊重，必须首先尊重对手。因此在谈判过程中，谈判者要处处表现出对对手的尊重。首先，应当尊重其人格，使用语言时要文明礼貌，而不要使用侮辱、攻击和谩骂的语言。其次，应尊重对手的身份和地位，在谈判中双方的身份和地位应该对等，即使有差距也不要太大，否则，身份和地位较低的人员与身份和地位较高的人员进行谈判时，后者会以为是对其不尊重，影响谈判进行，甚至造成谈判破裂。再次，应尊重对手的学识和能力，有时在谈判中对方会有意无意地搅乱谈判秩序或故意混淆一些本来很明确浅显的概念，这时也不要贬低、嘲笑或讥讽对方学识浅薄，只是从正面将问题予以澄清即可。

⑤ Knowledge needs and negotiation 求知的需要与谈判

Negotiators have the need for knowledge. If one party has any doubt about offer, terms, concepts, terms and conditions as well as reasons for concession proposed by the other party, he will clarify it by asking questions, which requires that the party who answers must be careful. In addition, a visiting party will explore the strength of the receiving party in many aspects, for example, by visiting the factory and chatting with workers and management personnel, the production and operation status of the receiving party will be known, which requires the receiving party to be more careful, so as not to disclose business secrets or business secrets.

谈判者都有求知的需要。如果谈判一方对另一方提出的报价、术语、概念、条款和让步理由有疑问时，会通过提问方式加以澄清，这就要求回答的一方必须小心应对。此外，来访的一方会对接待一方的实力进行多方面的探查,比如,通过参观工厂以及与工人和管理人员闲聊的方式了解接待一方的生产经营状况,这更要求接待一方谨慎应对,以免泄露经营秘密或商业秘密。

⑥ Aesthetic needs and negotiation 审美的需要与谈判

Negotiator should show the other party good qualities and mental outlook from the aspects of appearance, clothing, language, posture, etc. The receiving party should try his best to arrange a negotiation place that can bring good sensory enjoyment to people as a place for negotiation, so as to bring pleasant mood to visitors and create good conditions for promoting negotiation and reaching transactions.

谈判者要从外表、衣着、语言、姿态等各方面向对方展现自己的良好素质和精神面貌。接待一方,要尽量安排能给人带来良好感官享受的谈判场所作为洽谈地点,以便给来访者带来愉悦的心情,为促进谈判、达成交易创造良好条件。

⑦ Self-actualization needs and negotiation 自我实现的需要与谈判

The need of self realization of negotiators is reflected by the achievements of negotiation. The greater benefits negotiators get in the negotiation, the higher satisfaction of the need of self realizationis. The need of self realization can be said to be the highest need of negotiators, and also the most difficult need to meet. Restricted by the negotiation objectives of both parties, it can only meet the needs of self realization of the other party as much as possible on the premise of striving for the best negotiation interests for one party.

谈判者自我实现的需要是通过谈判取得的成绩来体现的,谈判者在谈判中获得的利益越大,自我实现需要的满足程度也越高。自我实现的需要可以说是谈判者最高的需求,也是最难满足的需要,因为受到双方谈判目标的制约,只能是在为自己一方争取最大谈判利益的前提下,尽量满足对方自我实现的需要。

Section 2　Game Theory

第 2 节　博　弈　论

1. History and researchers of game theory　博弈论的研究史和研究者

Game theory is that the two players use each other's strategies to change their confrontation strategies in equal games to achieve the goal of winning. Game theory thoughts have existed since ancient times. The ancient Chinese books such as *Sun Zi's Art of War* are not only a military work, but also the earliest game theory work. Game theory initially focused on winning and losing in chess, bridge, and gambling. People's grasp of the game situation only stayed on experience and did not develop into a theoretical development.

博弈论是双方在平等的对局中各自利用对方的策略变换自己的对抗策略，达到取胜的目的。博弈论思想古已有之，中国古代的《孙子兵法》等著作就不仅是一部军事著作，而且算是最早的一部博弈论著作。博弈论最初主要研究象棋、桥牌、赌博中的胜负问题，人们对博弈局势的把握只停留在经验上，没有向理论化发展。

Game theory considers the predictive and actual behavior of individuals in the game, and studies their optimization strategies. Modern research on game theory began in Zermelo, Borel, and Von Neumann.

博弈论考虑游戏中的个体的预测行为和实际行为，并研究它们的优化策略。近代对于博弈论的研究，开始于策梅洛、波莱尔及冯·诺依曼。

In 1928, Von Neumann proved the basic principles of game theory, thereby announcing the formal birth of game theory. In 1944, the epoch-making masterpiece *Game Theory and Economic Behavior* co-authored by von Neumann and Morganstein extended the two-player game to the structure of n-player games and systematically applied game theory to the economic field, thereby laying the foundation and theoretical systems.

1928 年，冯·诺依曼证明了博弈论的基本原理，从而宣告了博弈论的正式诞生。1944 年，冯·诺依曼和摩根斯坦共著的划时代巨著《博弈论与经济行为》将两人博弈推广到 N 人博弈结构并将博弈论系统地应用于经济领域，从而奠定了这一学科的基础和理论体系。

From 1950 to 1951, John Forbes Nash Jr used the fixed point theorem to prove the existence of equilibrium points, which laid a solid foundation for the generalization of game theory. Nash's seminal thesis *The Equilibrium Point of N-Player Game* (1950) and *Non-cooperative Game* (1951), etc. gave the concept of Nash equilibrium and the existence theorem of equilibrium. In addition, the research of Reinhard Zelten and John Hassani also promoted the development of game theory. The 1994 Nobel Prize in Economics was awarded to these three game theory experts in recognition of their pioneering contributions to the theory of equilibrium analysis in non-cooperative games, which had a significant impact on game theory and economics.

Today game theory has developed into a more comprehensive discipline.

1950—1951 年，约翰·福布斯·纳什利用不动点定理证明了均衡点的存在，为博弈论的一般化奠定了坚实的基础。纳什的开创性论文《N 人博弈的均衡点》(1950)、《非合作博弈》(1951)等，给出了纳什均衡的概念和均衡存在定理。此外，莱因哈德·泽尔腾、约翰·海萨尼的研究也对博弈论发展起到推动作用。1994 年诺贝尔经济学奖授予这 3 位博弈论专家，表彰他们在非合作博弈的均衡分析理论方面作出了开创性的贡献，对博弈论和经济学产生了重大的影响。

今天博弈论已发展成一门较完善的学科。

2. Basic contents of game theory　博弈论的基本内容

(1) Elements of Game Theory　博弈论的构成要素

① In-game player (Participant)　局中人（参与者）

In a competition or game, each participant with decision-making power becomes an in-game player. The phenomenon of a game with only two players is called a two-player game, and a game with more than two players is called a multi-player game.

在一场竞赛或博弈中，每一个有决策权的参与者成为一个局中人。只有两个局中人的博弈现象称为"两人博弈"，而多于两个局中人的博弈称为"多人博弈"。

② Strategy or behavior　策略或行为

Strategy or behavior refers to the collection of all strategies or behaviors that each participant can choose, that is, the means and methods that each participant can choose when making a decision.

策略或行为，指各参与者各自可选择的全部策略或行为的集合，即每个参与者在进行决策时可以选择的手段、方法等。

③ Information　信息

Information refers to the knowledge of participants in the game, especially the knowledge about the characteristics and actions of other participants.

信息，指参与者在博弈中的知识，特别是有关其他参与者的特征和行动的知识。

④ Payment function　支付函数

Payment function refers to the level of utility obtained by participants from the game, corresponding to each possible decision choice of each participant. The game has a result, which represents the gains and losses of each participant under the strategy combination. The result can be positive, negative or zero.

支付函数，指参与者从博弈中获得的效用水平，对应于各个参与者的每一种可能的决策选择。博弈都有一个结果，表示各个参与者在该策略组合下的所得和所失，这个结果可以是正值，也可以是负值或零。

⑤ Equilibrium 均衡

Equilibrium refers to the combination of optimal strategies or behaviors of all participants. 均衡，指所有参与者的最优策略或行为的组合。

(2) Game theory assumptions 博弈论的研究假设

① Player's assumption 对局中人的假设:

- Players are fully rational.
- Players attempt to maximize their utility/outcome.
- Players wll accept the highest payoffs.
- Players will only accept solutions that are at or greater than their security levels.
- Players know the "rules of the game".
- Players assume other parties to be fully rational.
- 局中人是完全理性的。
- 局中人试图最大化其效用/结果。
- 局中人将接受最高的回报。
- 局中人将只接受大于或等于其安全等级的解决方案。
- 局中人知道"游戏规则"。
- 局中人认为其他参与方是完全理性的。

② The number of players is fixed and known to all parties.

局中人的人数是固定的，参与各方都知道。

③ Each party recognizes a set of available options and develops tangible preferences among those options. Preferences remain constant throughout the conflict/negotiation interaction.

各方都认识到一组可用的选项，并在这些选项中发展出切实的偏好。在整个冲突/谈判互动中，偏好保持不变。

④ Each party knows or can estimate well the options and preferences of the other parties.

每一方都知道或可以很好地估计其他方的选择和偏好。

⑤ Communication is limited, highly controlled or not relevant to the conflict/negotiation interaction.

沟通受到限制，受到高度控制或与冲突/协商互动无关。

⑥ A decision must be possible that is maximally efficient, intersects with the solution set at a point that maximizes each party's own interests(Pareto optimal).

最高效的决策是可能的，与解决方案相交，各方利益达到最大化(帕累托最优)。

(3) Types of game　博弈的类型

Games are classified differently according to different criteria.

根据不同的基准，博弈有不同的分类。

① According to whether there is a binding agreement between the parties, games can be mainly divided into cooperative games and non-cooperative games. If there is, it is a cooperative game, if not, it is a non-cooperative game.

根据当事人之间有没有一个具有约束力的协议，博弈主要可以分为合作博弈和非合作博弈。如果有，就是合作博弈，如果没有，就是非合作博弈。

Zero-sum game is a non-cooperative game, which refers to the fact that the income of one party necessarily means the loss of the other party under strict competition. The sum of the income and loss of all parties in the game is always "zero", and there is no possibility of cooperation between the two parties. It can also be said that one's own happiness is based on the pain of the other, and the size of the two is exactly the same, so both sides try their best to achieve "I win, you lose" and "damage others for self-interest".

零和博弈，属非合作博弈，指参与博弈的各方，在严格竞争下，一方的收益必然意味着另一方的博弈，博弈各方的收益和损失相加总和永远为"零"，双方不存在合作的可能。也可以说，自己的幸福是建立在他人的痛苦之上的，二者的大小完全相等，因而双方都想尽一切办法实现"我赢你输""损人利己"。

Non-zero-sum game refers to the fact that the parties in the game are no longer the relationship of "I win, you lose". What one party gains does not necessarily mean what the other party loses, one's own happiness may not be based on the pain of the other, that is, "self-interest does not harm others", which implies that participants may have some kind of common interests, there is a possibility of cooperation, and they can obtain "win-win" or "multi-win" results. The "prisoner's dilemma" below is a representative model of non-zero-sum game, because there is at least one possible cooperation state among the four states of the two players in the model, the result is "win-win". Non-zero-sum game is divided into positive sum game and negative sum game according to whether "sum" is positive or negative.

非零和博弈，指博弈中各方不再是"我赢你输"的关系，一方所得并不一定意味着另一方所失，自己的幸福未必建立在他人的痛苦之上，即"利己不损人"，其中蕴含着参与者可能存在某种共同的利益，有合作的可能，能够获得"双赢""多赢"的结果。下述的"囚徒困境"是非零和博弈的代表模型，因为模型中博弈双方的四种状态中至少存在一种双方可能合作的状态，其结果是"双赢"。非零和博弈根据"和"为正数还是负数，分为正和博弈和负和博弈。

There is a plot in the movie *Beautiful Mind*:

In a hot afternoon, Professor John Nash gave classes to more than twenty students. Several workers were working downstairs outside the classroom window. The noise of the machine became harsh. So Nash went to the window and closed the window severely. "Professor, please don't close the window. It's too hot!" And Professor Nash replied with a serious face, "The quiet in class is much more important than your discomfort!" Then he turned around and said, "Come to class for you, it seems to delay not only your time, but also my precious time..." On the blackboard, he wrote the mathematical formula.

Just as the professor was writing the formula on the blackboard while talking to himself, a beautiful female student named Alisha (who later became Nash's wife) went to the window and opened it. In the movie, Nash looked at Alisha with reproachful eyes: "Miss..." And Alisha said to the workers outside the window, "Excuse me, hi! We have a little problem, close the window, it will be very hot here, open, but it is too noisy. I wonder if I can ask you to repair the other place first, about 45 minutes." A working worker said happily, "No problem!" Then he turned to his friends and said, "Guys, let's have a rest first!" Alisha turned around and looked at Professor Nash happily. Professor Nash also looked at Alisha with a smile, which was like lecturing and commenting on her practice, "You will find that in the variable calculus, there are many solutions to a difficult problem."

And Alisha's answer to the "problem of opening windows" made the original zero-sum game become another result: students did not have to bear the high temperature in the room, the professor could also lecture in a quiet environment, and the result was no longer zero, but + 2. From this we can see that many seemingly irreconcilable contradictions are not necessarily deadlocks. Those seemingly zero-sum games or negative sum games will also turn into positive sum games due to the clever design of participants.

电影《美丽心灵》中有一个情节：

烈日炎炎的一个下午，约翰·纳什教授给二十几个学生上课，教室窗外的楼下有几个工人正施工。机器的响声成了刺耳的噪音，于是纳什走到窗前狠狠地把窗户关上。马上有同学提出意见："教授，请别关窗子，实在太热了！"而纳什教授一脸严肃地回答说："课堂的安静比你舒不舒服重要得多！"然后转过身一边嘴里叨叨着"给你们来上课，在我看来不但耽误了你们的时间，也耽误了我的宝贵时间……"，一边在黑板上写着数学公式。

正当教授一边自语一边在黑板上写公式之际，一位叫阿丽莎的漂亮女同学(这位女同学后来成了纳什的妻子)走到窗边打开了窗子。电影中纳什用责备的眼神看着阿丽莎:"小姐……"而阿丽莎对窗外的工人说道:"打扰一下,嗨!我们有点小小的问题,关上窗户,这里会很热;开着,却又太吵。我想能不能请你们先修别的地方,大约45分钟就好了。"正在干活的工人愉快地说:"没问题!"又回头对自己的伙伴们说:"伙计们,让我们先休息一下吧!"阿丽莎回过头来快活地看着纳什教授,纳什教授也微笑地看着阿丽莎,既像是讲课,又像是在评论她的做法似地对同学们说:"你们会发现在多变性的微积分中,往往一个难题会有多种解答。"

而阿丽莎对"开窗难题"的解答,使得原本的一个零和博弈变成了另外一种结果:同学们既不必忍受室内的高温,教授也可以在安静的环境中讲课,结果不再是零,而成了+2。由此我们可以看到,很多看似无法调和的矛盾,其实并不一定是你死我活的僵局,那些看似零和博弈或者是负和博弈的问题,也会因为参与者的巧妙设计而转为正和博弈。

② From the time series of behavior, game theory is further divided into two categories: static games and dynamic games. Static games refer to the fact that in the game, the participants choose at the same time or not, but the latter actors do not know what specific actions the first actors did; dynamic game means that in the game, the actions of the participants have a sequence, and the later actors can observe the actions selected by the first actors. The "prisoner's dilemma" is a decision made simultaneously and belongs to a static game; while a decision or action such as a chess or card game has a sequence, it belongs to a dynamic game.

从行为的时间序列性,博弈论进一步分为静态博弈、动态博弈两类:静态博弈是指在博弈中,参与人同时选择或虽非同时选择但后行动者并不知道先行动者采取了什么具体的行动;动态博弈是指在博弈中,参与人的行动有先后顺序,且后行动者能够观察到先行动者所选择的行动。"囚徒困境"就是同时决策的,属于静态博弈;而棋牌类游戏等决策或行动有先后次序的,属于动态博弈。

③ According to the participants' understanding of other participants, it is divided into complete information games and incomplete information games. Complete information game means that during the game, each participant has accurate information about the characteristics, strategy space, and revenue function of other participants. Incomplete information game means that if participants do not know enough about the characteristics of other participants, the strategy space and the revenue function, or do not have accurate information about the characteristics, strategy space and the revenue function of all participants, the game played under the circumstances is an incomplete information game.

按照参与人对其他参与人的了解程度分为完全信息博弈和不完全信息博弈。完全信息博弈是指在博弈过程中，每一位参与人对其他参与人的特征、策略空间及收益函数有准确的信息。不完全信息博弈是指如果参与人对其他参与人的特征、策略空间及收益函数信息了解得不够准确或者不是对所有参与人的特征、策略空间及收益函数都有准确的信息，在这种情况下进行的博弈就是不完全信息博弈。

(4) A typical case of game theory

(Representative example in non-zero-sum games of game theory)

—Prisoner's dilemma

博弈论的典型案例(博弈论的非零和博弈中具代表性的例子)——囚徒困境

"Prisoner's dilemma" game model was proposed by Albert Tucker. Assume that two thieves, A and B, jointly committed a crime, privately entered a civil house and were caught by the police. The police put the two in two separate rooms for interrogation. For each suspect, the police's policy was: If both suspects confessed their crimes/admitted their guilt and handed over their stolen goods, the evidence is conclusive, both were found guilty and sentenced to 8 years each; if only one suspect confessed, the other did not confess and denied his guilt/refused to admit his guilt, the denied was sentenced to imprisonment for an additional two years for obstructing public duty (because of the evidence already available), the confessed is commuted/shortened/reduced sentence for 8 years because of his meritorious service and released/set free immediately. If they both denyed guilt/refused to admit guilt, the police cannot convict theft of the two because of insufficient evidence, but they can each be sentenced to one year in prison on the guilty of privately entering a civil house.

Every prisoner faces two choices: confession/honest/frankness or denial/repudiation. However, no matter what the associate chooses, the best choice for each prisoner is to confess, because, suppose the associate denies, if you confess, you will be released/set free, if you deny too, you will be sentenced for 1 year, so confession for you is better than denial; assume the associate confesses, if you confess too, you will be sentenced for 8 years; if you deny, you will be sentenced for 10 years. Compared with the 10-year sentence of denial, confession is better for you.

As a result, both suspects chose to be frank and each is sentenced for 8 years in prison. If both deny and sentence for each is given for 1 year, this result is obviously better for the group of the two.

The following table shows the payment matrix for this game.

A/B	Confess	Deny
Confess	8，8 (lose-lose, negative sum)	0，10 (win-lose, zero sum)
Deny	10，0 (lose-win, zero sum)	1，1 (win-win, positive sum)

"囚徒困境"(prisoner's dilemma)博弈模型是由阿尔伯特·塔克提出的。假设有两个小偷 A 和 B 联合犯事，私闯民宅，被警察抓住。警方将两人分别置于不同的两个房间内进行审讯，对每一个犯罪嫌疑人，警方给出的政策是：如果两个犯罪嫌疑人都坦白了罪行，交出了赃物，于是证据确凿，两人都被判有罪，各被判刑八年；如果只有一个犯罪嫌疑人坦白，另一个人没有坦白而是抵赖，则以妨碍公务罪(因已有证据表明其有罪)再加刑二年，而坦白者有功被减刑八年，立即释放；如果两人都抵赖，则警方因证据不足不能判两人的偷窃罪，但可以私入民宅的罪名将两人各判入狱一年。

每个囚徒都面临两种选择：坦白或抵赖。然而，不管同伙选择什么，每个囚徒的最优选择是坦白，因为，假设同伙抵赖，自己坦白的话被放出去，自己也抵赖的话被判一年，坦白比抵赖好；假设同伙坦白，自己也坦白的话被判八年，自己抵赖则被判十年，比起抵赖被判十年，坦白还是比抵赖好。

结果，两个嫌疑犯都选择坦白，各被判刑八年。如果两人都抵赖，各被判一年，显然这个结果对两人的小群体来说要更好。

下表给出了这个博弈的支付矩阵。

A/B	坦白	抵赖
坦白	8，8(双输，负和)	0，10(赢-输，零和)
抵赖	10，0(输-赢，零和)	1，1(双赢，正和)

On the whole, it is clear that it is most advantageous to deny both, but in reality this has become an impossible result. First, there is a contradiction between the interests of the group and the individual, for the group, 2 prisoners to be sentenced to 1 year is the best result, but for the individual, to confess and impeach the other, and to be set free, is the best result. Secondly, 2 prisoners who can not meet each other can not believe each other. If they deny, they may be sentenced to 10 years' imprisonment, so it is almost impossible to deny. The final result can only be that both of them confess, impeach each other, and each of them is sentenced to 8 years' imprisonment. However, this result is the worst for the group, which is "prisoner's dilemma". It reflects that the best choice of individuals is not the best choice of the group, and explains why it is difficult to maintain cooperation even when cooperation is beneficial to both sides.

从总体上来说，显然两者都抵赖是最为有利的，但在现实中这成为一种不可能的结果。首先，群体利益与个体利益之间存在着矛盾，对于群体而言，两个囚徒各获刑一年是最佳结果，但是对于每个囚徒个体而言，坦白检举对方而被释放才是最佳结果。其次，两个不能相互碰面的囚徒无法相信对方，如果自己抵赖，则可能会获刑十年，所以抵赖几乎是一件不可能的事情。最终的结果只能是两人都坦白，相互检举，最终各获刑八年，而这个结果对于群体来说，却是最差的结果，这就是"囚徒困境"。它反映个人最佳选择并非团体最佳选择，说明为什么甚至在合作对双方都有利时，保持合作也是困难的。

It can be seen that, due to the existence of "prisoner's dilemma", sometimes win-win cooperation is very difficult, but the "Prisoner's dilemma" model also shows us that cooperation may exist.

可见，由于"囚徒困境"的存在，有时合作共赢是很难的，但"囚徒困境"模型也让我们看到了合作的可能是存在的。

If the game is played only once, betraying each other is the most reasonable choice. But when two "Prisoners" play again and again, learn from each other, that is, "repeated prisoner's dilemma", the deduction of the game changes. It is a reasonable choice to exchange the present cooperation with others for the future cooperation. Theoretically, when the number of game repeats is close to infinity, the Nash equilibrium tends to Pareto optimality (the ideal state of resource allocation, the maximization of group interests).

这个游戏如果只玩一次，背叛对方是最合理的选择，但当两个"囚徒"一次又一次地玩，从中互相学习，即"重复的囚徒困境"，游戏的推演就发生了变化。用现在对他人予以的合作来换取今后他人给予的合作是一个合理的选择。理论上，游戏的重复次数接近于无限时，纳什均衡趋向于帕累托最优(资源分配的理想状态，群体利益最大化)。

(5) Nash equilibrium　纳什均衡

Nash equilibrium, also known as non-cooperative game equilibrium, is an important term in game theory, named after John Nash. In a game process, no matter what the other party's strategy choice is, one party will choose a certain strategy, which is called dominant strategy. If the strategic combination of the 2 players constitutes their respective dominant strategy, then the combination is defined as Nash equilibrium. A strategy combination is called Nash equilibrium. When each player's equilibrium strategy is to achieve the maximum of his expected return, at the same time, all other players follow this strategy.

纳什均衡，又称为非合作博弈均衡，是博弈论的一个重要术语，以约翰·纳什命名。在一个博弈过程中，无论对方的策略选择如何，当事人一方都会选择某个确定的策略，则该策略被称作支配性策略。如果两个博弈的当事人的策略组合分别构成各自的支配性策略，那么这个组合就被定义为纳什均衡。一个策略组合被称为纳什均衡，当每个博弈者的平衡策略都是为了达到自己期望收益的最大值，与此同时，其他所有博弈者也遵循这样的策略。

In "prisoner's dilemma" model, the Nash equilibrium is a combination of (confession, confession). Although in general, the combination of (repudiation, repudiation) is beneficial to both people, it is not the solution of the game because it does not constitute the Nash equilibrium. The Nash equilibrium of this game is obviously not the Pareto optimal solution considering the group interests. In terms of group interests, if both participants cooperate and remain silent, both of them will only be sentenced to 1 year, with higher overall interests, and the result is better than that two people betray each other and are respectively sentenced to 8 years. But according to the hypothesis, both of them are rational individuals and pursue their own personal interests only—the equilibrium situation is that both prisoners choose to betray. As a result, both of them have higher sentence than that of cooperation and lower overall interests than those of cooperation. This is where the "dilemma" lies. The model proves that in non-zero-sum game, the Pareto optimality of the group conflicts with the Nash equilibrium, and the Nash equilibrium often occurs.

在"囚徒困境"模型中，纳什均衡是(坦白、坦白)组合，尽管从总体上看, (抵赖、抵赖)组合是对两个人都有益的结果，但由于不构成纳什均衡，所以不是这个博弈的解。这场博弈的纳什均衡，显然不是顾及群体利益的帕累托最优解决方案。就群体利益而言，如果两个参与者都合作，保持沉默，两人都只会被判刑一年，总体利益更高，结果也比两人背叛对方、被各判八年的情况较佳。但根据假设，二人均为理性的个人，且只追求自己个人利益，均衡状况会是两个囚徒都选择背叛，结果二人判决均比合作为高，总体利益较合作为低。这就是"困境"所在。模型证明了：在非零和博弈中，群体的帕累托最优和纳什均衡是相冲突的，而且纳什均衡是较常发生的。

(6)　The difference between Nash's game theory and Von Neumann's game theory
　　　纳什的博弈论与冯·诺依曼的博弈论的区别

Von Neumann's game theory, simply speaking, is to use mathematical methods to guide the 2 parties' competitive or antagonistic behaviors. In this kind of behavior, in order to achieve their own goals (or interests), both sides of the game must consider various possible action plans of the opponent, and try to choose the most favorable or reasonable plan for themselves. In other words, what von Neumann solved was a non-cooperative, purely competitive, zero-sum game with only 2 players.

冯·诺依曼的博弈论，简单地讲就是用数学的方法，指导两方具有竞争或对抗性质的行为。在这类行为中，博弈的双方为了达到各自的目标(或者利益)，必须考虑对手各种可能的行动方案，并力图选取对自己最为有利或最为合理的方案。或者说，冯·诺伊曼所解决的是非合作的、纯竞争型的、只有两人的零和博弈的问题。

Nash developed Von Neumann's game theory, created a completely different "non-cooperative game" theory from Neumann's framework, and then made a clear distinction and definition between "cooperative game" and "non-cooperative game", proved the non-cooperative game and its equilibrium solution, and proved the existence of the equilibrium solution, namely the famous Nash equilibrium. He put forward a non-zero-sum game, that is to say, there is a state in the game where both sides can win-win, and one party's income does not need to be at the expense of another party's loss. In the "prisoner's dilemma" mentioned above, the 2 prisoners cooperate, do not tear down each other, do not report each other, do not confess, and deny, which corresponds to this state. Nash also studied "multiplayer game" and expanded Von Neumann's "two-player game" research.

纳什发展了冯·诺依曼的博弈论，开创了与诺依曼框架路线完全不同的"非合作博弈"理论，进而对"合作博弈"和"非合作博弈"做了明确的区分和定义，证明了非合作博弈及其均衡解，并证明了均衡解的存在性，即著名的纳什均衡。他提出了一种非零和博弈，也就是说在博弈中存在一种状态，双方能够共赢，一个人的所得并不需要以另一个人的损失为代价。比如，上述"囚徒困境"中，两个囚犯合作，不相互拆台，不互相检举，不坦白，都抵赖，所对应的状态。纳什还研究"多人博弈"，拓展了冯·诺依曼的"两人博弈"研究。

3. The application of game theory in negotiation　博弈论在谈判中的应用

(1) Application of complete information static game in international business negotiation
完全信息静态博弈在国际商务谈判中的应用

The prisoner's dilemma is the most frequently cited example in game theory. It illustrates the contradiction between individual rationality and collective rationality. The game between players in the prisoner's dilemma is a complete information static game. In China's foreign economic and trade negotiations, many export companies are like the players in prisoner's dilemma. They only care about their own interests and compete with other Chineses export companies to quote foreign companies at low prices for sales, launch price war against competitors. Knowing the result of doing so will be favourable to none, they are still obsessed.

囚徒困境是博弈论中被引用频率最高的例子,它说明了个人理性与集体理性之间的矛盾,囚徒困境中的局中人之间所进行的博弈属完全信息静态博弈。在我国对外经贸谈判中,很多外贸出口企业好比囚徒困境中的局中人,只顾自身利益,争相对外商从低报价竞销,出口企业之间大打价格战、明知这样做的结果是损人不利己,照样执迷不悟。

(2) Application of complete information dynamic game in international business negotiation

完全信息动态博弈在国际商务谈判中的应用

In the quotation phase of international business negotiations, the negotiating parties usually have to prepare several sets of action plans. After the quoting party completes the quotation, the counter-quoting party can take a targeted strategy from the plan prepared in advance, without blind selection.

在国际商务谈判的报价阶段,谈判双方通常都要准备几套行动方案。先报价的一方完成报价以后,还价的一方就可以从事先准备的方案中采取有针对性的策略,而不会盲目选择。

(3) Application of incomplete information static game in international business negotiation

不完信息静态博弈在国际商务谈判中的应用

In the auction mode of international trade, since each bidder only knows his own estimation of the auction target and does not know that of other bidders, so it is impossible for each bidder to know the earnings of other bidders. The higher bid price in an international auctionis, the greater chance of success of the auctionis, but the smaller the benefitis; the lower bid price is, the smaller chance of success of the auctionis, but once success of the auctionis made, the benefit is the greatest. Balancing opportunities and benefits, the compromise method is the best choice, so the equilibrium result of the auction is that of each player's best solution. It is that his bid price is half of his own estimation of the auction item.

在国际贸易的拍卖交易方式中,由于各竞拍方只知道自己对拍卖标的的估价,并不知道其他竞拍者的估价,所以每个竞拍者也不可能知道其他竞拍者的收益。国际拍卖中出价越高,拍中的机会越大,但得到的利益就越小;而出价越低,拍得的机会就越小,但一旦拍得,利益就最大。采用兼顾拍得机会和获益大小的折中方法,是其最佳选择。所以拍卖的均衡结果是每个博弈方的最佳方案,就是他的报价为自己对拍卖品估价的一半。

In the case of international public tendering and bidding, since the bids are submitted in a sealed manner, each bidder cannot know the bid prices of other bidders before the bid is opened, so the situation is similar to the aforementioned international auction.

在国际公开招标投标的情况下,由于投标书都是密封递交的,每个投标方在开标之前,都无法知道其他投标者的投标价,所以情况与上述国际拍卖相似。

(4) Application of incomplete information dynamic game in international business negotiation

不完全信息动态博弈在国际商务谈判中的应用

To a certain extent, international trade negotiations can be said that buyers and sellers are playing a dynamic game with incomplete information. Under normal circumstances, the buyer lacks understanding of the seller's purchase cost, and it is not easy to get hold of the bottom line of the selling price that the seller is willing to give; If the seller is lack of understanding of the market value of the goods, it is also difficult to figure out the bottom line that the buyer is willing to bid. There is also a situation who plays first will be passive. So, to be on safe side, the buyer and the seller often start from asking all the exorbitant prices and paying back the money on the spot and bargain slowly, so as to obtain more information about each other and strive for more benefits for themselves.

在一定程度上,国际贸易谈判可以说是买卖双方在进行不完全信息动态博弈。通常情况下,买方对卖方的进货成本缺乏了解,也不容易弄清楚卖方售价底线;卖方如对商品的市场价值缺乏了解,同样不容易弄清楚买方出价底线。还存在谁先出牌,谁可能被动的局面。所以,把稳起见,买卖双方经常从漫天要价、就地还钱开始,慢慢讨价还价,从而获得更多的关于对方的信息,以便为自己争取更多的利益。

In the above application examples, the relevant players are basically playing non-cooperative games.

以上应用例子中,相关博弈方基本上都在进行非合作博弈。

Section 3　Theory of Harvard Principled Negotiation

第3节　哈佛原则谈判理论

1. Research history and researchers of theory of Harvard Principled Negotiation
哈佛原则谈判理论的研究史和研究者

Increasing acceptance of win-win concept has brought forth development of totally new negotiation theories. A representative one is collaborative principled negotiation, also commonly known as Harvard Principled Negotiation founded in the late 1970s by Roger Fisher and William Ury, professors from Harvard University. The two professors developed their theoretical system and concept in their works, especially the famous book *Getting to Yes — Negotiating Agreement without Giving in* published by Houghton Mifflin in 1981. The book is regarded by a lot of scholars and negotiators as the "Bible" of negotiations and its viewpoints are widely quoted and practiced. Since its original publication in 1981, *Getting to Yes — Negotiating Agreement without Giving in* has been translated into 18 languages and has sold over 1 million copies in its various editions. The theory became more mature and perfect through the joint discussion and research of Roger Fisher, William Ury, Howard Raiffa and Bruce Patton.

双赢理念的日益深入人心，催生了全新的谈判理论的发展。有代表性的一种是合作原则谈判，又称哈佛原则谈判，由哈佛大学教授罗杰·费希尔(Roger Fisher)和威廉·尤里(William Ury)在20世纪70年代末创立。两位教授在其著作中发展了他们的理论体系和理念，尤其是由霍顿·米夫林出版社于1981年出版的著名的《谈判力——达成共识不妥协》一书，被许多学者和谈判者视为谈判的"圣经"，其观点被广泛引用和运用于实践。自1981年首次出版以来，《谈判力——达成共识不妥协》已被翻译成18种语言，各版销量超过100万册。经罗杰·费希尔、威廉·尤里、霍华德·雷法、布鲁斯·巴顿等人的共同探讨和研究，该理论更加成熟完善。

Harvard Principled Negotiation theory advocates that we should not study the negotiation process from the traditional point of view, nor adopt tricks, nor simply apply the so-called "skills", but treat the negotiator as a cooperator rather than an enemy according to the value and standards of fairness, seek common interests and reach an agreement, while being conducive to harmonious interpersonal relations, which enables both sides of the negotiation to get the desired results and not lose the grace.

哈佛原则谈判理论主张，不从传统的角度去研究谈判过程，不采用诡计，不简单地套用所谓的"技巧"，而是根据价值和公平的标准，把谈判对手视为合作者而不是敌人，在有利于融洽人际关系的同时，谋求共同利益，达成一致，这使谈判双方既能得到希望的结果，又能不失风度。

Harvard Principled Negotiation is a universal guide to the art of negotiating to solve personal and professional disputes, offering concise, step-by-step, and proven strategy for coming to mutually acceptable agreements in every sort of conflict — whether it involves parents and children, neighbors, bosses and employees, customers or corporations, tenants or diplomats. The most typical practical case of the theory is that it played a positive role in guiding US President Carter, Secretary of State Vance, National Security Assistant Brzezinski and others to deal with the Middle East affairs, and promoted Egypt Israel peace talk.

哈佛原则谈判理论是解决个人和职业争端的谈判艺术的通用指南,为在各种冲突中达成双方都能接受的协议提供了简明、循序渐进和行之有效的策略,无论涉及父母和子女、邻居、老板和雇员、客户或公司、租户还是外交官。该理论最典型的实用案例是:对当时美国总统卡特和国务卿万斯、国家安全事务助理布热津斯基等人处理中东事务,促成埃以和谈起到了积极的指导作用。

2. Contents of theory of Harvard Principled Negotiation　哈佛原则谈判理论的内容

The core of collaborative principled negotiation is to reach a solution beneficial to both parties by way of stressing interests and value, but not by way of haggling. The method of collaborative principled negotiation developed at the Harvard Negotiation Project is to decide issues on their merits rather than through a haggling process focused on what each side says it will and will not do. It suggests that you look for mutual gains whenever possible, and that when your interests conflict, you should insist that the result be based on some fair standards, independent of the will of either side. The method of collaborative principled negotiation is hard on the merits, soft on the people. It employs no tricks and no posturing. It shows you how to obtain what you are entitled to and still be decent. It enable you to be fair while protecting you against those who would take advantage of your fairness. When the interests of the two parties are contradictory, an objective criterion should be applied.

合作原则谈判的核心是通过强调利益和价值来达成对双方都有利的解决方案,而不是通过各执己见的讨价还价。哈佛谈判项目(Harvard Negotiation Project)开发的合作原则谈判方法,是根据问题本身的价值来决定问题,而不是通过一个讨价还价的过程,聚焦于双方说要做什么和不要做什么。它建议你在可能的情况下寻求互惠互利,当你们的利益发生冲突时,你应该坚持以一些公平的标准为基础,独立于任何一方的意愿。合作原则谈判的方法对道理原则是强硬的、刚性的,对人则是柔软的、温和的。它不耍花招,不摆架子。它向你展示了如何体面获得你应得的。它使你在公平的同时又能保护你不受那些利用你的公平的人的侵害。当双方的利益矛盾时,应该采用客观的标准。

Collaborative principled negotiation consists of four basic components.

No. 1　People: separate the people from the problem.

No. 2　Interests: focus on interests but not positions.

No. 3　Gaining: invent options for mutual gain.

No. 4　Criteria: introduce objective criteria.

The four components are interrelated with each other and should be applied to the whole course of the negotiation.

合作原则谈判由4个部分组成。

第一，对事不对人。

第二，着眼于利益而非立场。

第三，创造双赢方案。

第四，引入客观评判标准。

这4个组成部分相互联系，应用于整个谈判过程。

3. Application of theory of Harvard Principled Negotiation in negotiation
哈佛原则谈判理论在谈判中的应用

After the establishment of the Harvard Principled Negotiation theory, it quickly became an important guiding principle in negotiations for international dispute settlement and conflict resolution. It is also a universally applicable negotiation method. The four basic contents of the theory are also regarded as four basic principles providing basic guidance for negotiations.

哈佛原则谈判理论创立之后，迅速成为国际上处理纠纷、化解矛盾而进行谈判的重要指导原则，它也是一种普遍适用的谈判方法。该理论的4项基本内容也被视为4项基本原则，为谈判提供了基本指导。

(1) Separate people from problems　把人和问题分开

That is to say, in the negotiation, we should take different attitudes towards the negotiator and the issues discussed, make the relationship between them clear, adopt different ways to treat them, be friendly to people and adhere to the principle of things.

即，在谈判中，对谈判对手和所讨论的问题持不同的态度，明确两者之间的关系，采用不同的方式对待，对人友好，对事坚持原则。

Specific measures can be taken:

具体可采取：

First, state more, listen more and blame less. In the negotiation, the two sides may have differences, emotional confrontation, loss of reason, mutual accusation or even abuse because of different positions and interest demands, which will not help the solution of the problem. Contradiction is inevitable. We should be controlled as much as possible, keep calm and think rationally, distinguish the problem expounded by the opposite side from the other side, focus on the problem itself, and do not have to be excessively harsh on the other party. Objectively state, listen to and treat problems; understand the other's emotions and cherish each other's feelings.

第一，多阐述、聆听问题，少责备对手。谈判中，双方可能因为不同的立场和利益诉求，产生分歧，情绪对抗，失去理智，相互指责甚至谩骂，这样根本无助于问题的解决。矛盾在所难免，应尽量控制情绪，保持冷静，理性思考，把对方阐述的问题和对方本人区分开，聚焦于问题本身，而不必过分苛责对方。客观陈述、聆听和看待问题，理解对方的情绪，珍惜彼此的感情。

Second, we should increase the participation of both sides and face the problems together. Encourage the other party to actively participate in solving problems, discuss and draft solutions.

第二，提高双方的参与度，共同面对所出现的问题。激励对方积极参与到解决问题当中去，共同讨论、起草问题的解决方案。

Third, take care of each other's face. The other side's position may be behind the face which can not be lost, rather than our proposal which is not difficult to be accepted. We should be good at understanding and protecting the other side's mentality, avoid hurting the other side's feelings, and we can consider making some changes in language to achieve the effect.

第三，照顾对方的面子。对方所坚持的立场背后有可能是丢不起的面子，而非难以接受的我方的提议。应善于理解和保护对方的这种心态，避免伤害对方的感情，可考虑言语上做些改变，以达到效果。

(2) Focus on interests but not positions 聚焦于利益而非立场

That is to say, in negotiations, we should focus on the interests of both sides, seek common interests and coordinate conflicts, rather than sticking to our own views and sticking to our positions.

即，在谈判中，应把注意力集中在双方的利益诉求上，寻求共同利益，协调冲突，而非固执己见，死守立场。

Specific measures can be taken:
具体可采取：

First, grasp their own interests. Through in-depth and effective communication, accurately grasp the actual needs of the other party, clearly state your wishes and aspirations, and examine the different interests of both parties from different perspectives.

第一，把握各自的利益诉求。通过有深入有效的沟通，准确掌握对方的实际需求，清晰阐述你自己的意愿和愿望，从不同的角度审视双方的不同利益。

Second, find the interests behind the position. Put yourself in the other side's position, and find out the motivation and rationality of the other side's concerns and interest demands, as well as the differences and intersections between the other side's interest demands and your interest demands.

第二，发现立场背后的利益。换位思考，发现对方的关切和利益诉求的动因、合理性，以及对方的利益诉求跟你方利益诉求的不同点和交集点。

Third, seek common interests of both sides. On the basis of the above two measures, carefully analyze and identify the common interests of both sides.

第三，谋求双方的共同利益。在以上两项措施的基础上，认真细致地分析辨别双方的共同利益所在。

(3) Invent options for mutual gain 创造双赢的方案

That is to say, in the negotiation, both sides of the negotiation can achieve the expected goals, gain in psychology and be satisfied. Only when both sides are the winners of the negotiation, can they respectively gain interests in the subsequent cooperation and make the cooperation sustainable. Therefore, the key to negotiation is how to creatively seek and formulate a win-win solution acceptable to both sides.

即，在谈判中，使谈判双方都达到预期的目标，在心理上都有所收获，都满意。只有双方都是赢家的谈判，才会在随后的合作中各自取得利益，才能使合作持续下去。所以，谈判的关键是如何创造性地寻求和制订双方都能接受的双赢的解决方案。

Specific measures can be taken:

具体可采取：

First, we should give full play to our imagination and effectively expand the scope of choices and overall interests of solutions.

第一，充分发挥想象力，有效扩大解决方案的选择范围和总体利益。

Second, put forward the effective alternative solutions.

第二，提出有效解决问题的替代方案。

Third, separate the creation of the plan from the judgment of the plan, create as many plans as possible, and then make decisions. Do not jump to conclusions about the plan.

第三，将方案的创造与对方案的判断分开，尽可能多地创造方案，然后再决策，不要过早地对方案下结论。

Fourth, seek solutions that are easy for the other party to make decisions.

第四，寻求容易让对方作决定的方案。

(4) Introduce objective criteria 引入客观评判标准

That is to say, in the negotiation, when there is a very difficult conflict between the two sides, the two sides are in constant dispute and do not give in to each other, an objective, reasonable and feasible standard independent of the will of the two sides, recognized by the society shall be used.

即，在谈判中，遇到非常棘手、双方争执不下、互不让步的冲突问题时，使用独立于双方意志之外、社会公认、合乎情理、切实可行的客观标准。

Specific measures can be taken:

具体可采取：

First, establish objective standards. In international business negotiation, WTO rules, rules formulated by other international organizations, international trade practices, international economic laws, internationally recognized evaluation methods and commonly followed views on value can all become objective standards of international business negotiation.

第一，确立客观标准。国际商务谈判中，世界贸易组织规则、其他国际组织制定的规则、国际贸易惯例、国际经济法、国际公认的评估评价方式、普遍遵循的价值观念等都可以成为国际商务谈判的客观标准。

Second, we should build a fair and just step of interest division. For example, in the international investment negotiation, if the investors of the joint venture hold the same proportion of capital contribution, the two investors can determine through consultation and appoint the general manager by the way of term rotation.

第二，构建公平公正的利益分割步骤。比如，国际投资谈判中，如果合资企业的出资人持相同的出资比例，两位出资人可磋商确定，采用任期轮换的方式委派总经理。

Third, provide a reasonable basis for the adoption of objective standards. One party may have objections to the objective standards proposed by the other party. At this time, it is necessary to provide a reasonable basis for the adoption of the standards to win the recognition and acceptance of the other party, and ensure the smooth progress of negotiations.

第三，为客观标准的采用提供合理依据。一方可能对另一方提出的客观标准有异议，这时候需要为该标准的采用提供合理的依据，赢得对方的认可和接受，保证谈判的顺利进行。

Fourth, you should not succumb to pressure, but follow objective standards. When the other party puts pressure on the other party by means of the company's operating principles and ultimatums, you should dare to adhere to objective standards.

第四，不屈从于压力，而遵从客观标准。在对方以公司经营原则、最后通牒等方式施压时，要敢于坚持客观标准。

Terminology　本章术语

1. hierarchy of needs　需求层次
2. physiological needs　生理的需要
3. safety needs　安全的需要
4. love and belonging needs　爱和归属的需要
5. respect needs　尊重的需要
6. knowledge needs　求知的需要
7. aesthetic needs　审美的需要
8. self-actualization needs　自我实现的需要
9. game theory　博弈论
10. in-game player　局中人
11. payment function　支付函数
12. equilibrium　均衡
13. cooperative games and non-cooperative game　合作博弈与非合作博弈
14. zero-sum games and non-zero-sum games　零和博弈与非零和博弈
15. prisoner's dilemma　囚徒困境
16. static games and dynamic games　静态博弈与动态博弈
17. complete information games and incomplete information games　完全信息博弈与不完全信息博弈
18. payment matrix　支付矩阵
19. Nash equilibrium　纳什均衡
20. Harvard Principled Negotiation　哈佛原则谈判
21. collaborative principled negotiation　合作原则谈判

Exercises　本章练习

1. What does hierarchy of needs refer according to Maslow's theory?
   根据马斯洛的理论，需求层次指的是什么？
2. What are zero-sum game and non-zero game?
   什么是零和博弈与非零和博弈？

3. Have a try to describe the typical case of game theory —"prisoner's dilemma".
尝试描述博弈论的典型案例——"囚徒困境"。

4. How do you see so-called "dilemma" of prisoners in the case?
你如何看待本案中囚犯的所谓"困境"？

5. What are contributions of Nash to game theory comparing with Von Neumann?
与冯·诺伊曼相比，纳什对博弈论有何贡献？

6. Why is Harvard Principled Negotiation theory not only a negotiation theory, but also a practical negotiation method?
为什么说哈佛原则谈判理论不仅仅是谈判理论，更是实用的谈判方法？

Answers for Reference　参考答案

1. In the seven-level version of Maslow's hierarchy of needs, physiological needs, saefty needs, love and belonging (social) needs, respect needs, knowledge needs, aesthetic needs, and self-actualization needs, are arranged from low to high according to the importance in a pyramid shape,the bottom of the pyramid is the lowest level of needs, and the top of the pyramid is the highest level of needs,before the low level needs are met, the high level needs cannot be inspiring.

在 7 个层次马斯洛的需求层次理论中，生理的需要、安全的需要、爱与归属(社交)的需要、尊重的需要、求知的需要、审美的需要和自我实现的需要，按各自的重要性依次从低到高排列，呈金字塔状，金字塔底部是最低层次的需要，金字塔顶部是最高层次的需要，在低层次的需要得到满足之前，高层次的需要不能起到激励人的作用。

2. Zero-sum game is a non-cooperative game, which refers to the fact that the income of one party necessarily means the loss of the other party under strict competition. The sum of the income and loss of all parties in the game is always "zero", and there is no possibility of cooperation between the 2 parties. It can also be said that one's own happiness is based on the pain of the other, and the size of the two is exactly the same, so both sides try their best to achieve "I win you lose" and "damage others for self-interest".

零和博弈，属非合作博弈，指在严格竞争下，一方的收益必然意味着另一方的博弈，博弈各方的收益和损失相加总和永远为"零"，双方不存在合作的可能。也可以说，自己的幸福是建立在他人的痛苦之上的，二者的大小完全相等，因而双方都想尽一切办法实现"我赢你输""损人利己"。

Non-zero-sum game refers to the fact that the parties in the game are no longer the relationship of "I win you lose". What one party gains does not necessarily mean what the other party loses, one's own happiness may not be based on the pain of the other, that is, "self-interest does not harm others", which implies that participants may have some kind of common interests, there is a possibility of cooperation, and they can obtain "win-win" or "multi-win" results. The "prisoner's dilemma" below is a representative model of non-zero-sum game, because there is at least one possible cooperation state among the four states of the two players in the model. Non-zero-sum game is divided into positive sum game and negative sum game according to whether "sum" is positive or negative.

非零和博弈，指博弈中各方不再是"我赢你输"的关系，一方所得并不一定意味着另一方所失，自己的幸福未必建立在他人的痛苦之上，即"利己不损人"，其中蕴含着参与者可能存在某种共同的利益，有合作的可能，能够获得"双赢""多赢"的结果。"囚徒困境"是非零和博弈的代表模型，因为模型中博弈双方的四种状态中至少存在一种双方可能合作的状态。非零和博弈根据"和"为正数还是负数，分为正和博弈和负和博弈。

3. "Prisoner's dilemma" game model was proposed by Albert Tucker. Assume that two thieves, A and B, jointly committed a crime, privately entered a civil house and were caught by the police. The police put the two in two separate rooms for interrogation. For each suspect, the police's policy was: If both suspects confessed their crimes/admitted their guilt and handed over their stolen goods, the evidence is conclusive, both were found guilty and sentenced to 8 years each; if only one suspect confessed, the other did not confess and denied his guilt/refused to admit his guilt, the denied was sentenced to imprisonment for an additional two years for obstructing public duty (because of the evidence already available), the confessed is commuted/shortened/reduced sentence for 8 years because of his meritorious service and released/set free immediately; If they both denied guilt/refused to admit guilt, the police cannot convict theft of the two because of insufficient evidence, but they can each be sentenced to 1 year in prison on the guilty of privately entering a civil house.

Every prisoner faces 2 choices: confession/honest/frankness or denial/repudiation. However, no matter what the associate chooses, the best choice for each prisoner is to confess, because, suppose the associate denies, if you confess, you will be released/set free, if you deny too, you will be sentenced for 1 year, so confession for you is better than denial; assume the associate confesses, if you confess too, you will be sentenced for 8 years; if you deny, you will be sentenced for 10 years, compared with the 10-year sentence of denial, confession is better for you.

As a result, both suspects chose to be frank and each is sentenced for 8 years in prison. If both deny and sentence for each is given for 1 year, this result is obviously better for the group of the two.

The following table shows the payment matrix for this game.

A/B	Confess	Deny
Confess	8，8 (lose-lose,negative sum)	0，10 (win-lose,zero sum)
Deny	10，0 (lose-win,zero sum)	1，1 (win-win,positive sum)

"囚徒困境"(prisoner's dilemma)博弈模型是由阿尔伯特·塔克提出的。假设有两个小偷A和B联合犯事，被警察抓住。警方将两人分别置于不同的两个房间内进行审讯，对每一个犯罪嫌疑人，警方给出的政策是：如果两个犯罪嫌疑人都坦白了罪行，交出了赃物，于是证据确凿，两人都被判有罪，各被判刑八年；如果只有一个犯罪嫌疑人坦白，另一个人没有坦白而是抵赖，则以妨碍公务罪(因已有证据表明其有罪)再加刑二年，而坦白者有功被减刑八年，立即释放；如果两人都抵赖，则警方因证据不足不能判两人的偷窃罪，但可以私入民宅的罪名将两人各判入狱一年。

每个囚徒都面临两种选择：坦白或抵赖。然而，不管同伙选择什么，每个囚徒的最优选择是坦白，因为，假设同伙抵赖，自己坦白的话放出去，自己也抵赖的话判一年，坦白比抵赖好；假设同伙坦白，自己也坦白的话判八年，自己抵赖则判十年，比起抵赖判十年，坦白还是比抵赖好。

结果，两个嫌疑犯都选择坦白，各判刑八年。如果两人都抵赖，各判一年，显然这个结果对两人的小群体来说要更好。

这个博弈的支付矩阵。

A/B	坦白	抵赖
坦白	8，8(双输，负和)	0，10(赢-输，零和)
抵赖	10，0(输-赢，零和)	1，1(双 赢，正和)

4.

(1) Every prisoner faces 2 choices: confession or denial, this is "dilemma".
每个囚犯都面临两种选择：坦白或否认，这就是"两难"。

(2) In terms of group interests, if both participants cooperate and remain silent, both of

them will only be sentenced to 1 year, with higher overall interests, and the result is better than that two people betray each other and are respectively sentenced to 8 years. But according to the hypothesis, both of them are rational individuals and pursue their own personal interests only,the equilibrium situation is that both prisoners choose to betray,as a result, both of them have higher sentence than that of cooperation and lower overall interests than those of cooperation. This is where the "dilemma" lies.

就群体利益而言，如果两个参与者都合作，保持沉默，两人都只会被判刑一年，总体利益更高，结果也比两人背叛对方、被各判八年的情况较佳。但根据假设，二人均为理性的个人，且只追求自己个人利益，均衡状况会是两个囚徒都选择背叛，结果二人判决均比合作为高，总体利益较合作为低。这就是"困境"所在。

5. Nash developed Von Neumann's game theory, created a completely different "non-cooperative game" theory from Neumann's framework, and then made a clear distinction and definition between "cooperative game" and "non-cooperative game", proved the non-cooperative game and its equilibrium solution, and proved the existence of the equilibrium solution, namely the famous Nash equilibrium. He put forward a non-zero sum game, that is to say, there is a state in the game where both sides can win-win, and one party's income does not need to be at the expense of another party's loss. In the "prisoner's dilemma", the 2 prisoners cooperate, do not tear down each other, do not report each other, do not confess, and deny, which corresponds to this state. Nash also studied "multiplayer game"and expanded Von Neumann's "two player game" research.

纳什发展了冯·诺依曼的博弈论，开创了与诺依曼框架路线完全不同的"非合作博弈"理论，进而对"合作博弈"和"非合作博弈"做了明确的区分和定义，证明了非合作博弈及其均衡解，并证明了均衡解的存在性，即著名的纳什均衡。他提出了一种非零和博弈，也就是说在博弈中存在一种状态，双方能够共赢，一个人的所得并不需要以另一个人的损失为代价。比如，"囚徒困境"中，两个囚犯合作，不相互拆台，不互相检举，不坦白，都抵赖，所对应的状态。纳什还研究"多人博弈"，拓展了冯·诺依曼的"两人博弈"研究。

6. After the establishment of the Harvard Principled Negotiation theory, it quickly became an important guiding principle in negotiations for international dispute settlement and conflict resolution. It is also a universally applicable negotiation method. The four basic contents of the theory provide basic guidance for negotiations.It is not only theoretical but also practical.

哈佛原则谈判理论创立之后，迅速成为国际上处理纠纷、化解矛盾而进行谈判的重要指导原则，它也是一种普遍适用的谈判方法，该理论的四项基本内容为谈判提供了基本指导，它不仅是理论，而且还实用。

Chapter 4　International Business Negotiation Concept

第 4 章　国际商务谈判理念

Section 1　Chinese Negotiators' Idea —"Negotiation is an Art of Compromise between the Two Sides"

第 1 节　中国谈判者的"谈判是双方相互妥协的艺术"理念

Long Yongtu, the chief negotiator of China's re-entry into GATT and accession to WTO and former vice minister of the Ministry of Foreign Trade and Economic Cooperation of China; former director and secretary general of Boao Forum for Asia, former dean of Fudan University's school of international relations and public affairs and dean of Fudan University's institute of international issues, current co-chairman of the Global CEO Conference, chairman of Center for China and Globalization (CCG) and advisor of China Service Trade Association. At the end of 2003, he won the title of "CCTV2003 Economic Person"; at the end of 2011, he won the title of "CCTV2011 Economic Person". In July 2006, he received the honorary doctor's degree in economics from London School of Economics.

龙永图，中国复关及入世谈判的首席谈判代表，原中国外经贸部副部长；原博鳌亚洲论坛理事、秘书长；曾任复旦大学国际关系与公共事务学院院长、复旦大学国际问题研究院院长；现任全球 CEO 发展大会联合主席、中国与全球化智库(CCG)主席、中国服务贸易协会顾问。2003 年底获"CCTV2003 年度经济人物"称号；2011 年年底获"CCTV2011 年度经济人物"称号。2006 年 7 月，获英国伦敦政治经济学院名誉经济学博士学位。

In January 1992, he took the post of director of the international department of the Ministry of Foreign Trade and Economic Cooperation and began to participate in negotiations on China's re-entry into GATT. From February 1997 to March 2002, as the chief negotiator, he led and finally successfully concluded 15-year long negotiations on China's accession to WTO. After retiring as the chief negotiator of China's accession to the WTO, Long Yongtu shared his understanding of the negotiation in many seminars and speeches:

1992年1月出任外经贸部国际司司长，开始参加中国的复关谈判。1997年2月至2002年3月，作为首席谈判代表，在第一线领导并最终成功结束了长达十五年的中国加入世贸组织的谈判。卸任中国入世首席谈判代表之后，龙永图多次在的研讨会上和演讲时分享他对谈判的理解：

"The whole negotiation, especially the economic and trade negotiation, is a process of mutual concessions and consensus, a means of reaching an agreement, and an art of compromise. We should not only uphold our own interests, but also take into account the interests of the other party."

"整个谈判特别是经贸谈判，大都是一个互相让步、达成共识的过程，是达成协议的一个手段，是一种妥协的艺术，既要坚持自己的利益，也要顾及对方的利益。"

"Conversion thinking helps a lot in negotiating an agreement, change your mind, it's not that you are all right. If you only think about your own interests, it's impossible."

"换位思考对谈成协议有很大的帮助，换一种头脑，不是自己什么都对，如果你一门心思只想自己的利益，那是不可能的。"

"The easiest thing in negotiation is toughness. First of all, toughness does not need to study the suggestions and plans of the negotiating opponents, nor does it need to make very detailed preparations for the negotiation on your own. Because when you arrive at the negotiating room, you shoot the table, stare at your eyes, and keep tough to the end, this is the most worry-free thing. Secondly, if the negotiating opponent is a foreigner, especially a foreigner that everyone hates, then the tougher you are in the negotiation, the more you will score in domestic politics. Unfortunately, such a toughness will not achieve any goal of negotiation."

"谈判最容易的就是强硬。首先，强硬不需要研究谈判对手的建议、方案，也不需要在自己这方面为谈判做非常详尽的准备。因为到了会场上你拍桌子、瞪眼睛，一味强硬就完了，这是最省心的事情。其次，如果谈判对手是外国人，特别是大家比较恨的外国人，那么在谈判中你越强硬在国内政治上得分就越多。可惜，这样的强硬达不到任何谈判目的。"

"Actually, there are not so many harsh rhetorical arguments, negotiations are more heavy. Negotiations often use difficult and patient methods to find consensus and seek breakthroughs in differences."

"实际上，谈判没那么多唇枪舌剑，谈判更多的是很沉重的东西。谈判往往是用很艰难的、很耐心的方法去寻求共识，寻求对于分歧的突破。"

"The art of negotiation is the art of compromise, and compromise does not mean weakness."

"谈判的艺术就是妥协的艺术，而妥协并不就是意味着软弱。"

"The whole process of negotiation is the process of seeking compromise, which is to seek the balance of interests of both sides. In this process, it needs a lot of hard and meticulous work, rather than just being tough."

"谈判的整个过程就是寻求妥协的过程，是要寻求双方利益平衡点。在这当中，需要很多艰苦细致的工作，而不是一味强硬就可以的。"

"It's necessary to negotiate to join WTO, and the main negotiation object (pay attention to the object rather than the opponent) is the United States. 'Doing ideological work' with the US: to let China join the WTO is not only good for China, but also for the world and the US, that is to say, win-win and multi-win. The US feels that this is good for it, becomes active in the negotiation, and also makes a lot of concessions."

"加入世贸少不了谈判，而主要的谈判对象(注意是对象而非对手)非美国莫属。跟老美做'思想工作'：让中国加入WTO，不仅对中国有好处，对世界也有好处，对美国更有好处，也就是双赢、多赢，美国感觉这事对它有好处，谈判就积极了，也让了很多步。"

"Negotiation is the art of compromise between both sides. Any unilateral win is not called negotiation. It is conquest, or war."

"谈判是双方妥协的艺术，任何单方面的赢都不叫谈判，那是征服，或者说是战争。"

"No unilateral compromise can achieve a compromise balance."

"任何单方面的妥协都不可能实现一种妥协的平衡点。"

"To make the other side and you reach a certain compromise, we need to be rational and force both sides to compromise. It's very simple to start with ourselves. We should dare to compromise and be willing to compromise. The result of compromise is that both sides will benefit."

"使对方和你都做到一定的妥协，需要理性，逼迫双方妥协，很简单，从自己做起。要敢于妥协、甘于妥协，妥协的结果是双方都得到好处。"

Long Yongtu has been engaged in negotiation practice for a long time. He is a top-level negotiation expert who has made outstanding contributions to China's accession to the WTO. He is also a scholar who studies diplomatic negotiation, foreign trade negotiation, international relations and international issues. We regard his understanding of negotiation as an important negotiation concept of Chinese negotiators.

龙永图长期从事谈判实践，是中国加入 WTO 有突出贡献的顶级谈判专家，又是研究外交谈判和外经贸谈判以及国际关系和国际问题的学者，我们把他对谈判的理解，视为中国谈判者的重要谈判理念。

The formation of negotiation concept of Chinese business negotiators originates from profound Chinese cultural background, traditional business ethics and business philosophy. For a long time, Chinese businessmen have advocated "kindness is like water", "virtue carries things", "sea embraces all rivers, tolerance is great", "all embracing" and "harmony is precious". Fan Li, Zi Gong and Bai Gui in ancient times, Shanxi merchants, Anhui merchants and Chaoshan merchants in recent times, Ren Zhengfei and Li Ka-shing in modern times are all examples of that.

中国商务谈判者谈判理念的形成，源自深厚的中国文化背景、传统商业道德的熏陶和经营哲学思想的积淀。长期以来，中国商人崇尚"上善若水""厚德载物""海纳百川，有容乃大""兼容并包""和为贵"。古代的范蠡、子贡、白圭，近代的晋商、徽商、潮商等著名商帮，当代的任正非、李嘉诚等都是这方面的典范。

In ancient times

古代

"The ancestor of Taoistic merchants", an early Chinese business theorist, Fan Li, was a well-known figure during the Spring and Autumn period and the Warring States period. He assisted Gou Jian to completely defeat and revenge the humiliation upon Fuchai, the king of Wu, and recovered their country, and then helped Gou Jian to dominate the Central Plains northward. After he succeeded and became famous, he rapidly retreated farming and doing business, he created the glory of life, and made outstanding contributions to historical development.

One of Fan Li's ways of doing business is to do business in good faith without seeking huge profits. Fan Li is not only good at seizing opportunities in business, but also does not pursue huge profits. According to "Historical Records", Fan Li "Turn things when it is at right time, and pursue the interests of one tenth." This is a very humanized proposition, which is in line with the principle of "integrity" and "righteousness" in Chinese traditional business thoughts, moreover, small profits and large sales, not seeking huge profits, long-term flow of small water, accumulating over time, will become rich. This is one of the secrets of Fan Li's success.

"道商始祖"，中国早期商业理论家，范蠡，是春秋战国之际著名的人物，他协助勾践彻底击败吴王夫差而雪耻复国，继而助勾践北向称霸中原。功成名就之后，急流勇退，务农经商,创造了人生的辉煌,为历史发展作出了杰出的贡献。

范蠡经商之道之一是诚信经商,不求暴利。范蠡经商不仅善于抓住时机,并且不追求暴利。《史记》记载,范蠡"侯时转物,逐十一之利",这是非常人性化的主张,符合中国传统思想中经商求"诚信"、求"义"的原则,薄利多销,不求暴利,细水长流,日积月累,必成大富。这是范蠡成功的秘诀之一。

"The ancestor of Confucian merchants", Zigong, compared with other disciples of Confucius, the most special ponit is that Zigong was good at business and had outstanding talent in financial management and business. He was once in business between two states of Cao and Lu. He became the richest man among Confucius' disciples. Zigong's success in business did not depend on his own interests at the expense of others, but on his basic belief in Confucianism. In his self-cultivation of personality, he adhered to the moral cultivation principle of "gentle, good, respectful, thrifty, and humble", strived to be "poor without flattery, rich without arrogance", that is, even if he had money, he was self-effacing, not arrogant, and not ostentatious; when dealing with the relationship between himself and others, between himself and the society, he adhered to the loyalty and forgiveness principle of "I don't want be driven by others, I don't want to drive others", it was to deal with the relationship between people and himself in a compassionate and empathic way, to achieve mutual benefit and win-win results, and to give generously back to the society with the fraternity of "giving to the people and being able to help the people" (widely helping and relieving the people). Zigong's position of integrity, public interest and social responsibility was objectively conducive to the cohesion of people's minds, the coordination of relations, the establishment of a good image, the realization of sustainable development of commercial activities, and the maintenance of his own long-term interests.

"儒商鼻祖",子贡,与孔子其他弟子相比,最特殊的地方,是子贡善于经商之道,在理财经商方面具有卓越的天赋。他曾经经商于曹、鲁两国之间,富致千金,成为孔子弟子中的首富。子贡经商获得成功,不靠损人利己,而是秉持儒家基本信念。他在自我人格修养中坚持"温、良、恭、俭、让"(温和、良善、恭敬、节俭、谦让)的道德修养原则,努力做到"贫而无谄,富而无骄",也就是即使有钱,也不张扬、不骄横、不摆谱;在处理自身与他人、与社会的关系时,坚持"我不欲人之加诸我也,吾亦无欲加诸人"的忠恕之道,以同情的、换位思考的方式处理人我关系,实现互惠共赢,并以"博施于民而能济众"(广泛地帮助救济民众)的博爱胸怀,慷慨回馈社会。子贡这种坚持诚信、公心和社会责任的立场,客观上有利于凝聚人心、协调关系、树立良好形象,有利于实现商业活动的可持续发展,维持自身的长远利益。

"Saint Merchant", a great businessman in the Warring States period, Bai Gui, once said, "Pick up what others discard and give what others need", it means that "most of the things that others want to sell will be purchased by me, and most of the things that others want to buy and hoard will be sold to them by me". How to seize the opportunity is an important factor in the success of business, but if you want to do business for a long time, whether in ancient or modern times, there is one common golden rule: pay attention to integrity, guard against arrogance and greed. In his business activities, Bai Gui often looked at the overall situation of the business from the big point of view, never coveted small profits in front of his eyes in specific business operations, and never made profits through fraud by means of unfair competition such as intrigue. The way of business is that of man, doing business is being a man, which is the biggest secret of business success.

"商圣",战国时期大商人,白圭,曾说"人弃我取,人取我予",意思是"别人大都要抛售的东西就收购过来,而别人大都要收购囤积的东西就卖给他们"。如何把握时机,是商业成功的重要因素,但是要想把生意做得长久,无论是古代还是现代,都有一个共同的黄金法则:注重诚信,戒骄戒贪。白圭经商活动中常从大处着眼,通观生意全局,在具体的买卖经营上从不贪图眼前小利,也从不靠阴谋诡计等不正当竞争手段进行欺诈牟利。商道即人道,经商也就是做人,这才是经商成功的最大秘籍。

In recent times

近代

During the Ming and Qing dynasties, Shanxi merchants, the largest business group in China, were "the best of scholars, then officials" and handled the business of "goods delivered everywhere, exchange everywhere", whose business model is the most advanced, modern business methods, such as joint-stock system and capital operation, have sprouted in them. Anhui merchants were as famous as Shanxi merchants, and as a powerful force in the business community of China in the same era. Anhui merchants were solid, smart and "unique Confucian style", adhering to the principle of "being a man the first and doing business the second". They embodied the charm of Confucian ideal personality everywhere. Chaoshan merchants, known as "Oriental Jew", were full of adventure spirit, unique marine characteristics, strong centripetal force and international influence.

As the three famous commercial gangs in recent times of China, they had their own characteristics, but what they had in common was that they abided by the traditional Chinese commercial way, and they were honest and trustworthy, no cheating, made small profits and large sales, knew very well "still water runs long", and balanced the giving and the gaining.

明清时国内最大的商帮，晋商，"学而优则仕贾"，"货通天下、汇通天下"，经营模式最先进，股份制、资本运作等现代经营方式，已经在他们身上萌芽；与晋商齐名，作为同时代中国商界中一支劲旅的徽商，务实、精明且"儒风独茂"，恪守"做人第一，经商第二"的准则，处处体现着儒家理想人格的魅力；潮商，享有"东方犹太人"称誉，富于冒险精神，独具海洋特质，向心力强，具有国际性影响。

作为近代中国三大著名商帮，他们虽各领风骚，特色彰显，但共同之处是恪守中华传统商道，讲求诚实信用、童叟无欺、细水长流、薄利多销、有舍才有得。

In modern times

当代

Ren Zhengfei's "gray scale"

On May 16, 2019, the U.S. listed Huawei in the "entity list" and prohibited American enterprises from selling related technologies and products to Huawei, aiming to cut off Huawei's supply chain and make Huawei "no goods to sell". About a third of Huawei's core suppliers are US companies. Huawei have been buying chips from Qualcomm and Broadcom, wireless tower components from Intel, software from Oracle, and from small technology companies all over the United States. However, the United States has also announced a 90-day temporary general license to allow US companies not to cut off Huawei's supply during this period. In fact, adding Huawei to the entity list will cause more damage to the United States than Huawei, which will not only cause huge economic losses to American companies cooperating with Huawei, but also destroy the cooperation and mutual trust of global supply chain. Ren Zhengfei, the founder and CEO of Huawei, interviewed by German TV 1 on May 23, 2019, said "Huawei can survive independently even without American supply, but Huawei always respects American companies. For example, we have parts that can replace those parts of Qualcomm, but 50% of them continue to be bought from Qualcomm, we do not fully use our devices." Ren Zhengfei said that this was his decision. It was necessary to use American devices, not to enjoy all interests alone. "We will always embrace American companies, after the historical setbacks, our friendship with American companies will be tested even more. Only when we cooperate, we can push human civilization to new progress." Ren Zhengfei expressed that he believed in grayscale and compromise in philosophy, a compromise between "white" and "black" was "gray".

任正非的"灰度"

2019年5月16日,美国将华为列入"实体清单"(entity list),禁止美企向华为出售相关技术和产品,旨在切断华为供应链,令华为"无货可卖"。华为有约三分之一的核心供应商为美企,一直从美企高通和博通购买芯片,从英特尔购买无线发射塔部件,从甲骨文购买软件,同时还从美国各地的小型技术公司采购。但是,美国也宣布给予90天的临时通用许可证,在此期间,允许美企不对华为断供。实际上将华为加入实体清单,对美国的损害比对华为的损害更大,不仅会对与华为合作的美国公司造成巨大经济损失,也破坏了全球供应链的合作和互信。华为创始人、CEO,任正非,2019年5月23日,接受德国电视一台采访表示:"即使没有美国供应,华为也可以独立生存,但华为永远对美国公司充满敬仰。比如,我们有可以代替高通的零部件,但是50%继续购买高通的,并没有完全使用我们的器件。"任正非称,这是他定下的,必须要使用美国器件,不能自己一个人独吞利益。"我们永远都会拥抱美国公司,历史的挫折过去以后,会更加考验我们和美国公司的友谊。只有合作起来,才会把人类文明推向新的进步。"任正非表示,自己在哲学上信奉灰度,信奉妥协,"白"与"黑"之间有一个妥协是灰度。

Li Ka Shing's "create self, realize no self"

"What is the secret of making money that your father Li Ka Shing has taught you?" The reporter asked Richard Li. "My father never told me how to make money, only taught me some principles of life and doing things" Li said. The reporter was shocked and didn't believe it. Richard Li added, "My father told me that if you cooperate with others, if it is reasonable you get 70% of the whole of benefits, 80% can also be, we, family of Li, only need to get 60%." That is to say, if you cooperate with others, it's reasonable for you to take 70% of the whole of benefits, even if taking 80% is OK, but we should learn to be humble, we only take 60%, because in this way everyone is willing to cooperate with you." It is "ordinary people pursue profits only, supperman shares profits".

李嘉诚的"创造自我、实现无我"

记者问李泽楷:"你父亲李嘉诚究竟教会了你怎样的赚钱秘诀?"李泽楷说:"父亲从没告诉我赚钱的方法,只教了我一些做人处事的道理。"记者大惊,不信。李泽楷又说:"父亲叮嘱过,你和别人合作,假如你拿七分合理,八分也可以,我们李家只要拿六分就可以了。"也就是说,你跟别人合作,你拿他七分是合理的,你哪怕拿他八分的回报也是可以的,但是我们要学会谦让,我们只拿六分,因为这样谁都愿意跟你合作。这就是"只懂追逐利润,是常人所为;更懂分享利润,是'超人'所作"。

Section 2　Concept of "Win-Win Negotiation" in Western Academic Circle and Business Word

第 2 节　西方学界业界的"谈判双赢"理念

In the second half of the 20th century, greater benefits from free flow of people, goods, services and capital caused the rapid development of economic globalization and integration, having mingled all countries and areas into one interdependent and interrelated body. Resolving political disputes and conflicts especially economic disputes and conflicts by peaceful means based on equality and mutual benefit has prevailed in international affairs and also domestic affairs since countries started to view each other as partners and cooperators rather than adversaries and antagnists. Some scholars and social workers began advocating a brand new idea, which is a "win-win"concept. Among those outstanding figures are American scholars Roger Fisher, William Ury and British negotiator Bill Scott to name a few.

在 20 世纪下半叶，人员、货物、服务和资本自由流动带来的更大收益使得经济全球化和一体化飞速发展，已将所有国家和地区融合为一个相互依存、相互关联的机构。自从各国开始将彼此视为伙伴和合作者而不是对手和反抗者以来，通过基于平等和互利的和平手段解决政治特别是经济争端和冲突，已在国际事务和国内事务中盛行开来。一些学者和社会工作者开始倡导一个崭新的想法，这就是一个"双赢"的理念。在这些杰出人物中，有美国学者罗杰·费希尔、威廉·尤里和英国谈判代表比尔·斯科特。

The core of their thinking is mutual success and convergence of interests. By mutual success,they mean under the condition when one party tries to gain his utmost interests or at least takes action not detrimental to one's own interests, it may find one way or another to satisfy more or less the counterpart's interests as well. Seeking convenience of parties' interests is to conduct negotiations by exploring mutual benefits so that a better and bigger cake of common interests will be made jointly for mutual sharing. In the meantime, American attorney, Gerard Nierenberg, created his educational nonprofit negotiation institute in New York where he promoted his negotiation philosophy of" Everybody wins". Because of his success and popularity of his philosophy, he was recognized by Forbes magazine as "the Father of Negotiating Training". Based on the concept of "win-win", negotiation model has been developed. Practices have demonstrated its high effectiveness in dealing with disagreement and conflicts in negotiations, therefore, it has become the most widely accepted negotiation principle.

他们思想的核心是相互成功和利益汇合。相互成功，是指在一方设法获得最大利益或至少采取不损害自己利益的行动的条件下，也可能找到一种或另一种方式来或多或少地满足对方的利益。寻求各方利益的汇合是通过探索互利来进行谈判，以便共同创造更好更大的共同利益蛋糕，以实现共同分享。同时，美国律师杰拉德·尼尔伦伯格(Gerard Nierenberg)在纽约创建了他的教育性非营利性谈判学院，在那里他推广了"人人都赢"的谈判理念。由于他的成功和他哲学的普及，他被《福布斯》杂志誉为"谈判培训之父"。基于"双赢"理念的谈判模型已经开发出来。实践证明，它在处理谈判中的分歧和冲突方面具有很高的效力，因此，它已成为最广泛接受的谈判原则。

Win-win model is expressed as:

No.1 Determine each party's interests and needs.

No.2 Find out the other party's interests and demands.

No.3 Offer constructive options and solutions.

No.4 Announce the success of negotiations.

No.5 Declare failure of negotiations or negotiations in impasse.

双赢模式表示为

第一，确定各方的利益和需求。

第二，找出对方的利益和要求。

第三，提供建设性的选择和解决方案。

第四，宣布谈判成功。

第五，宣布谈判失败或陷入僵局。

A significant point that "win-win" model differs from "win-lose" model is that both parties will not only seek means to fulfill their own interests, but also hope the interests of the other party to be realized more or less. Negotiations guided by such concept are to be conducted in an atmosphere of mutual understanding and sincere cooperation and will be concluded with mutually accepted agreement to the satisfaction of both parties. The negotiation between Egypt and Israel on Sinai Peninsula provides an excellent example contrasting the striking effects of "win-lose" and "win-win" concepts.

"双赢"模式与"我赢你输(或我输你赢)"模式的不同之处在于，双方不仅要寻求实现自己利益的手段，而且希望或多或少地实现另一方的利益。以这种理念为指导的谈判应在相互理解和真诚合作的气氛中进行，并应在双方接受的协议下达成，使双方满意。埃及和以色列之间在西奈半岛上的谈判提供了一个很好的例子，"双赢"理念和"我赢你输(或我输你赢)"理念的效果形成了鲜明的对比。

The Middle East War of 1967 ended with Israel's occupation of 60000 square kilometers of Sinai Peninsula.As the mediators between the two countries, US and some other countries had striven for 11 years to help the two countries settle the dispute through negotiations. However, all efforts failed since both sides adhered firmly to their own stance and showed no flexibility. For Egypt, the occupied Sinai was an indisputable part of Egyptian territory. In view of the territorial integrity and national sovereignty,Egypt was entitled to recovering it without any conditions. For Israel, the occupation of Sinai was for the sake of Israel's security since several military attacks against Israel were launched from the Peninsula. In 1978, the peaceful negotiation was reopened at the Camp David in US, which was conducted this time by a completely new guideline of "win-win"concept. The two parties were encouraged to reexamine their own interests as well as the interests of their counterparts. It was found out that the Egypt's preliminary interest lied in the recovery of its territory, not threatening Israel's security, whereas Israel did not mean to expand its territory, rather to ensure its safety. Based on this mutual understanding, an acceptable accord was reached that Israel returned the occupied territory to Egypt, who in turn designated a part of the Sinai as nonmilitary zone. A dispute dragging for 11 years was resolved in a matter of 12 days.

1967年的中东战争以以色列占领西奈半岛6万平方公里而告终。作为两国的调停者，美国和其他一些国家努力11年，以通过谈判帮助两国解决争端。但是，由于双方坚持自己的立场，没有表现出任何灵活性，所有努力都失败了。对于埃及而言，被占领的西奈半岛是埃及领土上不可争议的一部分。为了领土完整和国家主权，埃及有权无条件追回。对于以色列来说，占领西奈半岛是为了以色列的安全，因为从半岛发动了好几次针对以色列的军事攻击。 1978年，和平谈判在美国的戴维营重新开始，这次是以全新的双赢理念为指南进行的，鼓励双方重新审视自己和对方的利益。人们发现，埃及的最初利益在于其领土的恢复，而不是威胁以色列的安全，而以色列并不是要扩大领土，而是要确保其安全。在这种相互了解的基础上，达成了可以接受的协议，即以色列将被占领领土交还给埃及，埃及又将西奈的一部分指定为非军事区。拖延了11年的纠纷仅用了12天就解决了。

The success of negotiations between Egypt and Israel was a great breakthrough in settling conflicts through peaceful means guided by "win-win"concept in the Middle East Peaceful negotiations. Israel and Palestine followed suit and put forward the celebrated "territory in exchange for peace", a negotiation principle for Middle East Peace Talk. The principle has been working effectively in negotiations between Palestine and Israel. It is inevitable that the"peace talks"in the Middle East suffer from periodical setbacks. However it is the wish of all people that "win-win"concept will lead the two sides to final and permanent peace in the region sooner or later.

埃及和以色列之间的谈判取得了成功，这是在中东和平谈判中以"双赢"理念为指导，通过和平手段解决冲突的重大突破。以色列和巴勒斯坦也紧随其后，提出了著名的"领土以换取和平"，这是中东和平对话的谈判原则。该原则在巴以之间的谈判中一直有效。中东的"和平谈判"不可避免地会遭受周期性的挫折，但是，所有人的希望是，"双赢"的理念或迟或早将带动双方在该地区实现最终和永久的和平。

The "win-win" theory has proved to be successful and effective in many tough negotiations because it takes into full consideration of both sides' interests, which contribute greatly to the mutual understanding of negotiating parties. Therefore it can produce twice the result with half the effort. Effective "win-win" model can be reality. However, not all people in all situations will be guided by "win-win" concept. They are sitll by virtue of deep-rooted one-dimension concept of "win-lose". Therefore, there is still a long way to go since it is a formidable task for people to establish a new concept.

事实证明，"双赢"理论在许多艰难的谈判中都是成功和有效的，因为它充分考虑了双方的利益，这极大地促进了谈判各方的相互了解，因此可以事半功倍。有效的"双赢"模式可以成为现实，但是，并非所有人在所有情况下都以"双赢"理念为指南，而是秉持根深蒂固的一维的"我赢你输(或我输你赢)"观念下的操守，因此树立新观念是一项艰巨的任务，还有很长的路要走。

Terminology　本章术语

1. art of compromise 妥协的艺术
2. win-win 双赢
3. multi-win 多赢
4. win-lose 我赢你输(或 我输你赢)

Exercises　本章练习

1. What is the essence of the Chinese negotiator's idea that "negotiation is an art of mutual compromise"?
中国谈判者的"谈判是双方相互妥协的艺术"理念的精髓是什么？

2. What is the core of the western concept of "win-win negotiation"?
西方"谈判双赢"理念的核心是什么？

Answers for Reference 参考答案

1. "Negotiation is the art of compromise between both sides. Any unilateral win is not called negotiation. It is conquest, or war."

"No unilateral compromise can achieve a compromise balance."

"Negotiations often use difficult and patient methods to find consensus and seek breakthroughs in differences."

"To make the other side and you reach a certain compromise, we need to be rational and force both sides to compromise. It's very simple to start with ourselves.

We should dare to compromise and be willing to compromise. The result of compromise is that both sides will benefit."

"谈判是双方妥协的艺术，任何单方面的赢都不叫谈判，那是征服，或者说是战争。"

"任何单方面的妥协都不可能实现一种妥协的平衡点。"

"谈判往往是用很艰难的、很耐心的方法去寻求共识，寻求对于分歧的突破。"

"使对方和你都做到一定的妥协，需要理性，逼迫双方妥协，很简单，从自己做起。要敢于妥协、甘于妥协，妥协的结果是双方都得到好处。"

2. The core of their thinking is mutual success and convergence of interests. By mutual success, they mean under the condition when one party tries to gain his utmost interests or at least takes action not detrimental to one's own interests, it may find one way or another to satisfy more or less the counterpart's interests as well. Seeking convenience of parties' interests is to conduct negotiations by exploring mutual benefits so that a better and bigger cake of common interests will be made jointly for mutual sharing.

他们思想的核心是相互成功和利益汇合。相互成功，是指在一方设法获得最大利益或至少采取不损害自己利益的行动的条件下，也可能找到一种或另一种方式来或多或少地满足对方的利益。寻求各方利益的汇合是通过探索互利来进行谈判，以便共同创造更好更大的共同利益蛋糕，以实现共同分享。

Chapter 5　Quality of International Business Negotiators

第 5 章　国际商务谈判者素质

The definition of "quality" in *Ci Hai* (a well-known Chinese lexicon and character dictionary, first published in 1936) is:

1. the original characteristics of human physiology;
2. the original nature of things;
3. the basic conditions necessary to complete certain activities.

Generally speaking, "quality" refers to a person's physique, quality, intelligence, ability and inner self-cultivation.

Negotiation is the communication among people. People are the subject of negotiation behavior. The quality of negotiators will have a significant impact on the negotiation results. High quality and strong ability negotiators are conducive to the success of negotiation. Generally speaking, the excellent quality of negotiators is not innate, but is acquired through postnatal long-term learning and practice. Excellent international business negotiators should have good political quality, moral quality, cultural quality, physical quality, psychological quality and professional quality, etc.

《辞海》，一本出版于 1936 年的著名词典，对"素质"的定义为：

1. 人的生理上的原来的特点；
2. 事物本来的性质；
3. 完成某种活动所必需的基本条件。

通常来讲，"素质"是指个人的体质、品质、才智、能力和内在涵养等。

谈判是人和人之间的沟通交流。人是谈判行为的主体。谈判人员的素质高低会对谈判结果产生重大影响。素质高、能力强的谈判人员有利于谈判取得成功。谈判者的优良素质一般不是天生的，而是在后天长期的学习和实践中锻炼而成。优秀的国际商务谈判者应具备良好的政治素质、品德素质、文化素质、身体素质、心理素质、专业素质等。

Section 1 Political and Moral Qualities of International Business Negotiators

第 1 节 国际商务谈判者的政治素质和品德素质

China's international business negotiators should have excellent political and moral qualities.

In general international business negotiations, although negotiators and teams represent enterprises to participate in negotiations for economic interests, the interests and image of the country are behind them. Therefore, Chinese international business negotiators must have excellent political and moral qualities. First, negotiators must be able to correctly handle the relationship among the interests of the state, enterprises and individuals, be loyal to the motherland at all times, resolutely safeguard national sovereignty and national dignity, put the interests of the state and enterprises first, and be honest and selfless. Those who are tempted by money, selfish with interests, accepting bribes, profiting at the expense of the public, and selling the interests of the state and enterprises are not suitable to participate in the negotiation as negotiators. Second, negotiators must be devoted to their duties, have high professional ethics and professionalism, and have a strong sense of career and responsibility when dealing with negotiation work. At the same time, they must have sincerity, patience, confidence and innovation spirit in negotiation. In addition, international business negotiation is an activity of both competition and cooperation, without tenacious enterprising spirit, negotiation is difficult to succeed. We should take honesty as the basis, adhere to mutual benefit and mutual patronage, and avoid arrogance and excessive humility. Third, negotiators must pay attention to daily behavior, strictly abide by team discipline, pay attention to personal integrity, resist temptation, and do not do things that are harmful to national standards and team image. At the same time, in the negotiation occasions, they should be dignified in appearance, proper in dress, elegant in manner, and generous in speech, so as to win the respect of each other.

中国的国际商务谈判人员应具备优秀的政治素质和道德品质。

在一般的国际商务谈判中，虽然是由谈判者个人和团队代表企业为经济利益参加谈判，但背后是国家的利益和形象，因此，中国的国际商务谈判人员必须具备优秀的政治素质和道德品质。第一，谈判人员必须能正确处理好国家、企业和个人利益之间的关系，任何时候都必须忠于祖国,坚决维护国家主权和民族尊严,把国家和企业利益放在首位,必须廉洁奉公、不谋私利。见钱眼开、见利忘义、收受贿赂、损公肥私,出卖国家和企业利益的人不适合作为谈判代表参与谈判工作。第二,谈判人员必须忠于职守,具备高尚的职业道德和崇高的敬业精神,对待谈判工作既要有强烈的事业心,又要有高度的责任感,同时,谈判人员在谈判中还要有诚心、耐心、信心和创新精神。另外,国际商务谈判是一项既竞争又合作的活动,没有顽强的进取精神,谈判难以取得成功。我们应以诚信为本,坚持互利互惠,忌妄自尊大和妄自菲薄。第三,谈判人员必须注意个人日常行为修养,谈判过程中严格遵守团队纪律,注重个人操守,抵制诱惑,不做有损国格和团队形象的事情。同时,在谈判场合,仪表端庄,服饰得体,举止优雅,谈吐大方,才能赢得对方的尊重。

Section 2　Cultural Quality of International Business Negotiators

第2节　国际商务谈判者的文化素质

International business negotiation is a process in which the parties of business activities in different countries or regions negotiate with each other on various elements of the transaction through information exchange in order to reach a certain transaction. Both sides of the negotiation come from different social and cultural backgrounds and have different cultural accomplishment. Culture influences the quality of the negotiator. Culture also influences the value trend, negotiation style, negotiation motivation, evaluation criteria of negotiators. To some extent, international business negotiation is not only confrontation of ideas and competition of strategies, but also a clash of cultures.

国际商务谈判是不同国家或地区的商务活动当事人为了达成某笔交易,彼此通过信息交流,就交易的各项要件进行协商的行为过程。谈判双方来自不同的社会文化背景,有着不同的文化修养。文化影响谈判者的素质。文化还影响谈判者的价值趋向、谈判风格、谈判动机、评价标准。某种程度上讲,国际商务谈判不仅是理念的交锋、策略技巧的较量,更是文化的碰撞。

1. Culture　文化

Culture is a unique phenomenon of human society, which is created by human beings and unique to human beings.

文化是由人所创造、为人所特有的人类社会特有的现象。

In a broad sense, culture is the sum of material wealth and spiritual wealth created by human beings in the process of social and historical practice, that is, the sum of material culture and spiritual culture. In a narrow sense, culture refers to spiritual culture.

广义的文化，是人类在社会历史实践过程中所创造的物质财富和精神财富的总和，即物质文化和精神文化的总和。狭义的文化，专指精神文化。

Material culture refers to the material civilization created by human beings, including living conditions such as means of transportation, clothing, food, daily necessities, living environment and production conditions such as means of production, science and technology, which is a visible dominant culture.

物质文化，指人类创造的物质文明，包括交通工具、服饰、食品、日常用品、居住环境等生活条件和生产工具、科学技术等生产条件，它是一种可见的显性文化。

Spiritual culture is national or ethical history, geography, local manners and feelings, traditional customs, life style, literature and art, behavioral norms, ways of thinking, values, etc. which is coagulated in the material and dissociated from the material. It is a generally recognized ideology that can be used for communication among people and inherited by human beings, and the sublimation of perceptual knowledge and experience to objective world, which belongs to invisible recessive culture. Spiritual culture includes behavioral culture, systematical culture and psychological culture. Behavior culture, is people's life style, behavior norms and customs, habits, etiquette, etc. established in interpersonal communication. Systematical culture, is the norms established by human beings in social practice to regulate their own behavior and mutual relations, such as family system, social system, enterprise system, political system, legal system, etc. Psychological culture, is people's social psychology and social ideology, including people's view of value, view on life, view on world, way of thinking, aesthetic taste and the resulting philosophy, religion, literature and art works, as the core of culture and the essence of culture.

精神文化，是凝结在物质之中又游离于物质之外的国家或民族的历史、地理、风土人情、传统习俗、生活方式、文学艺术、行为规范、思维方式、价值观念等。它是人类相互之间进行交流的普遍认可的一种能够传承的意识形态，是对客观世界感性上的知识与经验的升华，属于不可见的隐性文化。精神文化包括行为文化、制度文化和心理文化。行为文化，即人的生活方式、行为规范以及人际交往中约定俗成的风俗、习惯、礼仪礼节等。制度文化，即人类在社会实践中建立的规范自身行为和调节相互关系的准则，比如家庭制度、社会制度、企业制度、政治制度、法律制度等。心理文化，即人们的社会心理和社会意识形态，包括人们的价值观、人生观、世界观、思维方式、审美情趣以及由此而产生的哲学、宗教、文学艺术作品等，这是文化的核心，也是文化的精华部分。

Some anthropologists divide spiritual culture into three levels: high culture, which includes, philosophy, literature, art, religion, etc.; popular culture, which refers to customs, rituals, as well as lifestyle including food, clothing, housing and transportation, interpersonal relations, etc.; deep culture, which mainly refers to the definition of beauty and ugliness of values, time orientation, rhythm of life, ways to solve problems and personal roles related to gender, class, occupation and kinship. Both high culture and popular culture are rooted in deep culture, and a certain concept of deep culture is reflected in popular culture by a custom or lifestyle, and reflected in high culture by an art form or literary theme.

有些人类学家将精神文化分为三个层次：高级文化(high culture)，包括哲学、文学、艺术、宗教等；大众文化(popular culture)，指习俗、仪式以及包括衣食住行、人际关系等各方面的生活方式；深层文化(deep culture)，主要指价值观的美丑定义、时间取向、生活节奏、解决问题的方式以及与性别、阶层、职业、亲属关系相关的个人角色。高级文化和大众文化均植根于深层文化，而深层文化的某一概念又以一种习俗或生活方式反映在大众文化中，以一种艺术形式或文学主题反映在高级文化中。

2. Cultural quality　文化素质

Culture quality refers to the relatively stable and intrinsic basic quality of people in terms of culture, and indicates the quality, level and personality characteristics of people's comprehensive development in these knowledge and their corresponding abilities, behaviors and emotions. The knowledge here refers to not only the knowledge of science and technology learned from school, but also the knowledge of humanities and social sciences, including philosophy, history, literature, sociology, etc. Which are reflected by your language or words, by your hands and feet, and represent your cultural quality. In Chinese, it is also called cultural accomplishment, and it is a kind of cultural accomplishment that is acquired for a long time learning and rooted in the heart.

文化素质指人们在文化方面所具有的较为稳定的、内在的基本品质，表明人们在这些知识以及与之相适应的能力、行为、情感等方面综合发展的质量、水平和个性特点。这里所指的知识，不只是从学校学到的科学技术方面的知识，更多的是指人文社科类的知识，包括哲学、历史、文学、社会学等方面的知识。这些知识通过你的语言或文字的表达体现出来，通过你的举手投足反映出来，代表你所具有的文化素质。中文中也被称作文化修养，文化修养是经过长期而习得的、植根于内心的文化修养。

3. Cultural quality of international business negotiators　国际商务谈判者的文化素质

(1) Cultivation of Chinese culture
中国文化修养

The late premier Zhou Enlai once said, "there is no small matter in diplomacy". In fact, foreign trade is also "diplomacy", which means exchanges in the fields of foreign economics and trade. Foreign economics and trade negotiations and international business negotiations, similar to diplomatic negotiations, are all negotiations between Chinese and foreigners, but in foreign economics and trade negotiations, it is not Chinese diplomats, but Chinese business negotiators who negotiate on behalf of China with foreign businessmen, and their words and deeds reflect the features of Chinese businessmen, Chinese traditional business culture and Chinese business values all the time. Therefore, the cultural cultivation of Chinese business negotiators is very important and necessary.

已故的周恩来总理曾经说过，"外交无小事"。其实，外贸也是"外交"，是对外经贸交往的意思。外经贸谈判、国际商务谈判，类似于外交谈判，都是中国人跟外国人谈判，只不过在外经贸谈判中，不是中国外交官，而是中国商务谈判人员代表中国与外商谈判，言谈举止时时刻刻都体现中国商人的风貌、展示中国传统商业文化、反映中国的商业价值观，所以中国商务谈判者的文化涵养是非常重要和极其必要。

Chinese culture and Chinese business culture are extensive and profound. Chinese business negotiators should keep learning and making progress, should be familiar with and master Chinese civilization, Chinese culture and Chinese traditional virtues, business ethics, business philosophy, operation mode, negotiation style, etiquette norms, etc. as far as possible, In international business negotiations, Chinese international business negotiators can show the grace of Chinese culture through their own words and deeds, also actively introduce and publicize Chinese traditional culture to foreign businessmen in real time, tell Chinese stories well, be a good communicator of Chinese culture, win the respect of the other party for Chinese culture, and lay the foundation for the business negotiation parties to reach an agreement and make a successful deal.

中国文化和中国商业文化博大精深。中国的商务谈判者应该持续学习，不断进步，尽一切可能熟悉掌握中华文明、中国文化和中华传统美德、商业道德、经营哲学、运营模式、谈判风格、礼仪规范等。在国际商务谈判中，中国商务谈判者可通过自己的言谈举止展现中国文化风采，又可实时主动向外商介绍、宣传中国传统文化，讲好中国故事，当好中国文化的传播者，赢得对方对中国文化的尊重，为商务谈判双方达成一致、顺利成交奠定基础。

(2) Learning foreign culture and foreign business culture
外国文化和外国商业文化的学习

It is inevitable that there are cultural differences between the two parties in international business negotiation. Cultural differences are mainly reflected in the differences in negotiation style, negotiation mode, decision-making process, evaluation method, etc. due to the values, thinking mode, political and legal systems, religious beliefs, customs and business traditions between countries and nations. Chinese business negotiators should fully learn to understand the culture of the other country, while adhering to the Chinese cultural tradition, learn to tolerate, appreciate and respect, and even adapt to the culture of the other country when necessary, overcome cultural chauvinism and racism, abandon cultural prejudice, accept cultural differences, avoid cultural conflicts, and respect the other party. At the same time, it is likely to win the respect of the other party and make the negotiation go smoothly.

国际商务谈判的谈判双方之间的文化差异在所难免。文化差异主要体现在因国家和民族之间的价值观、思维方式、政治和法律制度、宗教信仰、风俗习惯、商业传统等的原因而形成的谈判风格、谈判方式、决策过程、评价方法等方面的不同。中国商务谈判者应充分学习了解对方国家的文化，在坚持中国文化传统的同时学会容忍、欣赏、尊重，甚至在必要时顺应对方国家的文化，克服文化上的沙文主义和种族主义，抛弃文化偏见，接受文化差异，避免文化冲突，尊重对方。与此同时很可能也就赢得了对方的尊重，使谈判顺利进行。

Section 3　Physical Quality of International Business Negotiators

第3节　国际商务谈判者的身体素质

Good physical quality is the basic requirement for negotiators. Healthy body, abundant energy and agile thinking are extremely important for negotiators, and the necessary conditions for them to be competent in negotiation work.

良好的身体素质是对谈判者的基本要求,健康的身体、充沛的精力、敏捷的思路对谈判人员极其重要,是胜任谈判工作的必要条件。

1. Physical quality　身体素质

Traditionally, physical quality/physical fitness refers to the speed, strength, endurance, sensitivity, flexibility and other functions of human body in activities. Speed diathesis refers to the ability of human body to move in unit time or respond to external stimulation quickly and slowly; strength diathesis refers to the strength produced when some muscles of the body contract; endurance diathesis refers to the ability of human body to carry out muscle activity and resist fatigue for a long time; sensitivity diathesis refers to the ability to change body position, change movement and adapt to circumstances; flexibility diathesis refers to elasticity and extension of muscles and ligaments of joints during human activities.

传统上,身体素质一般是指人体在活动中所表现出来的速度、力量、耐力、灵敏、柔韧等机能。速度素质,是人体在单位时间内移动的距离或对外界刺激反应快慢的一种能力;力量素质,是身体某些肌肉收缩时产生的力量;耐力素质,是指人体长时间进行肌肉活动和抵抗疲劳的能力;灵敏素质,是指迅速改变体位、转换动作和随机应变的能力;柔韧素质,指人体活动时各关节肌肉和韧带的弹性和伸展度。

Physical fitness also includes adaptability to environment, adaptability to changes and anti emergency ability. Adaptability to environment is manifested in the adaptation to the natural environment and the resistance to diseases. Adaptability to changes refers to the ability of people to deal with unexpected events and emergencies, or how to make appropriate response at the fastest speed when the external environment changes. Emergency handling capacity refers to the handling capacity of any event that endangers national security, public security and social order, threatens the safety of citizens' lives and property, and may cause serious consequences.

身体素质还包括适应能力、应变能力和抗突发事件能力等方面。适应能力表现在对自然环境的适应和疾病的抵抗方面。应变能力是指人对意外性事件、突发性事件进行应急处理的能力,或在外界环境发生变化时,如何以最快的速度作出恰如其分的反应的能力。紧急事件处理能力是指对任何需要立即予以处置的危及国家安全、危害公共安全和社会秩序、威胁公民生命和财产安全,并有可能造成严重后果的事件的处理能力。

2. Physical quality of international business negotiators　国际商务谈判者的身体素质

Negotiation is not a task that can be easily accomplished by simply opening your mouth or tapping your keyboard. Many negotiations have requirements on time and tasks, which not only consume physical energy but also mental energy. International business negotiations are likely to leave negotiators exhausted physically and mentally due to various factors, such as frequent long-distance flights and transfers, jet lag, shortened itinerary due to cost constraints, being hard and busy for decorations and arrangements of exhibition booth, being busy, tired and even hungry and thirsty in continuous reception of visiting customers, in addition, the other negotiators being possibly vexatious, unreasonable, nitpicking, changeable and so on. Generally, international business negotiation consumes more energy and physical strength than domestic business negotiation, and international business negotiators need a strong body and a good physical fitness.

谈判工作并不是简单地动动嘴口头谈谈或动动手指敲敲键盘通信谈谈就能轻易完成的任务。很多谈判在时间和任务上都有要求，不仅消耗体力更消耗脑力。国际商务谈判因种种因素很可能让谈判人员身心俱疲，比如，经常长途飞行和转机、时差、行程受成本的制约而缩短、布置展场辛苦忙碌、连续接待来访客户疲惫甚至忍饥挨饿或忙不过来喝一口水，还有，谈判对手胡搅蛮缠、无理取闹、吹毛求疵、变化无常等等。通常国际商务谈判比一般的国内商务谈判更加耗费精力和体力，国际商务谈判人员更需要一个强健的体魄和良好的身体素质。

3. How to maintain good physical fitness for international business negotiators
   国际商务谈判者保持良好身体素质的方法

The strength of physical quality is one of the important signs to measure a person's physical condition.

Physical quality is often latent in people's life, study and work, and naturally also in physical exercise. The strength of a person's physical quality is related to heredity, but it is more closely related to the acquired nutrition and physical exercise. Through correct methods and proper exercise, the level of physical quality can be improved from all aspects.

身体素质的强弱，是衡量一个人体质状况的重要标志之一。

身体素质经常潜在地表现在人们的生活、学习和工作中，自然也表现在体育锻炼方面。一个人身体素质的好坏与遗传有关，但与后天的营养和体育锻炼的关系更为密切。通过正确的方法和适当的锻炼，可以从各个方面提高身体素质水平。

(1) Attach great importance to physical health.
(2) Adhere to long-term physical exercise and arrange appropriate exercise intensity.

(3) Keep good eating habits and a balanced diet.
(4) Make the mood happy and stable.
(5) Get enough sleep.
(6) Take physical examination regularly.
(1) 思想上高度重视身体健康。
(2) 坚持长期身体锻炼,安排合适的锻炼强度。
(3) 保持良好的饮食习惯和营养平衡的膳食。
(4) 让心情愉悦、情绪稳定。
(5) 保证充足的睡眠。
(6) 定期参加体检。

Section 4　Psychological Quality of International Business Negotiators

第4节　国际商务谈判者的心理素质

In the process of negotiation, there may be all kinds of resistance and confrontation, but also unexpected situations. Negotiators must have good psychological quality to withstand all kinds of pressure and face different challenges to win the negotiation.

在谈判过程中可能会遇到各种阻力和对抗,还可能会产生突发情况,谈判人员必须具备良好的心理素质,才能承受各种压力和面对不同的挑战,赢得谈判。

1. Psychological quality　心理素质

In short, psychological quality is the synthesis of psychological potential, psychological energy, psychological characteristics, psychological peculiarity and psychological behavior, which is based on physiological quality and gradually occurs, develops and forms under the influence of postnatal environment, education, practical activities and other factors. It is the external expression of emotional core.

简单地说,心理素质是以生理素质为基础,在后天环境、教育、实践活动等因素的影响下逐步发生、发展和形成的心理潜能、心理能量、心理特点、心理特质与心理行为的综合,是情绪内核的外在表现。

Psychological potential means that everyone is born with a certain potential; everyone is eager to give full play or realize his potential; everyone can give full play or realize his potential as long as he works hard.

心理潜能指每个人生来都具有一定的潜能；每个人都亟欲把自己的潜能发挥出来或得到实现；每个人只要自己努力都可以充分发挥或实现自己的潜能。

Psychological energy, also known as mental power or mental ability. Man is a system, which is composed of body system and mental system. These two subsystems have power (energy). The former is physical ability, and the latter is mental ability. This kind of psychological energy is not only the embodiment of human psychological quality, but also the energy function regulated by consciousness. Its strength can also reflect a person's psychological quality level.

心理能量，亦称心理力量或心理能力。人是一个系统，由身体系统与心理系统构成，而这两个子系统是有力量(能量)的，前者为体力即身体之能力，后者为心力即精神之能力。这种心理能量乃是人的心理素质的体现，也是用意识来调节的能量作用，其大小强弱也能够反映出一个人的心理素质水平。

Psychological characteristics refer to the inherent attributes of people's psychological activities. For example, some people have the psychological characteristics of passiveness, while some people have the psychological characteristics of activeness. In addition, psychological phenomena also have their own characteristics, such as the directness and concreteness of perception, the indirectness and generality of thinking, the fluctuation and infection of emotion, the purpose and regulation of will and so on. Psychological characteristics are also concrete signs of psychological quality.

心理特点指人的心理活动固有的属性，比如，有的人具有受动性的心理特点，而有的人具有能动性的心理特点。另外，心理现象也具有各自的特点，比如，感知的直接性与具体性，思维的间接性与概括性，情感的波动性与感染性，意志的目的性与调控性等。心理特点也是心理素质的具体标志。

Psychological peculiarity is not inherent in psychological activities, but acquired. There are different levels of psychological peculiarity among people. Almost every psychological phenomenon has certain peculiarities, such as the agility, persistence, accuracy and reserve of memory, the flexibility, profundity, independence and criticism of thinking, the tendentiousness, diversity, fixity and efficacy of emotion, the consciousness, decisiveness, persistence and self-control of will, etc. The quality of psychological peculiarity can best show the level of human psychological quality.

心理特质，并非心理活动本身所固有，而是后天习得的。人与人之间各具有不同水平的心理特质。几乎每一种心理现象都具有一定的品质，如记忆的敏捷性、持久性、准确性、备用性，思维的灵活性、深刻性、独立性、批判性，情感的倾向性、多样性、固定性、功效性，意志的自觉性、果断性、坚持性、自制性等。心理特质的优劣最能表现出人的心理素质的水平。

Psychological behavior. People's simple behavior or complex behavior, in the final analysis, are dominated by people's psychology, and all of them are external manifestations of people's psychology. Therefore, in this sense, all human behaviors can be called psychological behaviors. This kind of psychological behavior is the symbol of psychological quality, through which we can test the level of psychological quality. In addition, the four components of psychological quality, such as psychological potential, energy, characteristics, peculiarity, will be obviously or not obviously reflected in behavior. It can be seen that psychological behavior is an important component of psychological quality.

心理行为。人们无论简单的行为还是复杂的行为，归根结底都受人的心理的支配，都是人的心理的外部表现。因此，从这个意义上说，人的一切行为都可以称为心理行为。这种心理行为是心理素质的标志，通过它可以检验心理素质水平的高低。而且，前述心理素质的四个组成因素如心理潜能、能量、特点、特质，也都会明显地或不明显地在行为上反映出来。可见，心理行为是构成心理素质的一个重要成分。

The level of psychological quality is measured from the following aspects:

The quality of personality, the size of cognitive potential, the strength of psychological adaptability, the size and direction of internal motivation, the quality of mental health and behavior performance.

心理素质水平的高低从以下方面进行衡量：

性格品质的优劣、认知潜能的大小、心理适应能力的强弱、内在动力的大小及指向、心理健康状况的好坏、行为表现的优劣。

High level of psychological quality is usually manifested as the following.

Good personality: self-knowledge, self-confidence, self-improvement, self-discipline, optimism, cheerful, strong, calm, kind, gregarious, enthusiastic, dedicated, responsible, serious, diligent, etc.

Normal intelligence: normal feeling, perception, memory, thinking, imagination and attention.

Strong psychological adaptability: self-awareness, interpersonal communication, psychological adaptation, competition and cooperation, ability to bear setbacks, adjust emotions and control behaviors.

Positive and strong internal motivation: reasonable need, moderate motivation, extensive interest, appropriate ideal, scientific belief.

Healthy mentality: normal intelligence, positive mood, good personality, interpersonal harmony, appropriate behavior, good social adaptation.

Appropriate behavior: in line with roles, groups, social norms, ethics and regulations.

心理素质水平高，通常表现为以下方面。

良好的个性：自知、自信、自强、自律、乐观、开朗、坚强、冷静、善良、合群、热情、敬业、负责、认真、勤奋等。

正常的智力：感觉、知觉、记忆、思维、想象、注意力正常。

较强的心理适应能力：自我意识、人际交往、心理应变、竞争与协作、承受挫折、调适情绪、控制行为。

积极而强烈的内在动力：合理的需要、适度的动机、广泛的兴趣、适当的理想、科学的信念。

健康的心态：智力正常、情绪积极、个性良好、人际和谐、行为适当、社会适应良好。

适当的行为表现：符合角色、群体、社会规范、道德和法规。

2. Psychological quality of international business negotiators
国际商务谈判者的心理素质

In real practice, the psychological quality of the negotiators plays a crucial role, particularly the personal characteristics and capabilities.

在实际工作中，谈判者的心理素质起着至关重要的作用，尤其是个人的特点和能力。

According to Jeffrey Edmund Curry, American business expert and scholar of negotiation science, it is highly desirable that a negotiator has the following range of character issues to achieve satisfactory negotiation results.

按美国商务专家和谈判学者杰弗里·埃德蒙·库里所说，谈判人员非常希望具有以下一系列个性心理特征，以取得令人满意的谈判结果。

(1) Shrewdness

The successful negotiator must be capable of allowing the other side to see only what serves the strategy best, and this requires a ethical mixture of honesty and cunning. People who "wear their hearts on their sleeves" or insist on transparency in all dealings will make sorry negotiators in the global marketplace. For this reason, shrewdness heads the list for desirable characteristics.

(1) 精明

成功的谈判者必须能够让对方只看到最适合(你所采用的)战略的东西,而这需要诚实和狡猾的道德结合。那些在所有交易中"把心放在袖子上(即把心里的真实想法表达出来)"或坚持透明的人,将成为全球市场上令人遗憾的谈判者。出于这个原因,精明名列必需的个性特征榜单的榜首。

(2) Patience

Patience is an indispensable attribute. Negotiations can be quite taxing—each offer brings a counter offer, every maneuver brings a counter maneuver and delays eat up time and energy. Corrupt officials, petty management and incompetent staff member all must be handled with care and patience.

(2) 耐心

耐心是必不可少的。谈判是很费劲的,每个发盘都会带来一个还盘,每个动作都会带来一个反动作,拖延会消耗时间和精力。腐败官员、琐碎的管理人员和无能的工作人员都必须小心和耐心地应付。

(3) Adaptability

Negotiations seldom go completely according to plans, nor will they always change in preconceived patterns. The negotiator must be able to respond quickly and decisively to unforeseen developments. Negotiations are concerned with each side getting the other to change positions. An inflexible strategy and limited tactics will almost instantly bring negotiations to an unproductive close. So, the negotiator must be highly adaptable.

(3) 适应性

谈判很少完全按计划进行,也不会总是按预先设想的方式进行,谈判人员必须能够对不可预见的事态发展作出迅速和果断的反应。谈判涉及双方让对方改变立场。一个僵硬的战略和有限的战术几乎将立即导致谈判徒劳无功地结束。因此,谈判者必须有很强的适应能力。

(4) Endurance

While negotiation is primarily a mental activity, it can be physically demanding. The negotiator must be available for all sessions and the typical eight-hour work days will be rare. Adding in travel fatigue, climatic changes, jet lag, foreign food, late-night socializing and work stress,you have the makings of burnout. So physical fitness and endurance are highly desirable.

(4) 耐久性

虽然谈判主要是一种心理活动,但也可能有体力上的要求。谈判者必须能参加所有的会议，典型的 8 小时工作日很少。再加上旅行疲劳、气候变化、时差、外国食物、深夜社交和工作压力，你就精疲力竭了。所以身体素质和耐力是非常需要的。

(5) Gregariousness

The "relationship" will play a huge role in finalizing a contract. A competent negotiator is gregarious. Just as many deals are made across the dinner table as are made across the conference table. The ability to hold a good, off-business-topic conversation with a counterpart will only advance the negotiator's position.

(5) 爱交友

这种"关系"将在合同的最终敲定中发挥巨大作用。能干的谈判者善于交际。正像餐桌上的交易和会议桌上的交易一样多。与对方进行良好的非业务话题对话的能力只会提升谈判者的地位。

(6) Concentration

International business can make substantial demands on its practitioners. Time zone changes, language problems can all be major distractions from the goals set forth the strategy. The potential danger for "losing track" is enormous. Counterparts will often attempt to put as many points as possible "on the table" in an effort to cloud the main issue. You will lose if you are distracted from it.

(6) 专注

国际商务会对其从业人员提出实质性要求。时区的变化、语言问题都可能是让你偏离设定了策略的目标的主要因素。潜在的"迷失方向"的危害是巨大的。对手们往往会试图把尽可能多的观点"摆在桌面上"，试图掩盖主要问题。如果你心不在焉，你会输的。

(7) The ability to articulate

Good negotiators must be practiced listeners as well as articulate speakers. Everything about them from their demeanor, their clothes and their body language to how they handle subordinates will be inspected critically. A negotiator must also have a keen sense of what is motivating his counterparts in order to communicate the proper image.

(7) 表达能力

优秀的谈判者既要善于倾听，也要善于表达。从他们的举止、衣着和肢体语言到他们如何对待下属，他们的一切都将受到严格的审查。谈判者还必须敏锐地意识到是什么激励了他的对手，以便传达正确的形象。

(8) Sense of humor

Negotiating can be a very stressful affair and there will be moments when it hardly seems worth the effort. A negotiator must be equipped with a highly developed sense of humor in order to weather persistent storms like the negotiating delays, logical problems, absurd social settings, and the discomforts of travel. Viewing such problems with a humorous eye can help keep negotiations on track.

(8) 幽默感

谈判可能是一件压力很大的事情,有时似乎不值得努力。谈判者必须具备高度发展的幽默感,才能经受住持续不断的风暴,如谈判延误、逻辑问题、荒谬的社会环境和旅行的不适。用幽默的眼光看待这些问题,有助于使谈判走上正轨。

According to Liu Yuan, Chinese scholar on negotiation, an efficient and competent international business negotiator should have certain ability and good psychological quality, mainly including four aspects.

(1) Quick and clear reasoning ability and strong self-control ability.

(2) The ability to convey accurate information.

(3) Strong willpower, indomitable spirit, and self-confidence and determination to never give up until the goal is achieved.

(4) Keen insight, high foresight and adaptability.

In addition, the leaders who preside over the negotiation must be able to command the overall situation, have a long-term vision, be able to strategize, be good at deciding the "force deployment" and scheme design in advance according to contents and counterparts of the negotiation, and make necessary changes at any time to adapt to the changes of the situation on the negotiation table.

根据中国谈判学者刘园的观点,一个高效率称职的国际商务谈判人员应具备一定的能力和良好的心理素质,主要包括4个方面。

(1) 敏捷清晰的推理能力和较强的自控能力。

(2) 传达准确的信息的能力。

(3) 坚强的毅力、百折不挠的精神,以及不达目的决不罢休的自信心和决心。

(4) 敏锐的洞察力、高度的预见和应变能力。

此外,主持谈判的领导人员必须能统率全局,有长远的眼光,能运筹帷幄,善于针对谈判内容的轻重、对象的层次,事先决定"兵力部署"和方案设计,并随时做出必要的改变,以适应谈判桌上形势的变化。

Section 5　Professional Quality of International Business Negotiators

第5节　国际商务谈判者的专业素质

Professional quality refers to the professional knowledge and ability of international business negotiators.

专业素质指国际商务谈判者应具备的专业知识和专业能力。

1. Professional knowledge　专业知识

Professional knowledge is sometimes called knowledge quality. International business negotiators should master professional and relevant knowledge in depth and breadth. They must have expertise and be versatile.

专业知识有时也被称作知识素质。国际商务谈判人员理应从深度和广度掌握专业的相关知识，必须有专长，又是多面手。

Negotiation on international cargo trade is a segment of international cargo trade. Taking negotiation on international cargo trade as an example, there is a saying in China that "what to sell, what to shout" and "what to sell, what to shout" across borders is not easy! In the negotiation on international cargo trade, if you are an exporter, you need to be very familiar with the goods you are dealing in, including its specifications, performance, efficacy, size, color, style, materials, production process, manufacturing process, technical requirements, quality standards, price level and change trend, supply of raw materials, market demand, competitive products and competitors, etc, and then you can make an eloquent introduction and promote your goods to the importers at the negotiation table. You also need to understand the relevant terms, rules, practices, operation procedures and methods of international trade business, that is, you need to be able to speak the jargon of international trade business. In most cases, you need to communicate with the other party in English or the language of the other party's country. Moreover, foreign trade and economics policy have a strong policy nature, so you need to understand the relevant regulations and policies of China and foreign countries in international trade, and trade related such as customs supervision, foreign exchange control, inspection and quarantine, monetary finance,

finance and taxation, as well as international conventions, treaties and international practices in international goods trading and related transportation, insurance, settlement, intellectual property, etc. In addition, if you are dealing with negotiation counterparts with different cultural backgrounds, you also need to understand the negotiation concept, negotiation style, thinking mode, decision-making process, customs, etiquette and taboo of the other parties, and you need to learn negotiation science, psychology, behavioral science, etc. It's really not easy for you!

国际货物贸易谈判是国际货物贸易经营的一个环节。以国际货物贸易谈判为例,中国有句俗话——"卖什么吆喝什么",但跨国境"卖什么吆喝什么"并不容易!在国际货物贸易谈判中,如果作为出口商,你得非常熟悉你所经营的商品,包括它的规格、性能、功效、尺寸、颜色、款式、用料、生产流程、制作工艺、技术要求、质量标准、价格水平及变化趋势、原料供应情况、市场需求状况、竞争产品和竞争对手动态等,才有可能在谈判桌上对进口商口若悬河地介绍、推销你的商品。你还得懂与国际贸易业务有关的术语、规则、惯例、操作流程、方式方法,即,你得会说国际贸易业务的行话。绝大多数情况下你都得用英语或对方国家的语言跟对方沟通交流。而且,对外经贸政策性强,所以你得懂中国和外国与国际贸易相关的海关监管、外汇管理、检验检疫、货币金融、财政税收方面的法规政策,还有国际货物买卖以及相关的运输、保险、结算、知识产权等方面的国际公约、条约和国际惯例。另外,如果你是在跟来自不同文化背景的谈判对手打交道,你还得了解对方的谈判理念、谈判风格、思维方式、决策程序、风俗习惯、礼仪礼节和禁忌等,你还得学谈判学、心理学、行为科学等,确实不容易!

The requirements for the knowledge and quality of international business negotiators can be summarized as follows.

对国际商务谈判人员的知识素质的要求可概括如下。

An international business negotiator must be an all-round expert. All-around means that you should have a full command of knowledge in all relevant aspects. Expert means you should have a specialized ability of certain field, For example, you are proficient in a few foreign languages speaking, or you are quite familiar with the international business laws, or you are rich in experience of business operating and/or customs clearance.

Some scholars use a kind of T-type knowledge structure to describe the intellectual qualities which qualified international business negotiators should have, that is to say, horizontally negotiators should have a broad range of knowledge and also be proficient in expertise vertically.

国际商务谈判者必须是一个全方位的专家,全方位意味着你要全面掌握各方面的知识。专家意味着你要有某一领域的专门能力，比如说你精通几门外语，或者你对国际商法相当熟悉，或者你有丰富的业务运营和(或)清关经验。

一些学者用一种 T 字形知识结构来描述合格的国际商务谈判人员应具备的知识素质，即，在横向，谈判人员应具有广泛的知识面，在纵向，谈判人员应精通专业知识。

2. Professional ability 专业能力

Professional ability is sometimes called ability/competence quality, which refers to the ability to apply professional knowledge to solve professional problems. In short, it is the ability to apply the above knowledge to solve practical problems in international business negotiation and international business operation.

专业能力有时也被称作能力素质，是指应用专业知识解决专业问题的能力。简单而言，就是应用上述知识于国际商务谈判和国际商务经营当中解决实际问题的能力。

In fact, the education of typical foreign-related economics and trade majors such as international economics and trade, international trade, international business and business English in Chinese universities has gradually been carried out in accordance with the training mode of compound talents, which is mainly reflected in the curriculum system. Most of the professional knowledge mentioned above has been reflected in the curriculum system, such as for majors of international trade and business English, the teaching of Foreign trade and related knowledge and the teaching of foreign language are equally important. It is a routine operation to take foreign trade courses in foreign languages, especially in English, and a second foreign language and a third foreign language are also offered. However, the students are still lack of ability, and there are many things that need to be improved in school education. For example, teachers are lack of experience in international business negotiation practice and international business operation. Their teaching are mostly on paper. However, the current mechanism does not really encourage teachers to learn from business practice, and then feed back to education practice. In addition, colleges and universities generally have internship arrangements, but the internship term is short, and the cooperation between schools and enterprises or other relevant institutions is relatively loose, so students can not learn the real things. These are all the disadvantages that restrict students to transform knowledge into ability. We need to reform the system and mechanism and remove the obstacles. The international models we can refer to include the co-op program in Canada and the apprenticeship model in Germany.

实际上，中国各高校对国际经济与贸易、国际贸易、国际商务、商务英语等典型的涉外经贸专业学生的教育，已经逐渐按照复合型人才培养方式进行，主要体现在课程体系设置，前面提到的专业知识大多已经体现在课程体系中，比如，对于国际贸易专业和商务英语专业，外经贸及相关知识教学与外语教学并重。用外语尤其英语上外经贸专业课已是常规操作，还开设第二外语、第三外语。但是，学生还是能力不足，学校教育需要改进的地方不少，比如，教师欠缺国际商务谈判实务、国际商务经营的经验，多为纸上谈兵，而现行机制并不真正鼓励教师到实践中去学习，然后反哺到教育实践。还有，各高校一般皆有安排，但实习的学期少、时间短，而且学校与企事业等相关机构的合作相对比较松散，学生学不到真东西。这些都是制约学生将知识转化为能力的弊端，需要从体制机制上改革，破除障碍。国际上可供我们参照的样板有加拿大的 co-op 项目、德国的学徒制模式等。

Terminology　本章术语

1. political quality　政治素质
2. moral quality　品德素质
3. cultural quality　文化素质
4. physical quality　身体素质
5. psychological quality　心理素质
6. professional quality　专业素质
7. professional knowlege　专业知识
8. professional ability　专业能力

Exercises　本章练习

Why must international business negotiators have good quality? What qualities are generally included?

国际商务谈判者为什么必须具备良好的素质？一般包括那些素质？

Answers for Reference 参考答案

Negotiation is the communication among people. People are the subject of negotiation behavior. The quality of negotiators will have a significant impact on the negotiation results. High quality and strong ability negotiators are conducive to the success of negotiation. Generally speaking, the excellent quality of negotiators is not innate, but is acquired through postnatal long-term learning and practice. Excellent international business negotiators should have good political quality, moral quality, cultural quality, physical quality, psychological quality, professional quality, etc.

谈判是人和人之间的沟通交流。人是谈判行为的主体。谈判人员的素质高低会对谈判结果产生重大影响。素质高、能力强的谈判人员有利于谈判取得成功。谈判者的优良素质一般不是天生的,而是在后天长期的学习和实践中锻炼而成。优秀的国际商务谈判者应具备良好政治素质、品德素质、文化素质、身体素质、心理素质、专业素质等。

Chapter 6　International Business Negotiation Strategy

第6章　国际商务谈判策略

From preparation, formal start to agreement, negotiation has experienced a complicated and ever-changing process, which is generally divided into five stages: preparation stage, opening stage, quotation stage, negotiation stage and transaction stage. In the long-term negotiation practice, people have summed up a lot of negotiation strategies in various stages, which have been widely used.

谈判从准备、正式开始到达成协议，要经历一个错综复杂、千变万化的过程，一般分为5个阶段：准备阶段、开局阶段、报价阶段、磋商阶段、成交阶段。人们在长期的谈判实践中，就各个阶段总结出很多有关谈判的策略，这些策略一直被广泛运用。

Section 1　Preparation Strategy

第1节　准备阶段策略

"No preparation, no success". To a great extent, the preparation before negotiation determines whether the negotiation can proceed smoothly, whether the agreement can be signed and whether the transaction can be reached.

"凡事预则立，不预则废"，谈判前的准备工作做得如何，在很大程度上决定着谈判能否顺利进行，协议能否签订，交易能否达成。

1. Negotiation information and intelligence collection　谈判信息和情报搜集

Negotiation information and intelligence refer to the conditions and situations closely related to negotiation activities, including the preparation of relevant policies and regulations, market information, information of negotiation opponents, scientific and technological information, financial information, catalog samples and quotations, etc.

谈判信息情报,指跟谈判活动有密切联系的条件、情况等,包括有关政策法规、市场信息、谈判对手的资料、科技信息、金融信息、目录样品及报价单等的准备情况。

(1) Policies and regulations 政策法规

It includes the political situation, laws and regulations, customs and other tax policies, foreign exchange control policies, import and Export Quota Licensing System of relevant countries or regions.

它包括有关国家或地区的政治状况、法律规定、关税及其他税收政策、外汇管制政策、进出口配额许可证制度等。

(2) Market information 市场信息

It includes international market supply and demand information, market distribution, market potential, market capacity, main competitors and competitive product information.

它包括国际市场供求信息、市场分布情况、市场潜力、市场容量、主要竞争对手及竞争产品信息等。

(3) Information of negotiation counterpart 谈判对手的资料

It includes the type, strength, operation, credit status and transaction intention of the counterparties.

它包括谈判对手的类型、实力、经营情况、信用状况、成交意愿等。

(4) Financial information 金融信息

It includes international financial market interest rate, exchange rate, international settlement procedures, formalities, fees, international investment and financing methods, practices, balance of international payments regulations, etc.

它包括国际金融市场利率、汇率、国际结算程序、手续、费用、国际投融资方式、做法、国际收支规定等。

(5) Scientific and technological information 科技信息

It refers to the development status and trend of science and technology related to the negotiation object, including relevant data, indicators, specifications, performance, quality, supporting and after-sales services, product life cycle, etc. It is necessary to collect and analyze scientific and technological information in advance when introducing advanced technology and equipment.

它指与谈判标的有关的科技发展现状及趋势,具体包括有关数据、指标、规格、性能、质量、配套及售后服务、产品生命周期等。在引进先进技术和设备时，提前搜集、分析科技信息很有必要。

(6) Catalogue, sample and quotation, etc. 目录、样品及报价单等

It is necessary to prepare enterprise brochures, catalogues, samples, quotations and a sufficient number of business cards in advance when participating in international commodity exhibitions and overseas marketing.

参加国际商品展会和出访海外进行市场推销，有必要提前准备好企业宣传册、目录、样品、报价单，以及足够数量的商业名片。

2. Negotiation team formation 谈判团队组建

(1) Size of negotiation team 谈判队伍的规模

The specific number of negotiation teams shall be determined according to the goals and costs of negotiation, and shall be based on the reasonable and efficient principle.

谈判队伍的具体人数，根据谈判的目标和成本确定，以合理高效为原则。

(2) Composition of negotiators 谈判人员的组成

Generally, negotiation leaders, technicians, business personnel, legal personnel, financial personnel, translators, recorders, etc. or personnel with one specialty and multiple abilities, should be considered.

一般要考虑配备谈判领导人员、技术人员、商务人员、法律人员、财务人员、翻译人员、记录人员等，或一专多能的人员。

(3) Division and cooperation of negotiators 谈判人员的分工与配合

The leaders of the above-mentioned negotiation members are usually the main negotiators and the core of the negotiation team. They lead the work of the negotiation team, master the negotiation process, supervise the negotiation process, listen to the suggestions and explanations of the professionals, coordinate the opinions of the negotiation team, decide the important matters in the negotiation process, sign contracts with the outside on behalf of the enterprise, and report the negotiation work to the higher leaders.

Technical, commercial, legal, financial, translation and other professionals use their own expertise to participate in the negotiation.

A recorder, such as a stenographer or typist, is responsible for recording negotiations accurately, completely, in a timely manner.

During the negotiation, the language and actions of the negotiation members coordinate and echo each other. For example, the verbal agreement among the negotiation members, "yes" and "that's it", and, for example, keeping eyes on the speaker, and nodding head, etc. are strong supports for the speaker, which will enhance the weight and credibility of the speaker, and contribute to the success of the negotiation.

上述谈判组成人员中的领导人员通常是主谈人，是谈判队伍的核心，领导谈判班子的工作，掌握谈判进程，监督谈判程序，听取专业人员的建议、说明，协调谈判班子的意见，决定谈判过程的重要事项，代表本企业对外签约，向更高层领导汇报谈判工作。

技术、商务、法律、财务、翻译等专业人员运用各自的专长参与谈判工作。比如记录人员，其职责是准确、完整、及时地记录谈判内容。

谈判中谈判成员之间语言和动作的相互协调、相互呼应，比如，谈判成员之间口头上的附和，"对""就是这样"，还有，眼睛注视正在发言的主谈人，点头等，是对发言人的有力支持，会增强发言人说话的分量和可信度，有助于谈判取得成功。

3. Negotiation plan determination　谈判方案确定

Negotiation plan refers to the arrangement made by the negotiators for the negotiation objectives, agenda and place before the negotiation, which is the guide and direction of the negotiators' actions.

谈判方案，指谈判人员在谈判前预先对谈判目标、谈判议程和谈判地点等所做的安排，是谈判者行动的指导和方向。

(1)　Negotiation goals　谈判目标

①　Top goal/Highest goal　最高目标

Top goal, also known as the optimal expectation goal, refers to the highest goal one party pursues in the negotiation, and also the maximum that the other party can bear. If it exceeds this goal, it is often in danger of negotiation breaking down. In practice, the optimal expectation goal is generally the ideal direction that is expected but not accessible, and there is little possibility of realization. Negotiation is the redistribution of the interests of both parties. No negotiator is willing to give all his own interests to others, and no negotiator can expect to lead in the negotiation. However, it does not mean that the optimal expectation goal has no effect in the negotiation. The optimal expectation goal is the topic at the beginning of the negotiation. If a negotiator introduces his optimal expectation goal at the beginning, he is likely to achieve the lower level goal, that is, the actual demand goal/desirous goal, due to the influence of negotiation psychology, interests, reputation and other factors.

Of course, the optimal expectation goal is not an absolute failure. There is a chance to achieve the optimal expectation goal in the negotiation between two negotiators with high trust.

最高目标，也称最优期望目标，指自己一方在谈判中所追求的最高目标，也往往是对方所能忍受的最大限度。如果超过这个目标，往往要面临谈判破裂的危险。实践中最优期望目标一般是可望而不可即的理想方向，很少有实现的可能。谈判是双方利益重新分配的过程，没有哪个谈判者心甘情愿地把自己的利益全部让给他人，同样任何一个谈判者也不可能指望在谈判中独占鳌头。尽管如此，这不意味着最优期望目标在谈判中没有作用，最优期望目标是谈判开始的话题。如果一个谈判者一开始就推出他的最优期望目标，由于谈判心理、利益、信誉等因素的影响，他很可能达到低一层次的目标，即实际需求目标。

当然，最优期望目标不是绝对达不到，信任度极高的两个谈判对象之间的谈判，达到最优期望目标的机会是存在的。

② Actual demand goal/Desirous goal 实际需求目标

The actual demand goal is the negotiation goal, which is incorporated into the negotiation plan by the negotiator, taking into account all aspects of the situation, on the basis of subjective and objective factors, after scientific demonstration, prediction and accounting. It is the negotiation goal that the negotiator mobilizes all kinds of enthusiasm, uses all kinds of negotiation means and strives to achieve. The goal of this level has a strong driving force for negotiators. Compared with the highest goal, the goal of this level is more realistic.

实际需求目标，是谈判者考虑到各方面情况，根据主客观因素，经过科学论证、预测和核算后，纳入谈判计划的谈判目标；是谈判者调动各种积极性，使用各种谈判手段，努力达到的谈判目标。这一层次的目标对谈判者有着强烈的驱动力。相对于最高目标，这一层次的目标更现实一些。

③ Acceptable goal 可接受目标

Acceptable goal refers to the scope of concession in negotiation, which can meet part of the needs of one party and realize part of economic benefits. Before negotiation, negotiators should fully estimate the occurrence of this situation and formulate corresponding negotiation measures.

可接受目标，指在谈判中可做出让步的范围，它能满足谈判一方的部分需求，实现部分经济利益。谈判者在谈判前应充分估计到这种情况的出现，并制定相应的谈判措施。

④ Bottom goal/Minimum goal 最低目标

The minimum goal is the minimum requirement, the bottom line and the goal of negotiation that must be achieved. If it cannot be achieved, it is better to break the negotiation than to bargain or compromise.

最低目标，是谈判的最低要求，是底线，是必须实现的目标。若不能实现，则宁愿谈判破裂也没有讨价还价、妥协让步的可能。

In the case of multiple negotiation topics, each topic has four levels of objectives, so there are multiple objectives for multiple topics. Negotiators should comprehensively consider, weigh and formulate objectives accordingly, one of which pursues high-level objective, the other may have to accept low-level objective. For example, in terms of commodity price (profit) and quantity, whether exporters want to sell more at low price (small profit) or sell less at high price (huge profit), they need to consider and make choice.

在有多个谈判议题的情况下，每个议题都有 4 个层次的目标，那么多个议题就存在多重目标。谈判者应综合考虑、权衡、相应制定目标，其中一个议题追求高层次目标，其他的议题可能就得接受低层次目标。比如，出口商在商品价格(利润)和数量方面，是追求低价(薄利)多销还是高价(暴利)少销，他们需要对此考虑和做出决定。

(2) Negotiation agenda 谈判议程

Negotiation agenda refers to the order of business in negotiation. In the negotiation agenda, it is necessary to determine the negotiation topics and explain the arrangement of negotiation time.

谈判议程，指谈判的议事日程。谈判议程中需要确定谈判议题和说明谈判时间的安排。

① Topics/Issues 议题

Topics refer to issues related to negotiations that need to be negotiated and discussed. When determing negotiation topics, the name, number and order of topics should be determined.

议题，指与谈判有关的需要展开磋商、讨论的问题。确定谈判议题，包括确定议题的名称、个数、顺序。

② Timing/Schedule 时间安排

Timing includes the following questions. When will the negotiation take place? How long does it last? Do you arrange any recreational activities? What are they? Where are they held? If the negotiation is carried out in stages, it is necessary to determine the stages and the time spent in each stage.

时间安排包括以下问题。谈判在何时举行？为时多久？是否安排调剂性的娱乐活动？有哪些？在哪儿举行？若谈判分阶段进行，还需确定分为几个阶段和每个阶段所花的时间等。

(3) Place 谈判地点

Place of negotiation, is the place where the negotiation is held.

Determining the place of negotiation, includes the choice of the main venue, the away venue, or the third party venue, the arrangement of negotiation rooms, the arrangement of negotiation tables and chairs, and the accommodation arrangement of negotiators in the negotiation place, etc.

谈判地点，即举行谈判的场所。

确定谈判地点，包括选择主场、客场，还是第三方场所，谈判间的布置，谈判桌椅的安排，以及谈判人员在谈判地的食宿安排等。

4. Simulated negotiation　模拟谈判

Simulation negotiation generally has the following segments.

模拟谈判一般有以下几个环节。

(1) Hypothesis/Assumption　拟定假设

Hypothesis making is to recognize (i.e., conjecture) something as a fact according to certain established facts or common sense.

According to the content of the hypothesis, it can be divided into three categories: one is the hypothesis of external objective things; the second is the hypothesis of the other party; and the third is the hypothesis of one's own side.

Hypotheses are not facts, but may be wrong. You should be fully prepared for the unexpected results of hypotheses. In addition, if possible, the hypothesis should be carefully verified.

拟定假设是根据某些既定的事实或常识，将某些事物承认(即臆测)为事实。

根据假设的内容，可把假设划分为三类，一是对外界客观事物的假设，二是对对方的假设，三是对己方的假设。

假设不是事实，有可能是错的，要对假设产生的意外结果有充分的心理准备。另外，如有可能，要对假设，小心求证。

(2) Imagination practice　想象练习

On the basis of formulating assumptions, imagine the process, results and possible actions of the negotiation.

Imagination practice is the thinking activity of the individual or collective of the negotiator, which can be carried out by the negotiator himself, that is, individual imagination, or by gathering of the members of the negotiation team, who make brainstorm, imagine together, discuss collectively, express their opinions freely and fully, and form a high-level plan and countermeasure. Common imagination or collective imagination, is commonly known as salon imagination or discussion conference.

在拟定假设的基础上,想象谈判的过程、结果和可能采取的行动。

想象练习,是谈判者个人或集体的思维活动,可由谈判者个人进行,即个人想象,也可把谈判团队成员聚集在一起,开展头脑风暴,共同想象,集体讨论,自由充分地发表意见,形成高水平的方案和对策。共同想象或集体想象,通常又称为沙龙式模拟或研讨会。

(3) Rehearsal/ Exercise 实际演习

Rehearsal/Exercise, also known as dramatic simulation or role play, is different from imagination practice. Dramatic simulation is a real performance. Each negotiator plays a specific role in simulated negotiation. With the development of the plot, the whole process of negotiation will be displayed in front of each negotiator. Through dramatic simulation, the negotiation preparation will be more full and accurate, so that each negotiator can find their best position in the negotiation and it will provide an opportunity for negotiators to analyze the motivation of negotiation of his own side and the way of thinking, which will ultimately contribute to the success of negotiation.

实际演习,也称为戏剧式模拟或角色扮演。跟想象练习不同,戏剧式模拟是真实地进行演出。每个谈判者都在模拟谈判中扮演特定的角色。随着剧情发展,谈判全过程将展现在每个谈判者面前。通过戏剧式模拟使谈判的准备更充分、更准确,使每个谈判者找到自己在谈判中的最佳位置,能为分析己方的谈判动机及思考问题的方法等提供一次机会,最终将有助于谈判的成功。

Section 2　Strategy in Opening Stage

第 2 节　开局阶段策略

The opening stage mainly refers to the time period after the negotiation parties meet and before they discuss the specific and substantive transaction contents, when they introduce each other, exchange greetings and talk about topics other than the negotiation contents. The opening of the negotiation is the starting point of the formal negotiation, and the effect of the opening determines the trend and development of the whole negotiation to a large extent, so a good opening will be a solid foundation of the success of negotiation. Negotiators should attach great importance to the opening.

开局阶段主要是指谈判双方见面后，在讨论具体、实质性的交易内容之前，相互介绍、寒暄以及就谈判内容以外的话题进行交谈的那个时间段。谈判的开局是正式谈判的起点，开局的效果在很大程度上决定着整个谈判的走向和发展趋势，因此一个良好的开局将为谈判成功奠定坚实的基础，谈判人员应给予高度重视。

In the opening stage, the main task of the negotiators is to create a negotiation atmosphere, exchange views and make opening statements.

在开局阶段，谈判人员的主要任务是创造谈判气氛、交换意见和做开场陈述。

1. Create a good negotiation atmosphere 创造良好的谈判气氛

The pre contact before the two sides meet and the communication during the negotiation will have an impact on the negotiation atmosphere. However, the impact at the beginning of the negotiation is the strongest, which lays the foundation for the negotiation. Therefore, in order to create a friendly, cooperative and relaxed negotiation atmosphere, negotiators should pay attention to the following points.

谈判双方见面之前的预先接触、谈判中的交流，都会对谈判气氛产生影响，但是，谈判开始瞬间的影响最为强烈，它奠定了谈判的基础。因此为创造友好、合作、轻松的谈判气氛，谈判者应注意以下几点。

(1) Before the negotiation, you should calm down to imagine the situation of the negotiating party again.

谈判前应静下心来再次设想谈判对手的情况。

(2) Pay attention to the dress and appearance, shape the image in line with your own identity, and give a good impression to the other.

注意服饰仪表，塑造符合自己身份的形象，给予对方良好的印象。

(3) Appear in front of the other with an open and honest attitude, stand up and greet with him, and look friendly and trustworthy.

以开诚布公的态度出现在对方面前，可站立寒暄致意，目光表现出友善、可信。

(4) Act and speak with ease and without panic.

行动和说话轻松自如不慌张。

(5) It's appropriate to talk about a light digression.

可适当谈论轻松的题外话。

2. Exchange views 交换意见

Later, both parties can sit down and exchange views on negotiation objectives, agenda and schedule.

随后谈判双方可落座，就谈判目标、谈判议程、谈判计划交换意见。

3. Make opening statement 开场陈述

Then the two sides set forth their own views and principles on relevant issues, with the focus on the interests of one's own side.

After the two sides have made their respective statements, they will make a statement that can lead both sides to seek common interests, that is, the initiative. When making initiative, the two sides put forward various ideas and solutions to the problem, and then build a bridge to the road of transaction between the ideas and the reality in line with commercial standards.

然后双方分别阐明自己对有关问题的看法和原则，重点是自己一方的利益。

双方分别陈述后，再做一种能把双方引向寻求共同利益的陈述，即倡议。倡议时，双方提出各种设想和解决问题的方案，然后再在设想和符合商业标准的现实之间，搭起一座通向成交道路的桥梁。

Section 3　Strategy in Quotation Stage

第3节　报价阶段策略

After the opening stage of non specific and non substantive introduction, the negotiation will turn to the main topic of the transaction content and start to quotation/offer. Offer, not only refers to the asking price in terms of commodity price, but also refers to the requirements put forward by one party to the other in terms of quantity, quality, packaging, price, payment, transport, insurance, commodity inspection, claim, dispute resolution and other transaction terms, of which price is the core of transaction negotiation.

The strategies in the quotation stage are mainly reflected in the order of quotation, how to quote and how to treat the other party's quotation.

在非具体内容、非实质性介绍寒暄的开局阶段之后，谈判将转向交易内容的正题，开始报价。报价，不仅指在商品价格方面的要价，还包括谈判一方对另一方提出的自己在数

量、质量、包装、价格、支付、运输、保险、商品检验、索赔、纠纷解决等交易条款方面的要求，其中价格是交易谈判的核心。

报价阶段的策略主要体现在报价的先后顺序、如何报价和如何对待对方的报价方面。

1. Order of quotation　报价的先后顺序

There are advantages and disadvantages in quoting first.

Advantages: set a baseline or framework for the negotiation, and the final negotiation will be reached within this scope. For example, the seller's quotation for men's cotton shirts is CIF New York US$100/dozen. The negotiation result is unlikely to exceed this price. Of course, if both parties have basic understanding of the market situation, unless the negotiation breaks down, the final transaction price will not be too far below this price.

Disadvantages: who offers first, his bottom card has actually been disclosed to the other party, and the other party can modify the psychological price prepared previously. For example, the buyer's original psychological price is CIF New York US$110/dozen. After hearing the seller's offer of CIF New York US$100/dozen, the buyer should cut down the seller's offer of US$100 or accept the seller's offer of US$100 along the way.

According to trade practice, the seller usually offers first, or, who initiates the negotiation, who offers first.

先报价，有利也有弊。

利：为谈判划定一个基准线或框架，最终谈判将在这个范围内达成。比如，男式棉质衬衫，卖方报价 CIF 纽约 100 美元/打，磋商结果不太可能超过这个价位，当然，如双方都对市场行情有基本了解，除非谈判破裂，最终成交价也不至于低于这个价位太远。

弊：先报价一方等于向对方透露底牌，对方可以据此修改原先准备好的心理价位。比如，买方原来的心理价位是 CIF 纽约 110 美元/打，在听到卖方的报价 CIF 纽约 100 美元/打之后，买方应该会就 100 美元的卖方报价再压价或者顺水推舟接受 100 美元的卖方报价。

按贸易惯例，一般由卖方先报价，或者，谁发起谈判，谁先报价。

2. How to quote　如何报价

Even for a veteran on negotiating, pricing is rather difficult, which is "brain-burnt", and needs long-term learning and experience accumulation to be proficient at.

即使是一个谈判老手，定价也相当困难，很"烧脑"，需要长期的学习和经验积累熟练掌握：

(1) composition of price(cost, fees,profit,tax and so on)

价格构成(成本、费用、利润、税收等)

(2) different influencing factors(quantity, quality, packing, destination, delivery term, seasonal demands, fluctuations in exchange, payment mode, commission and so on)

不同的影响因素(数量、质量、包装、目的地、交货期、季节性需求、汇率波动、付款方式、佣金等)

(3) various ways of pricing(cost oriented pricing, demands oriented pricing, competition oriented pricing)

多种定价方式(成本导向定价、需求导向定价、竞争导向定价)

(4) goals(maximize current profit, keep a good relationship with the business counterpart, expand and consolidate market share, cope with competitors)

目标(最大化当前利润,保持与业务对手的良好关系,扩大和巩固市场份额,应对竞争对手)

(5) strategies of pricing of the enterprise(for a new product, for a group of products, for different areas, for different grades and etc.)

企业定价策略(新产品、一组产品、不同地区、不同档次等)

3. How to treat the other party's quotation 如何对待对方的报价

(1) In the process of the other party's quotation, do not disturb the other party, listen carefully, and try to record the quotation content of the other party completely, accurately and clearly.

在对方报价的过程中,切忌干扰对方,应认真听取,并尽力完整、准确、清楚地记下对方的报价内容。

(2) After the other party's quotation, if there is something you don't understand, you can ask the other party to answer. If necessary, summarize your understanding of the other party's quotation and repeat it to confirm whether your understanding is accurate. Strive to let the other party make a detailed explanation of price composition, quotation basis, calculation basis, method, etc. After that, make a counter-offer or acceptance.

在对方报价结束后,如果有没听明白的地方,可要求对方解答,如有必要,将自己对对方报价的理解归纳总结,进行复述,以确认自己的理解是否准确无误。争取让对方对其价格的构成、报价依据、计算基础以及方式方法等作出详尽的解释。之后,再进行还价或接受。

Section 4　Strategy in Negotiation Stage

第4节　磋商阶段策略

In general, after one party's offer, the other party may not accept it unconditionally, but make a counter-offer, and then the offerer and offeree makes offer and counter-offer over and again, until they make a deal after many times. Of course, the negotiation may break down. After the quotation, the stage before the transaction is the negotiation stage, also known as the bargaining stage. This stage is the key stage of negotiation, the most difficult and tense stage, or the stage of advocating interests, resolving differences and making concessions to each other.

一般情况下，在一方报价之后，另一方可能不会无条件地接受，而是还价，再报价，再还价，往复多次之后，才成交，当然也可能谈判破裂。报价之后，成交之前的这个阶段，就是磋商阶段，也叫讨价还价阶段。这个阶段是谈判的关键阶段，也是最困难，最紧张的阶段，还是主张利益、解决分歧、相互让步的阶段。

Generally speaking, the negotiation strategy used in this stage is related to the status and strength of negotiators. The strong side will often take the initiative to attack and use strategies to force the other side to make concessions, meanwhile the weak side might try to prevent the other side from attacking or make concessions.

一般而言，这个阶段所运用的谈判策略，与谈判者的地位、实力有关。强势的一方常常会主动进攻，运用策略迫使对方让步，同时弱势的一方可能力图阻止对方进攻或妥协让步。

1. The strategy of forcing the other side to give in　迫使对方让步的策略

The strategy of forcing the other side to give in is also called offensive strategy.
迫使对方让步的策略也叫进攻策略。

(1) Manufacturing and leveraging competition　制造和利用竞争

When one side of the negotiation has competitors, its negotiation ability will be greatly reduced. Making and using competition is the most effective strategy to force the other side to give in in negotiation. Before the negotiation, several potential negotiation counterparts can be inspected and contacted. During the negotiation, the situation of competitors of some negotiation counterparts can be properly disclosed, which makes the negotiation counterparts have pressure and sense of crisis. In addition, the negotiation with other negotiation counterparts should not be concluded too early, so as to keep the competition situation. Even if the other party does not actually have a competitor, it can cleverly create a false image to confuse the other party.

当谈判的一方存在竞争对手时，其谈判的能力会大减。制造并利用竞争是谈判中迫使对方让步最有效的策略。谈判前，可多考察、接触几家潜在的谈判对象。谈判中，可适当地透露一些谈判对象的竞争对手的情况，让谈判对象有压力、产生危机感。另外，不过早地结束与其他谈判对象的谈判，让竞争局面一直保持。即使对方实际上没有竞争对手，也可巧妙地制造假象迷惑对方。

(2) Adopt every possible means/Carrot and stick 软硬兼施

The hardliners who sing "red face" on your own side come out first, take a tough stand and press each other step by step, so as to overwhelm the other party in momentum, even provoke the other party and force the other party to give in. The "white faced" moderates on your side will come to the stage next, with a moderate tone, sincere attitude, cordial words, and launch "reasonable" conditions.

己方"唱红脸"的强硬派先出场，立场强硬，步步紧逼，从气势上压倒对方，甚至激怒对方，迫使对方让步。己方"唱白脸"的温和派再登场，以缓和的语气、诚恳的态度、亲切的言语，推出"合情合理"的条件。

(3) Ultimatum 最后通牒

If neither could convince the other, and the other party is unwilling to make concessions and accept the terms of your own transaction, in order to force the other party to make concessions, you can issue an ultimatum to the other party, that is, if the other party does not accept the terms of your own transaction and reach an agreement within a certain period of time, you will announce that the negotiation is broken down and withdraw from the negotiation.

在双方争执不下，对方不愿让步并接受己方交易条件时，为了逼迫对方让步，己方可以向对方发出最后通牒，即，如果对方在某个期限内不接受己方的交易条件并达成协议，己方就宣布谈判破裂并退出谈判。

2. Strategies to stop the attack   阻止进攻的策略

The strategy to stop the attack is also called defensive strategy.
阻止进攻的策略也叫防守策略。

(1) Restrictive strategy 限制策略

① Limitation of power 权力限制

When the other party is aggressive and demands you to agree to the other party's terms of transaction immediately, you can use the excuse "within my power, I can't agree to your request". If the other party chooses to terminate the negotiation and find a competent supervisor to start the negotiation again, he will have to suffer the loss of human resources, financial resources and time.

在对方咄咄逼人，要求己方立即答应对方的交易条件时，可用托词"在我的权力范围之内，没法答应贵方要求"。对方若选择终止谈判，寻找有权限的上司重新开始谈判，不得不遭受人力、财力和时间上的损失。

② Information restriction 资料限制

When the other party requests an explanation of a question or a concession of a request, you can use the tone of apology to inform the other party that you are really sorry that the information in this regard is not available, or is not prepared, or belongs to your business secrets, so you can't reply for the time being.

当对方要求己方就某一问题做解释或就某一要求做让步时，己方可用抱歉的语气告知对方，实在对不起，这方面的资料暂时没有，或没有备齐，或属于本方的商业秘密，因此暂时不能答复。

③ Other restrictions 其他方面的限制

It has also been suggested that due to the influence of technology, manpower, environment, time and other factors, you can not meet the requirements of the other party.

己方还可提出因技术、人力、环境、时间等因素的影响，而没法满足对方的要求。

(2) Show weakness for pity 示弱以求怜悯

In general, people always sympathize with the weak and don't want the weak to be killed. In the negotiation, the defensive side can use this characteristic of human nature as a defensive strategy to prevent the other side from attacking. For example, when you are cornered by the other party in the negotiation, you can open your real hope and requirements in the negotiation to seek the understanding and tolerance of the other party, and even show the obvious attitude of the weak to ask the other party to give up the request.

一般情况下，人们总是同情弱者，不愿将其置于死地。谈判中防守方可以利用人性的这一特点作为防守策略，阻止对方进攻。比如，在谈判中被对方逼得走投无路时，把己方对本次谈判的真实希望和要求和盘托出，求得对方的理解和宽容，甚至表现出明显的弱者的姿态，请求对方高抬贵手，放弃要求。

(3) Tit for tat 以牙还牙，以攻对攻

In the negotiation, the defensive side sometimes also needs to consider defensive counterattack to attack the other and give him tit for tat. When the other side forces you to give in on a certain issue, you can consider this issue together with other issues, attack on other issues and ask the other side to give in. For example, if the other party asks for a price concession, you can ask for a payment concession, increasing the proportion of the deposit, paying off the balance before delivery, etc.

谈判中防守方有时也要考虑防守反击,以攻对攻,以牙还牙。在对方就某一问题逼迫己方让步时,己方可将这个问题与其他问题联系在一起加以考量,在其他问题上进攻,要求对方让步。比如,对方要求己方做价格让步,己方可要求对方做支付的让步,提高定金的比例,发货前须付清余款等。

3. Concession strategy 让步策略

If it is necessary to make concessions and your side is willing to make concessions, you can still use appropriate concession strategies, otherwise, it will be a vain concession.

在需要让步并且己方也愿意让步的情况下,仍可运用适当的让步策略,否则让也白让。

(1) Do not make unnecessary concessions, you should let the other party feel the sincerity of your concessions and the efforts you have made, and cherish the concessions you have made.

不做无谓的让步,应让对方感受到己方让步的诚意和所付出的努力,珍惜所得到的让步。

(2) Concessions should be made in key links with reasonable rhythm and range, and smaller concessions can bring greater satisfaction to the other party.

让步要让在关键环节,节奏合理,幅度适当,较小的让步带给对方较大的满足感。

(3) You should strive to let the other party make concessions on issues that you think important. You can make concessions on issues that you think less important or not important.

在己方认为重要的问题上,力求对方先让步;在己方认为次重要或不重要的问题上可以做出让步。

(4) Concessions should be cautious, and trustworthy. Think before act. Concessions that have been made should not be taken back.

让步要谨慎,也要守信。三思而后行,已做出的让步不宜再收回。

Section 5　Strategy in Transaction Stage

第 5 节　成交阶段策略

The transaction stage is the final stage of formal negotiation and the stage when both parties are determined to conclude the transaction according to the final transaction terms reached through negotiation. There are three main objectives in this stage. The first is to try to reach an agreement as soon as possible; the second is to try to ensure that the agreed transaction terms remain unchanged, and the third is to strive for the final benefit.

The following strategies can be adopted in the closing stage.

成交阶段是正式谈判的最后阶段,是双方下决心按磋商达成的最终交易条件成交的阶段。这一阶段主要有三个目标,一是力求尽快达成协议,二是尽量保证谈妥的交易条件不变,三是争取最后的利益收获。

成交阶段可采用以下策略。

1. Off negotiation room transaction　场外交易

When the negotiation enters into the stage of transaction, both parties have reached an agreement on most issues, and only have differences on one or two issues, transaction. Transaction outside the negotiation room can be considered, and the negotiation can be transferred to banquets, golf courses and other places of entertainment. In a relaxed, friendly and harmonious atmosphere, the tense situation between the two sides can be eased. Both sides can freely talk about topics of interest, exchange personal feelings, resolve problems left over from the negotiation table, and even make large-scale concessions to each other to reach an agreement.

谈判进入成交阶段,双方已在绝大多数议题上取得一致意见,仅在某一两个问题上存在分歧而影响成交时,可考虑采取场外交易,把谈判转到宴会或高尔夫球场及其他娱乐场所。在轻松、友好、融洽的气氛下,双方剑拔弩张的紧张局面得以缓和,双方可自在地谈论自己感兴趣的话题,交流私人感情,化解谈判桌上遗留的问题,甚至会大度地相互作出让步而达成协议。

2. Final concession　最后让步

Before the deadline or the last moment of negotiation, one of the negotiating parties takes the initiative to make the final concession, which is helpful for both parties to reach an agreement.

谈判一方在谈判的最后期限或最后时刻到来之前，主动做最后让步，有助于双方达成协议。

3. Don't forget the final profit　不忘最后获利

Some smart negotiators still use the last moment to strive for the last harvest, when they are about to sign a contract, and suddenly make a small request for the other party to make a small concession.

有些精明的谈判者，在即将签约的时候，还利用最后时刻争取最后一点收获，突然提出一个小的请求，要求对方再做出一个小的让步。

4. Celebration for both parties　为双方庆贺

At the time of signing the contract, you should celebrate for both sides and emphasize that it is through the joint efforts of both sides that the negotiation results can be achieved, so as to meet the psychological balance and comfort of both sides.

在即将签约之时，要为双方庆贺，强调是经过双方的共同努力才取得谈判成果，以满足双方的心理平衡和安慰。

5. Review the agreed transaction terms before signing the contract
　　签约之前复核已谈妥的各项交易条款

The formal agreement is binding on both parties of the transaction. The breaching party will bear the liability for breach of contract and compensate the observant party. Therefore, before transforming the negotiation result into a formal agreement, it is necessary to carefully check the negotiated transaction terms to ensure that they are correct without any ambiguity or error.

正式协议对交易双方都有约束力，违约方将承担违约责任，赔偿守约方。所以，在将谈判的成果转变为正式协议之前，应认真核对已谈妥的各项交易条款，保证正确无误，没有任何歧义和误差。

Terminology 本章术语

1. preparation stage 准备阶段
2. opening stage 开局阶段
3. quotation stage 报价阶段
4. negotiation stage 磋商阶段
5. transaction stage 成交阶段
6. negotiation strategy 谈判策略
7. top goal 最高目标
8. actual demand goal/desirous goal 实际需求目标
9. acceptable goal 可接受目标
10. bottom goal/minimum goal 最低目标
11. simulated negotiation 模拟谈判
12. hypothesis/assumption 拟定假设
13. imagination practice 想象练习
14. rehearsal/exercise 实际演习
15. ultimatum 最后通牒
16. off negotiation room transaction 场外交易

Exercises 本章练习

1. What are included in information and intelligence collection?
   谈判信息和情报收集包括哪些内容？
2. What should be done in the preparation stage?
   在准备阶段应该做些什么？
3. What are the issues covered by the negotiation plan?
   谈判方案涵盖哪些事项？
4. What does the highest goal work for?
   最高目标起什么作用？
5. What segments are generally there in simulation negotiation?
   模拟谈判一般有哪些环节？

6. What should be done in the opening stage?
   在开局阶段应该做些什么？

7. What are advantages and disadvantages in quoting first? Which party usually offers first according to trade practice?
   先报价的优点和缺点是什么？按贸易惯例，一般哪一方先报价？

8. How to quote?
   如何报价？

9. What are strategies of forcing the other side to give in?
   迫使对方让步有哪些策略？

10. What strategies could be used for stopping the attack?
    可以使用什么策略来阻止攻击？

11. What strategies should we master about concession?
    让步应掌握哪些策略？

12. What is off negotiation room transaction?
    什么是场外交易？

Answers for Reference　参考答案

1. Negotiation information and intelligence refer to the conditions and situations closely related to negotiation activities, including the preparation of relevant policies and regulations, market information, information of negotiation opponents, scientific and technological information, financial information, catalog samples and quotations, etc.

谈判信息情报，指跟谈判活动有密切联系的条件、情况等，包括有关政策法规、市场信息、谈判对手的资料、科技信息、金融信息、目录样品及报价单等的准备情况。

2. The following things should be done in the preparation stage. 准备阶段应该做以下事情。
   (1) Negotiation information and intelligence collection 谈判信息和情报搜集
   (2) Team formation 谈判团队组建
   (3) Plan determination 谈判方案确定
   (4) Simulated negotiation 模拟谈判

3. Negotiation plan refers to the arrangement made by the negotiators for the negotiation objectives, agenda and place before the negotiation, which is the guide and direction of the negotiators' actions.

谈判方案，指谈判人员在谈判前预先对谈判目标、谈判议程和谈判地点等所做的安排，是谈判者行动的指导和方向。

4. The highest goal, also known as the optimal expectation goal, refers to the highest goal one party pursues in the negotiation, and also the maximum that the other party can bear. If it exceeds this goal, it is often in danger of negotiation breaking down. In practice, the optimal expectation goal is generally the ideal direction that is expected but not accessible, and there is little possibility of realization. Negotiation is the redistribution of the interests of both parties. No negotiator is willing to give all his own interests to others, and no negotiator can expect to lead in the negotiation. However, it does not mean that the optimal expectation goal has no effect in the negotiation. The optimal expectation goal is the topic at the beginning of the negotiation. If a negotiator introduces his optimal expectation goal at the beginning, he is likely to achieve the lower level goal, that is, the actual demand goal/desirous goal, due to the influence of negotiation psychology, interests, reputation and other factors.

Of course, the optimal expectation goal is not an absolute failure. There is a chance to achieve the optimal expectation goal in the negotiation between two negotiators with high trust.

最高目标，也称最优期望目标，指自己一方在谈判中所追求的最高目标，也往往是对方所能忍受的最大限度，如果超过这个目标，往往要面临谈判破裂的危险。实践中最优期望目标一般是可望而不可即的理想方向，很少有实现的可能。谈判是双方利益重新分配的过程，没有哪个谈判者心甘情愿地把自己的利益全部让给他人，同样任何一个谈判者也不可能指望在谈判中独占鳌头。尽管如此，这不意味着最优期望目标在谈判中没有作用，最优期望目标是谈判开始的话题，如果一个谈判者一开始就推出他的最优期望目标，由于谈判心理、利益、信誉等因素的影响，他很可能达到低一层次的目标，即实际需求目标。

当然，最优期望目标不是绝对达不到，信任度极高的两个谈判对象之间的谈判，达到最优期望目标的机会是存在的。

5. Simulation negotiation generally has the following segments.
模拟谈判一般有以下几个环节。
(1) Hypothesis/Assumption　拟定假设
(2) Imagination practice　想象练习
(3) Rehearsal/Exercise　实际演习

6. In the opening stage, the main task of the negotiators is to create a negotiation atmosphere, exchange views and make opening statements.
在开局阶段，谈判人员的主要任务是创造谈判气氛、交换意见和做开场陈述。

7. There are advantages and disadvantages in quoting first.

Advantages: set a baseline or framework for the negotiation, and the final negotiation will be reached within this scope. For example, the seller's quotation for men's cotton shirts is CIF New York US$100 / dozen. The negotiation result is unlikely to exceed this price. Of course, if both parties have basic understanding of the market situation, unless the negotiation breaks down, the final transaction price will not be too far below this price.

Disadvantages: who offers first, his bottom card has actually been disclosed to the other party, and the other party can modify the psychological price prepared previously. For example, the buyer's original psychological price is CIF New York US$110/dozen. After hearing the seller's offer of CIF New York US$100/dozen, the buyer should cut down the seller's offer of US$100 or accept the seller's offer of US$100 along the way.

According to trade practice, the seller usually offers first, or, who initiates the negotiation, who offers first.

先报价，有利也有弊。

利：为谈判划定一个基准线或框架，最终谈判将在这个范围内达成。比如，男式棉质衬衫，卖方报价 CIF 纽约 100 美元/打，磋商结果不太可能超过这个价位，当然，如双方都对市场行情有基本了解，除非谈判破裂，最终成交价也不至于低于这个价位太远。

弊：先报价一方等于向对方透露底牌，对方可以据此修改原先准备好的心理价位。比如，买方原来的心理价位是 CIF 纽约 110 美元/打，在听到卖方的报价 CIF 纽约 100 美元/打之后，买方应该会就 100 美元的卖方报价再压价或者顺水推舟接受 100 美元的卖方报价。

按贸易惯例，一般由卖方先报价，或者，谁发起谈判，谁先报价。

8. Even for a veteran on negotiating, pricing is rather difficult, which is "brain-burnt", and needs long term learning and experience accumulation to be proficient at.

即使是一个谈判老手，定价也相当困难，很"烧脑"，需要长期的学习和经验积累熟练掌握：

(1) composition of price(cost, fees, profit, tax and so on)

价格构成(成本、费用、利润、税收等)

(2) different influencing factors(quantity, quality, packing, destination, delivery term, seasonal demands, fluctuations in exchange, payment mode, commission and so on)

不同的影响因素(数量、质量、包装、目的地、交货期、季节性需求、汇率波动、付款方式、佣金等)

(3) various ways of pricing(cost oriented pricing, demands oriented pricing, competition

oriented pricing)

多种定价方式(成本导向定价、需求导向定价、竞争导向定价)

(4) goals(maximize current profit, keep a good relationship with the business counterpart, expand and consolidate market share, cope with competitors)

目标(最大化当前利润,保持与业务对手的良好关系,扩大和巩固市场份额,应对竞争对手)

(5) strategies of pricing of the enterprise(for a new product, for a group of products, for different areas, for different grades and etc.)

企业定价策略(新产品、一组产品、不同地区、不同档次等)

9. The strategies of forcing the other side to give in

迫使对方让步的策略

(1) Manufacturing and leveraging competition 制造和利用竞争

(2) Adopt every possible means/Carrot and stick 软硬兼施

(3) Ultimatum 最后通牒

10. The strategies could be used to stop the attack are as follows.

用于阻止进攻的策略如下。

(1) Restrictive strategy 限制策略

(2) Show weakness for pity 示弱以求怜悯

(3) Tit for tat 以牙还牙,以攻对攻

11. If it is necessary to make concessions and your side is willing to make concessions, you can still use appropriate concession strategies, otherwise, it will be a vain concession.

在需要让步并且己方也愿意让步的情况下,仍可运用适当的让步策略,否则让也白让。

(1) Do not make unnecessary concessions, you should let the other party feel the sincerity of your concessions and the efforts you have made, and cherish the concessions you have made.

不做无谓的让步,应让对方感受到己方让步的诚意和所付出的努力,珍惜所得到的让步。

(2) Concessions should be made in key links with reasonable rhythm and range, and smaller concessions can bring greater satisfaction to the other party.

让步要让在关键环节,节奏合理,幅度适当,较小的让步带给对方较大的满足感。

(3) You should strive to let the other party make concessions on issues that you think important. You can make concessions on issues that you think less important or not important.

在己方认为重要的问题上,力求对方先让步,在己方认为次重要或不重要的问题上可以做出让步。

(4) Concessions should be cautious, and trustworthy. Think before act. Concessions that have been made should not be taken back.

让步要谨慎，也要守信。三思而后行。已做出的让步不宜再收回。

12. When the negotiation enters into the stage of transaction, both parties have reached an agreement on most issues, and only have differences on one or two issues, transaction, transaction outside the negotiation room can be considered, and the negotiation can be transferred to banquets, golf courses and other places of entertainment. In a relaxed, friendly and harmonious atmosphere, the tense situation between the two sides can be eased, both sides can freely talk about topics of interest, exchange personal feelings, resolve problems left over from the negotiation table, and even make large-scale concessions to each other to reach an agreement.

谈判进入成交阶段，双方已在绝大多数议题上取得一致意见，仅在某一两个问题上存在分歧，相持不下，而影响成交时，可考虑采取场外交易，把谈判转到宴会或球场及其他娱乐场所。在轻松、友好、融洽的气氛下，双方剑拔弩张的紧张局面得以缓和，双方可自在地谈论自己感兴趣的话题，交流私人感情，化解谈判桌上遗留的问题，甚至会大度地相互作出让步而达成协议。

Chapter 7 International Business Negotiation Skills

第 7 章 国际商务谈判技巧

Negotiation is completed by means of information exchange between the two sides of the negotiation. In the negotiation, information transmission and reception need to be completed by means of listening, narration, questioning, answering, watching, debating and persuasion between the negotiators. The negotiators must pay attention to the use of negotiation skills at any time on the negotiation table, so as to accurately grasp the behaviors and thoughts of the other side.

谈判是借助谈判双方的信息交流来完成的,谈判中信息传递与接收需要通过谈判者之间的听、叙、问、答、看、辩及说服等方法来完成。谈判者在谈判桌上必须随时注意谈判技巧的运用,以便准确地把握对方的行为与思想。

Section 1 Listening Skills

第 1 节 听的技巧

Communication refers to the exchange of information and knowledge between the sender and the receiver through certain channels in the process of interaction, which is a conscious activity process. Language communication is the most basic way for human beings to exchange information with each other, and listening is the most basic and important way to obtain the other's information, so listening is the premise and necessary guarantee of communication. Carnegie said:"If you want to be a good conversationalist, be a dedicated listener first." Franklin said: "The key to a successful conversation is to listen more and never pretend to understand." Dorothy Dix said:"The shortcut to fame is to lend your ears, not your tongue to everyone."

Negotiation is a process of communication. The main way for us to understand and grasp the other's views and standpoints is listening. Among all negotiation and communication skills, we put listening skills in the first place.

Listening is not simply to listen with the ears, but also an art. It is not only to listen to the speaker's words with the ears, but also to feel the verbal and non-verbal information expressed in the conversation process of the other party with all one's heart.

沟通是指人们在互动过程中，发送者通过一定渠道与接收者进行信息、知识的交流，这是一个有意识的活动过程。语言交流是人类互相交换信息的最基本方式，倾听则是获取对方信息的最基础和最重要的方式，所以倾听是沟通的前提和必要的保障。卡耐基说："如果你希望成为一个善于谈话的人，那就先做一个致力于倾听的人。"富兰克林说："与人交谈取得成功的重要秘诀就是多听，永远不要不懂装懂。"多罗西娅·迪克斯也说："成名的捷径就是把你的耳朵而不是舌头借给所有人。"

谈判是沟通交流的过程，我们了解和把握对方观点与立场的主要手段和途径就是倾听。在各项谈判沟通技巧中，我们把倾听的技巧放在第一位介绍。

倾听不是简单地用耳朵来听，它也是一门艺术，不仅仅是要用耳朵来听说话者的言辞，还需要一个人全身心地去感受对方在谈话过程中表达的言语信息和非言语信息。

Listening skills 倾听技巧

1. Concentration is the most basic and important content in listening art.

2. Lean forward, take the initiative to look at the speaker, look softly and attentively, cooperate with some actions, expressions and simple words, and give response to the other party at the right time, such as raising eyebrows or smiling or nodding with approval or "um", "right" and "yes", showing interest or attention to the conversation, so as to encourage the speaker.

3. Try to avoid environmental interference that may lead to unclear hearing.

4. Don't rush to interrupt, refute, argue, judge, evaluate, draw a conclusion, express opinions and study countermeasures.

5. Don't listen and think about what the speaker will say next.

6. Avoid preconceived, and prejudiced listening.

7. Good memory is worse than bad writing; take notes on important content.

8. You can find gaps to clarify the content by asking questions.

9. Listen and pay attention to the key points.

These are just some of the basic listening skills.

1. 专心致志是倾听艺术中最基本最重要的内容。

2. 身体前倾，主动与讲话者进行对视，目光柔和专注，配合一些动作、表情和简单的言语，适时给予对方回应，比如，扬一下眉或微笑或赞同地点头或"嗯""对""是的"，表示出对谈话感兴趣或重视，以鼓励讲话者。

3. 尽量避免环境干扰导致听不清。
4. 不急于打断、反驳、争论、判断、评价、下结论、发表观点、研究对策。
5. 不要边听边琢磨讲话者下面会讲什么。
6. 忌先入为主，带偏见和成见地听。
7. 好记性不如烂笔头，重要内容做笔记。
8. 可寻找空隙通过提问澄清内容。
9. 听话听音，抓重点。

以上仅是倾听的一些基本技巧，不一而足。

It should be noted that English is the common spoken language in the field of international economics and trade, and in international business circle. Mastering English is the basic requirement for the students majoring in international economics and trade, international business, business English and other typical foreign affairs majors. It is the basic skill that relevant practitioners should have. For them, international business negotiation is a part of their work and common practice. Although they have good English language ability, it's not easy to listen effectively in international business negotiations, because almost all they hear in international business negotiations are problems of business, professional terms, commodity knowledge, project content, etc. expressed in English. Only a simple English language ability is not enough. So students and relevant personnel are required to keep sober. English is just a tool, to rely on, but not to lean on. They must continue to learn to accumulate to fill the gap. Compound talents can meet the requirements of the industry.

特别需要注意的是，英语是国际经贸界、国际商务圈的普通话、通用语。熟练掌握英语是对国际经济与贸易、国际商务、商务英语等典型涉外经贸、商务专业学生的基本要求，是相关从业人员应当具备的基本功。对他们而言，国际商务谈判是工作的一部分，是"家常便饭"。尽管他们具备还不错的英语语言能力，但要在国际商务谈判当中做到有效倾听却很不容易，因为他们在国际商务谈判中听到的几乎全是用英语表达的业务问题、专业术语、商品知识、项目内容等。只有单纯的英语语言能力是远远不够的。因此学生和有关从业者应当保持清醒。英语就是个工具而已，可依靠，不可依赖。他们还必须不断学习积累补缺。复合型人才才适应得了行业要求。

Section 2　Narration Skills

第 2 节　叙的技巧

"Narration" is based on one's own standpoint, point of view, plan, etc. to express specific views on various issues or to elaborate on objective things through statements, so as to make the other party understand. "Narration" is a kind of active elaboration, which is one of the methods of transmitting information and communicating emotions.

Generally speaking, negotiators should be sincere, clear-cut, vivid and fluent in language, clear and compact in their statements of problems, views and opinions. In the process of negotiation, the narration consists of two parts: entry and elaboration. The negotiator must grasp the corresponding skills.

"叙"是基于己方的立场、观点、方案等，通过陈述来表达对各种问题的具体看法，或是对客观事物的具体阐述，以便让对方有所了解。"叙"是带有主动性的阐述，是传递信息、沟通情感的方法之一。

一般而言，谈判者在叙述问题、表达观点和意见时，应当态度诚恳，观点明确，语言生动、流畅，层次清晰、紧凑。谈判过程中叙述大体包括入题、阐述两个部分，谈判者须把握相应的技巧。

1. Entry skills　入题技巧

When the two sides of the negotiation just enter the negotiation place, they will inevitably feel constrained, especially the novice negotiators. They often have uneasy psychology in the important negotiation. The appropriate skills of the negotiation will help to ease the tension, eliminate the embarrassment and start the negotiation easily.

谈判双方在刚进入谈判场所时，难免会感到拘谨，尤其是谈判新手，在重要谈判中往往会产生忐忑不安的心理，运用适当的入题技巧有助于缓解紧张，消除尴尬，轻松地开始谈判。

(1) Detour into question　迂回入题

It can avoid being too straightforward and affecting the harmonious atmosphere of the negotiation by using circuitous approach. The specific methods of detour are as follows.

谈判时采用迂回入题，可避免过于直白而影响谈判的融洽气氛。迂回入题的具体方法如下。

① From the extraneous into the question.

Take the season, weather, international news, sports, culture, art, fashion, travel information, social celebrities, etc. as topics.

② From the introduction of your basic situation into the question.

Including production conditions, product quality, business situation, market environment, reputation, etc.

③ From introduction of the members of your negotiation team.

Generally, the position, education background, experience, etc. of the members of the negotiation team of your own side can be briefly introduced.

① 从题外话入题。将有关季节、天气、国际新闻、体育、文化、艺术、时尚、旅行见闻、社会名人等作为话题。

② 从介绍己方的基本情况入题。包括生产条件、产品质量、经营状况、市场情况、口碑声誉等。

③ 从介绍己方谈判团队成员入题。通常可简略介绍己方谈判组成员的职务、学历、经历等。

(2) In large-scale negotiations, we should first discuss general principles and then details.

在大型谈判中，先谈一般原则，再谈细节问题。

(3) In the phased negotiation, before the start of each phase of negotiation, we should first discuss the issue of this phase and then discuss the specific content.

在分阶段谈判中，每阶段的谈判开始之前，先谈本次的议题，再谈具体内容。

2. Elaboration skils　阐述技巧

After the entry, the next step is for both parties to elaborate their own views, which is also skillful.

谈判入题后，接下来是双方阐述各自观点的环节，阐述也有讲究。

(1) According to the situation, let the other party talk first.

根据情况，让对方先谈。

When you don't know much about the market situation and product pricing, or you haven't decided which product to buy, or you don't have the rights to directly decide whether to buy or not, you should try to ask the other party to first explain what kind of product can be provided, how the product performance is, what the product price is, and so on, and then carefully express your opinions. Sometimes even if you have a better understanding of the market and product pricing, you have a clear purchase intention in mind, and you can directly decide whether to purchase or not, you may as well let the other party first elaborate the interest requirements, offer and introduce the product, and then put forward your own requirements on this basis.

当己方对市场态势和产品定价情况不太了解，或者己方尚未确定购买何种产品，或者己方无权直接决定购买与否的时候，要争取让对方首先说明可提供何种产品，产品的性能如何，产品的价格如何等，然后再审慎地表达意见。有时即使己方对市场和产品定价比较了解，心中有较为明确的购买意图，而且能够直接决定购买与否，也不妨先让对方阐述利益要求、报价和介绍产品，然后在此基础上提出自己的要求。

(2) Key points of your opening statement
己方开场阐述的要点

① Start with a clear idea and clarify the theme to be solved in this negotiation, so as to focus the attention of both sides and unify the understanding of both sides.

② Show the benefits that your side should get through negotiation, especially the vital benefits to your side.

③ Show your basic standpoint.

④ The introduction should be principled, not specific, and as concise as possible.

⑤ The opening presentation should be expressed in a sincere and relaxed way, so that the other party can understand your intention and create a harmonious atmosphere for negotiation.

① 开宗明义，明确本次谈判所要解决的主题，以集中双方的注意力、统一双方的认识。

② 表明己方通过谈判应得到的利益，尤其是对己方至关重要的利益。

③ 表明己方的基本立场。

④ 开场阐述应该是原则性的，而不是具体的，尽可能简明扼要。

⑤ 开场阐述应以诚挚和轻松的方式来表达，让对方明白己方的意图与创造和谐的谈判气氛。

(3) Key points of general elaboration
通用的阐述要领

① The speech is closely related to the theme, objective and true in description, proper in wording and not extreme.

② The language is accurate, standard, concise and rational, and the explanation is easy to understand.

③ Pay attention to intonation, speed, voice level, proper pause, necessary repetition, topic conversion, etc.

④ Correct mistakes in time.

① 发言紧扣主题，叙述客观真实，措辞得体，不走极端。
② 语言准确规范、简明扼要，具有条理性，解释说明通俗易懂。
③ 注意语调、语速、声音高低、适时的停顿、必要的重复、话题的转换等。
④ 发现错误并及时纠正。

Section 3　Asking Skills

第3节　问的技巧

In negotiation, "asking" is often used as a means to analyze the needs of the other party, master the psychology of the other party and express your feelings. Paying attention to and flexibly using the skill of asking questions can not only cause the discussion of both sides, obtain information, but also control the direction of negotiation. "Asking" generally includes three important factors: content, time and method, that is, what to ask, when to ask and how to ask.

谈判中经常运用"问"作为探析对方需要、掌握对方心理、表达自己感情的手段。重视和灵活运用问的技巧，不仅可以引起双方的讨论，获取信息，还可以控制谈判的方向。"问"一般包含三个重要因素：内容、时间、方式，即，问什么、何时问、怎么问。

1. What to ask　问什么

According to the content of the questions, the "questioning" can be divided into the following types.

根据提问的内容可以将"问"划分为以下类型。

(1) Closed questioning　封闭式发问

A closed question refers to a question that can bring out a specific answer (such as "yes" or "no") in a specific field. For example, "Do you think there is no possibility of improvement of after-sales service?" "Do you think our product is good enough?" Closed questions can provide the questioner with specific information, and the person who answers such questions does not need too much thinking to give a reply. However, this kind of questions sometimes has a considerable degree of threat.

封闭式发问指在特定的领域中能带出特定的答复(如"是"或者"否")的问句。例如，

"您是否认为售后服务没有改进的可能？""您认为我们的商品是否足够好？"等。封闭式问句可令发问者获得特定的信息，而答复这种问句的人并不需要太多的思索即能给予答复。但是，这种问句有时具有相当程度的威胁性。

(2) Questioning for clarification 澄清式发问

A clarification question is a kind of questions put forward again in response to the other party's reply, so that the other party can further clarify or supplement its original reply. For example, "You just said that you can choose the current business, does that mean you have full power to negotiate with us?" The function of clarifying questions lies in that it can ensure that all parties in the negotiation can communicate on the basis of "the same language", and it is also an effective method of information feedback for the other's words, which is an ideal way for both parties to cooperate closely.

澄清式发问是针对对方的答复重新提出问题，以使对方进一步澄清或补充其原先答复的一种问句。例如，"您刚才说对目前进行的这笔买卖可以取舍，这是不是说您有全权跟我们谈判？"澄清式问句的作用在于它可以确保谈判各方能在叙述"同一语言"的基础上进行沟通，而且是针对对方的话语进行信息反馈的有效方法，是双方密切配合的理想方式。

(3) Questioning with emphasis 强调式发问

The purpose of the emphasis question is to emphasize one's own point of view and one's own stance. For example, "Isn't this agreement notarized before it takes effect?" "How can we forget that we enjoyed our last cooperation?" "In accordance with your request, isn't our view clear?"

强调式发问旨在强调自己的观点和立场。例如，"这个协议不是要经过公证之后才生效吗？""怎么能够忘记我们上次合作得十分愉快呢？""按照贵方要求，我们的观点不是已经阐述清楚了吗？"等。

(4) Exploratory questioning 探索式发问

Exploratory questioning is a kind of questioning methods which is extended or exemplified in response to the other party's reply to explore new questions and find new methods. For example, "Does this work?" "You said that the contract can be fulfilled as scheduled. Is there any fact to explain?" "What if we use this program?" Exploratory questioning can not only further explore more sufficient information, but also show that the questioner attaches great importance to the reply of the other party.

探索式发问是针对对方答复要求引申或举例说明，以便探索新问题、找出新方法的一种发问方式。例如，"这样行得通吗？""您说可以如期履约，有什么事实可以说明吗？"

"假设我们运用这种方案会怎样？"探索式发问不但可以进一步发掘较为充分的信息，还可以显示发问者对对方答复的重视。

(5) Questioning with help 借助式发问

Asking question with help is a way of asking with the help of the third party's opinions to influence or change the other party's opinions. For example, "Does Mr. XX pay attention to whether you can fulfill the contract as scheduled?" "What does Mr. XX think?" When taking this way of asking questions, it should be noted that the third party who puts forward his opinions must be familiar to the other party, and the other party is very respectful to the third party. This kind of questions will have a great impact on the other party, otherwise quoting a person who the other party does not know very well and is not respectful to as a third party, will probably cause the other party's antipathy. Therefore, this way of asking questions should be cautious.

借助式发问是一种借助第三者的意见来影响或改变对方意见的发问方式。例如，"某某先生对您方能否如期履约关注吗？""某某先生是怎么认为的呢？"采取这种提问方式时，应当注意提出意见的第三者必须是对方所熟悉的，而且是对方十分尊重的人，这种问句会对对方产生很大的影响，否则引用一个对方不很知晓且谈不上尊重的人作为第三者，很可能会引起对方的反感，因此这种提问方式应当慎重使用。

(6) Forced choice questioning 强迫选择式发问

The purpose of forced selective questioning is to give your own opinions to the other party and let the other party choose to answer within a specified range. For example, "It is in line with international practice to pay commission. We usually get 3%~5% commission from French suppliers. Please pay attention to it." It is reasonable to say that before raising this question. The questioner should at least obtain the promise that the other party will pay commission. However, this kind of question removes this premise and directly forces the opponent to make a choice within the given narrow range. It can be said that it is aggressive or even intolerant. This kind of question should be used with special caution. Generally, it should be used when you have full initiative, otherwise it is easy to deadlock or even break the negotiation. It should be noted that when using the forced choice style of asking questions, you should try to be soft in tone and appropriate in wording, so as not to leave the other party with the bad impression of being domineering and imposing on others.

强迫选择式发问旨在将己方的意见抛给对方，让对方在一个规定的范围内进行选择回答。例如，"付佣金是符合国际惯例的，我们从法国供应商那里一般可以得到3%~5%的佣金，请贵方予以注意。"按理说，在提出这一问题之前，发问者至少应该先取得对方将付佣金的承诺，但是，这种提问把这一前提去掉，直接强迫对手在给出的狭小范围内进行选择，可谓咄咄逼人。运用这种提问方式要特别慎重，一般应在己方掌握充分的主动权的情况下使用，否则很容易使谈判出现僵局甚至破裂。需要注意的是，在使用强迫选择式发问时，要尽量做到语调柔和、措辞达意得体，以免给对方留下专横跋扈、强加于人的不良印象。

(7) Demonstrative questioning 证明式发问

The purpose of demonstrative questioning is to make the other party prove or explain the question through your questioning. For example, "Why do you want to change the original plan? Please explain the reason, OK?"

证明式发问旨在通过己方的提问，使对方对问题作出证明或解释。例如，"为什么要更改原已定好的计划，请说明道理，好吗？"

(8) Multi-level questioning 多层次式发问

The multi-level question is a question with many subjects, that is, a question contains many contents. For example, "What about the local water quality, power resources, transportation and natural resources?" "Could you talk about the background of the agreement, the performance of the agreement, the liability for breach of contract and the views and attitudes of both parties?" This kind of questions contains too many themes, which makes it difficult for the other party to grasp it completely. It is better to include only one theme for a question, no more than three.

多层次式发问是含有多种主题的问句，即一个问句中包含有多种内容。例如，"当地的水质、电力资源、运输状况以及自然资源情况怎么样？""你是否就该协议产生的背景、履约情况、违约责任以及双方的看法和态度谈一谈？"这类问句因含有过多的主题，而使对方难以周全把握，一个问题最好只包括一个主题，最多不超过三个。

(9) Induced questioning 诱导式发问

The purpose of induced questioning is to open channels for water diversion, give strong hints to the other party's answers, and make the other party's answers meet the expected purpose of your side. For example, "The other party should be liable for breach of contract, right?" "When it comes to the present, I think the discount we have given you can be set at 4%. You will certainly agree, won't you?" This kind of questions almost makes the other party have no choice, but reply according to the answer designed by the questioner.

诱导式发问旨在开渠引水，对对方的答案给予强烈的暗示，使对方的回答符合己方预期的目的。例如，"对方如果违约是应该承担责任的，对不对？""谈到现在，我看我方给您方的折扣可以定为4%，您方一定会同意的，是吗？"这类提问几乎使对方毫无选择余地，而按发问者所设计好的答案回答。

(10) Consultative questioning 协商式发问

Consultative questioning refers to asking questions to the other party in a consultative tone in order to make the other party agree with your own views. For example, "Is it appropriate to set our discount at 3%?" The tone of this kind of questions is peaceful and the other side is easy to accept. Even if the other side does not accept the terms of your own side, the negotiation atmosphere can still be harmonious and the two sides still have the possibility of continuing cooperation.

协商式发问指为使对方同意自己的观点，采用商量的口吻向对方发问。例如，"给我方的折扣定为3%是否妥当？"这种提问，语气平和，对方容易接受，而且即使对方没有接受己方的条件，但谈判的气氛仍能保持融洽，双方仍有继续合作的可能。

2. When to ask　何时问

(1) Ask questions after the other party has finished speaking
在对方发言完毕之后提问

(2) Ask questions during pauses and breaks
在对方发言停顿和间歇时提问

(3) Ask questions at the debate time set on the agenda
在议程规定的辩论时间提问

(4) Ask questions before and after your speech
在己方发言前后提问

3. How to ask 怎么问

(1) Prepare questions in advance.
预先准备好问题。

(2) Avoid asking questions that may prevent the other party from making concessions.
避免提出可能会阻碍对方让步的问题。

(3) No forced questioning
不强行追问。

(4) Don't ask the other party questions in the judge's voice, and don't keep asking questions.
既不以法官的口吻问对方，也不接连不断地提问题。

(5) After asking questions, you should keep your mouth shut and concentrate on waiting for the other party to answer.

提问后应闭口不言，专心致志等待对方作答。

(6) Ask questions with sincerity.

以诚恳的态度提问。

(7) Questions should be as brief as possible.

问句应尽量简短。

(8) Don't ask hostile or personal questions about the other party.

不提带有敌意的或有关对方个人隐私的问题。

(9) Don't ask question directly blaming the other party on quality and reputation.

不提直接指责对方品质和信誉方面的问题。

(10) Don't ask questions on purpose to express yourself.

不为了表现自己而故意提问。

(11) Pay attention to speed when asking questions.

提问应注意语速。

(12) When asking questions, you should also pay attention to the mood of the other party.

提问还应注意对方的心情。

Section 4　Answering Skills

第4节　答的技巧

If you are asked a question, you will have to give an answer. Asking is an art and answering is skillful. If asking is improper, it will be bad for negotiation; if you don't answer well, you will also be passive. Negotiators are responsible for every word, and your words will be regarded as promises by the other party. Accordingly they will bring certain mental burden and pressure to the responders. Therefore, the level of a negotiator depends on his answers to questions to a great extent.

The answer in negotiation is a process of proving, explaining, refuting or promoting one's own point of view. Generally, you should answer the other's questions in a realistic and positive way. However, the questions are often variable, put forward after careful consideration and design by the other party, which may contain strategies or traps. If you answer all the questions in a positive way, Which is not always the best way to answer, so you must use certain skills to answer them.

有问必有答。问有艺术，答也有技巧。问得不当不利于谈判，答得不好同样也会使己方陷入被动。谈判者对每一句话都负有责任，都将被对方认为是承诺，因而会给答复的人带来一定的精神负担和压力。因此，一个谈判者水平的高低，在很大程度上取决于其答复问题的水平。

谈判中的回答，是一个证明、解释、反驳或推销己方观点的过程。通常，应当针对对方的问题实事求是地正面作答，但是，由于提问往往变数很多，是对方深思熟虑、精心设计之后才提出的，可能含有谋略或陷阱，如果对所有的问题都正面回答，并不一定是最好的答复的方法，所以答复也必须运用一定的技巧。

1. Give yourself time to think before you answer.

回答之前给自己留有思考时间。

2. Response to the questioner against his real psychology.

For example, for question "Put a 2.5kg chicken into a bottle that can only hold 0.5kg water. How can you take out the chicken?" answer "How you put it in, and how I will take it out."

针对提问者的真实心理答复。比如，针对"把一只2.5千克重的鸡装进一只只能装0.5千克水的瓶子里，用什么办法把它拿出来？"回答"您怎么放进去的，我就会怎么拿出来。"

In this question, the questioner's real psychology is purposely making difficulties for the answerer.

在这个问题中，提问者的真实心理是有意刁难回答的人。

3. Not all questions need to be answered. Some questions are not worth answering. Sometimes you can use the diplomatic language "no comment".

并非任何问题都要回答，有些问题并不值得回答，有时可以使用外交辞令"无可奉告"。

4. Avoid the front and move to the side, change the topic of conversation.

避正答偏，顾左右而言他。

5. Don't answer questions you don't know.

不知道的问题不回答。

6. Some questions can be solved by answering to other questions.

有的问题可通过答非所问来解决。

7. Use questions instead of answers to deal with questions that are difficult to answer or you don't want to answer, and leave the questions to the other party.

用以问代答来应付一时难以回答或不想回答的问题，将问题抛给对方。

8. For the questions that are unprepared or can be answered but you are unwilling to answer, the way of shirking responsibility is adopted. For example, "I have not investigated this question. I am not clear, but I have heard about it…"

对毫无准备或即使能回答但不愿回答的问题，采取推卸责任方式，比如，"对这个问题我没有调查过，不清楚，但曾经听说过……"

9. In order to delay thinking about the answers, ask the questioner to repeat the questions or leave by excuse.

为拖延时间思考答案，可要求提问者重复问题或借故离开。

Section 5　Watching Skills

第5节　看的技巧

Negotiation is not only the exchange of language, but also the exchange of behavior, which is called "listening to his words and observing his actions". The "action" here refers to the silent language such as posture, movement, facial expression, etc. The information transmitted by the silent language can sometimes replace or even exceed the role played by the voice language, because the information transmitted by them is authentic.

This section briefly introduces the information conveyed or the meanings represented by the negotiator's actions, postures, facial expressions, etc.

谈判不仅是语言的交流，也是行为的交流，就是所谓"听其言观其行"。这里的"行"，指姿势、动作、面部表情等无声语言，通过无声语言所传递的信息，有时可以代替甚至超过有声语言所起的作用，因为它们所传递的信息真实可信。

本节就谈判者的动作、姿势、面部表情等所传递的信息或所代表的意义做简单介绍。

1. Facial expressions 面部表情

(1) Message from eyes 眼睛传达的信息

The eye is called "the window of the soul", which has the function of reflecting people's deep psychology. The information conveyed by the eyes mainly includes the following aspects.

眼睛被称为"心灵的窗户"，具有反映人们深层心理的功能。眼睛所传达的信息主要有以下几方面。

① According to the length of staring at the speaker, you can judge the listener's psychological feeling. When talking with people, the time of eye contact with the other's face should account for 30%~60% of the total conversation time under normal circumstances. If it exceeds this average value, you can think that he is more interested in the speaker than the conversation content. If it is lower than this average value, he is not interested in both the speaker and the conversation content.

根据目光凝视讲话者时间的长短来判断听者的心理感受。跟人交谈时，视线接触对方脸部的时间，在正常情况下应占全部谈话时间的 30%～60%。超过这一平均值，可认为对谈话者本人比对谈话内容更感兴趣，低于这个平均值，则表示对谈话者和谈话内容都不感兴趣。

② Different blinking frequencies have different meanings. Ordinary people blink 5~8 times per minute. If the blink times per minute exceed this range, it means he is active and interested in something.

不同的眨眼频率有不同的含义。一般人每分钟眨眼 5～8 次，如果一个人每分钟眨眼次数超过这个范围，则表示他神情活跃，对某事物感兴趣。

③ When listening to the other, it's an attempt to cover up when he hardly looks at the other.

倾听对方谈话时，几乎不看对方是试图掩饰的表现。

④ The message conveyed by the pupils of the eye. If the pupil is enlarged and bright, it means that the person is in a state of joy and excitement, if the pupil is narrowed, his expression is dull, his eyes are dull and his face is sad, it means that the person is in a state of negativity, vigilance or anger. If someone wears colored glasses on the negotiation table, he should be on guard. He may be making a cover up so that the negotiation opponent can't notice his pupil changes.

眼睛瞳孔所传达的信息。瞳孔放大，炯炯有神，表示此人处于欢喜、兴奋状态，瞳孔缩小，神情呆滞，目光无神，愁眉苦脸，则表示此人处于消极、戒备或愤怒的状态。谈判桌上如果有人戴有色眼镜，应加以提防，他可能在做掩饰，让谈判对手察觉不到他的瞳孔变化。

⑤ Information conveyed by flickering eyes. Flickering in the eyes is an abnormal act, usually considered as a means of concealment, or an expression of dishonesty in personality.

眼神闪烁不定所传达的信息。眼神闪烁不定是一种反常的举动，通常被认为是一种掩饰的手段，或是人格上不诚实的表现。

⑥ Looking at the other person with wide eyes is a sign of great interest in the other person.

睁大眼睛看着对方是对对方有很大兴趣的表示。

(2) Message from eyebrows 眉毛传达的信息

When people are in a state of surprise or panic, their eyebrows rise, that is, the so-called eyebrows of happiness; when they are in a state of anger or annoyance, their eyebrows pull down or stand upside down, that is to say, sword eyebrows; when they move up and down quickly, they express kindness, agreement or pleasure; when they frown tightly, they show that people are in a state of embarrassment, unhappiness or disapproval; when the person raises his eyebrows ,it expresses inquiry or question.

人们处于惊喜或惊恐状态时，眉毛上耸，即所谓喜上眉梢；处于愤怒或气恼状态时，眉角下拉或倒竖，即常说的剑眉倒竖；眉毛迅速上下运动，表示亲切、同意或愉快；紧皱眉头，表示人们处于困窘、不愉快、不赞同的状态；眉毛向上挑起，表示询问或疑问。

(3) The message of the action of the mouth 嘴的动作所传达的信息

Closing his mouth tightly, often shows resolute will.

Pouting is the expression of dissatisfaction and readiness to attack.

When suffering failure, he often bites his lips, punishes himmself, and sometimes it is interpreted as guilt.

Pull up the corner of the mouth to show listening, and pull down the corner of the mouth to show dissatisfaction and stubbornness.

紧紧地抿住嘴，往往表现出意志坚决。

噘起嘴是不满意和准备攻击对方的表现。

遭受失败时，往往咬嘴唇，自我惩罚，有时也可解释为内疚的心情。

嘴角向上拉，表示在倾听，嘴角向下拉表示不满和固执。

Closely related to the movement of the mouth is the posture of smoking, and the message of smoking is as follows.

When smoking and spitting it up, it means positive self-confidence; when spitting it down, it means negative mood, depression and doubt.

Smoking slowly spitting out from the corner of the mouth, generally reflects the mood and thinking of the smokers at this time, who is trying to find an unexpected way out of the chaotic emotions.

A constant shaking of cigarette ash indicates conflict or uneasiness.

The ashes burning for a long time, but seldom being taken up to smoke, indicates that he is thinking nervously or waiting for the tension to subside.

Snuffing out the cigarette end before he takes a few puffs, indicates that the smoker wants to end the conversation as soon as possible or has made up his mind to do something.

Tilting head, smoke from nostrils, shows a sense of self-confidence and superiority, as well as a relaxed and self satisfied mood.

与嘴的动作紧密联系的是吸烟的姿势,吸烟所传达的信息如下。

吸一口烟并向上吐,表示积极自信;将烟朝下吐时,表示情绪消极、意志消沉、有疑虑。

烟从嘴角缓缓吐出,一般反映出吸烟者此时的心境和思维,力求找到一条走出纷乱情绪的意想不到的途径。

不停地磕烟灰,表明内心冲突或不安。

烟灰烧了很长,却很少拿起来抽,表明在紧张思考或等待紧张情绪的平息。

没抽几口就把烟头掐灭,表明吸烟者想尽快结束谈话,或已下决心要做一件事。

斜仰着头,烟从鼻孔吐出,表现出自信和优越感,以及一种悠闲自得的心情。

2. Movement language of upper limbs   上肢的动作语言

Clench his fist to show the feeling of challenge or self tension.

Hitting the desktop with his fingers or pen in his hand, or scribbling on the paper, often indicates that he is not interested in the topic of the other party, or disagrees or he is impatient.

The fingers of both hands closing together and setting on the front upper part of the chest, showing a spire shape, indicates full of confidence.

Connecting hands between chest and belly is a reflection of modesty, reserve or a little uneasiness.

Crossing his arms over his chest is a sign of conservatism or defense; crossing his arms over his chest and holding them tightly are often signs of hostility.

拳头紧握,表示向对方挑战或自我紧张的情绪。

用手指或手中的笔敲打桌面,或在纸上乱涂乱画,往往表示对对方的话题不感兴趣、不同意或不耐烦。

两手手指并拢并置于胸的前上方呈塔尖状,表示充满信心。

手与手连接放在胸腹部,是谦逊、矜持或略带不安的心情的反映。

双臂交叉于胸前表示保守或防卫;双臂交叉于胸前并握紧往往是怀有敌意的标志。

The standard handshake posture is to hold the other's palm slightly with fingers, and the other party also uses the same posture. The handshake time is no more than seconds. If the handshake of both parties is inconsistent with the standard posture, there are additional meanings besides greetings and politeness, mainly including the following situations.

First, if you feel sweaty hands and feet, it means that the other party is in a state of excitement, tension or emotional instability.

Second, if the other party shakes hands strongly, it indicates that the other party has a lively and enthusiastic character. If the handshake is not forceful, on one hand, it may be that the person is cowardly and lacks courage, on the other hand, it may be that the other party is arrogant and reserved and likes to put on airs.

Third, gazing at the other for a moment before shaking hands, and then reaching out to shake hands, to some extent, means this person wants to defeat the other psychologically and put the other at a psychological disadvantage.

Fourth, when he puts the palm upward to shake hands with the other party, it often shows that he is weak in character and in a passive, inferior or dominated state, and means to lean on the other party. Putting the palm downward to shake hands with the other party indicates that he wants to gain initiative, advantage or dominant position, and it has the meaning of being superior.

Fifth, holding the other's hand tightly with both hands and swing it up and down, often expresses a warm welcome, sincere thanks, or seeking help from others or affirming contractual relationship.

标准的握手姿势，是用手指稍稍用力握住对方的手掌，对方也用同样的姿势，用手指稍稍用力回握，用力握手的时间在1～3秒钟，如果双方握手与标准姿势不符，便有除了问候、礼貌以外的附加意义，主要包括以下几种情况。

第一，如果感觉对方手脚出汗，表示对方处于兴奋、紧张或情绪不稳定的心理状态。

第二，如果对方用力握手，则表明对方具有好动、热情的性格。如果对方握手不用力，一方面可能是此人个性懦弱，缺乏气魄，另一方面可能是对方傲慢矜持、爱摆架子的表现。

第三，握手前先凝视对方片刻，再伸手相握，某种程度上，这人是想在心理上先战胜对方，将对方置于心理上的劣势地位。

第四，掌心向上与对方握手，往往表现其性格软弱，处于被动、劣势或受人支配的状态，有一种向对方投靠的意思。掌心向下与对方握手，则表示想取得主动、优势或支配地位，有居高临下的意思。

第五，用双手紧握对方一只手并上下摆动，往往表示热烈欢迎，也表示真诚感谢，或有求于人或肯定契约关系等含义。

3. Movement language of lower limbs 下肢的动作语言

Shaking the foot and slapping the floor with the tip of the foot, shaking the legs, all indicate restlessness, helplessness, impatience or desire to get rid of some kind of tension.

Sitting with legs crossed, for men, often means to suppress their emotions from the psychological point of view, such as to reserve an attitude towards someone or something, to show vigilance, prevention, and try to suppress their own tension or fear, for women, if the two knees are close together, it means that they refuse the other or a defensive psychological state.

Sitting with your legs apart shows that he is confident and willing to take the challenge.

When one leg is put on the other leg, it usually means refusing the other and protecting its sphere of influence from others.

Frequent changes in leg position indicate emotional instability, restlessness or impatience.

摇动足部用足尖拍打地板，抖动腿部，都表示焦躁不安、无可奈何、不耐烦或欲摆脱某种紧张感的意思。

双腿交叉而坐，对男性而言，往往表示从心理上压制自己的情绪，如对某人或某事保留态度，表示警惕、防范，尽量压制自己的紧张或恐惧。对女性来讲，如果再将两膝盖并拢，则表示拒绝对方或一种防御的心理状态。

分腿而坐，表明很自信并愿意接受对方的挑战。

一条腿架到另一条腿上就座，一般表示拒绝对方并保护自己的势力范围，使之不受他人侵犯。

如果频繁变换架腿姿势，则表示情绪不稳定、焦躁不安或不耐烦。

Section 6 Debating Skills

第 6 节 辩的技巧

"Debate" can best reflect the distinguishing characteristic of negotiation, and the bargaining in negotiation is concentrated on "debate". The debate in the negotiation is different from listening, speaking, asking, answering and watching. It has the duality of mutual dependence and confrontation between the two sides of the negotiation. It is a comprehensive application of human language art and thinking art, with strong skills.

"辩"最能体现谈判的特征，谈判中的讨价还价就集中体现在"辩"上。谈判中的辩与听、叙、问、答、看等不同，它具有谈判双方相互依赖、相互对抗的二重性，是人类语言艺术和思维艺术的综合运用，具有较强的技巧性。

The basic debating skills are as follows.

辩的基本技巧如下。

1. Clear point of view and firm position.

观点明确，立场坚定。

2. Calm mind, quick thinking, strict argument and strong logic.

头脑冷静，思维敏捷，论辩严密，逻辑性强。

3. Master big direction, big premise and big principle, and do not entangle in details.

掌握大方向大前提大原则，不纠缠于细枝末节。

4. To grasp the scale of attack, you should stop at the right time.

把握进攻尺度，适可而止，不穷追不舍。

5. The attitude is objective and fair, the wording is accurate and strict, and personal attack with slander, insult and vitriol is forbidden.

态度客观公正，措辞准确严密，忌用诽谤、侮辱和尖酸刻薄的语言进行人身攻击。

6. Be not frivolous, indulgent or complacent when you are in an advantage; be calm, not angry or depressed when you are in a disadvantage.

处于优势时，不轻狂，不放纵，不得意忘形；处于劣势时，沉着冷静，从容不迫，不怄气，不沮丧。

Section 7　Persuasion Skills

第7节　说服的技巧

Persuasion is a very important work, often throughout the negotiation. Sometimes even if your motivation is good and your point of view is correct, you can't persuade the other party, or even you may be refuted by the other party. If you want to persuade others, you should not only uphold good motivation and master the correct point of view, but also master subtle communication skills and persuasion skills.

说服是一项很重要的工作，常常贯穿于谈判的始终。有时候即使己方动机良好、观点正确，却不能说服对方，甚至还可能被对方驳倒。要想说服他人，不仅要秉持良好的动机，掌握正确的观点，还要掌握微妙的沟通技术、说服技巧。

1. Establish a good interpersonal relationship and gain the trust of the other party.

建立良好的人际关系，取得对方的信任。

2. Use issues of common interest (including work, life, hobbies and the third party familiar to both parties) as a bridge to win the recognition of the other party.

用双方共同感兴趣的问题(包括双方工作、生活、兴趣爱好上的共同点以及双方共同熟悉的第三者)作为桥梁，争取对方的认同。

3. Explain to the other party the sufficient reasons for accepting the opinions, and analyze the possible impact on both parties caused by the opinions.

向对方说明接受所提意见的充分理由，分析所提意见可能导致的对双方的影响。

4. Simplify the process of persuasion.

For example, when a written agreement is needed, a draft of the principle agreement can be prepared in advance, telling the other party that it only needs to sign the draft of the principle agreement. The formal agreement will be ready within one week, and then sent to the other party for formal signing.

简化对方接受说服的程序。

例如，在需要书面协议的场合，可提前准备一份原则性的协议书草案，告知对方只需在这份原则性的协议书草案上签字即可，正式的协议书会在一周内备妥，到时再送给对方正式签署。

5. Consider the objective reasons for the existence of the other party's views or behaviors, think for the other party, and enhance the trust of the other party.

考虑对方观点或行为存在的客观理由，为对方着想，增强对方的信任感。

6. Create a harmonious and good atmosphere, and eliminate the other party's vigilance. Do not blindly imagine the opposition and non cooperation attitude of the other party, and then refute and persuade the other party.

创造和谐良好的氛围，消除对方的戒心。不盲目设想对方抱有反对和不合作的态度，然后批驳劝说对方。

7. The persuasion language should be considered, and the coercion or fraud should not be used for persuasion.

说服用语要推敲，忌用胁迫或欺诈的手法进行说服。

8. If the other party has strong self-esteem and is unwilling to admit mistakes, it is advisable to give the other party a step down first.

如果对方自尊心强，不愿承认错误，不妨先给对方一个台阶下。

9. It's hard for the other party to persuade for the time being, and he doesn't change his views face to face, you might leave the other party some time to think and choose.

对方一时难以说服，没有当面表示改变看法，不妨留给对方一定的思考和选择的时间。

10. When it is difficult for the other party to accept positive persuasion, instead of forcing the other party to debate, you may take a circuitous approach.

当对方很难接受正面说服时，不强迫对方进行辩论，而采取迂回的方法。

11. When the other party intentionally creates difficulties, you should not make too many explanations; you can be silent.

对方有意刁难，不宜做过多的解释，可以沉默。

Terminology 本章术语

1. listening 听
2. narration 叙
3. questioning 问
4. answering 答
5. watching 看
6. debating 辩
7. persuasion 说服
8. detour into question 迂回入题
9. closed questioning 封闭式发问
10. questioning for clarification 澄清式发问
11. questioning with emphasis 强调式发问
12. exploratory questioning 探索式发问
13. questioning with help 借助式发问
14. forced choice questioning 强迫选择式发问
15. demonstrative questioning 证明式发问
16. multi-level questioning 多层次式发问
17. induced questioning 诱导式发问
18. consultative questioning 协商式发问
19. actions/movements 动作
20. postures 姿势
21. facial expressions 面部表情
22. silent language 无声语言

23. voice language 有声语言
24. movement language 动作语言

Exercises　本章练习

1. What communication skills should negotiators command?
   谈判者应该掌握哪些沟通技巧？
2. What do you think of "listening is the premise and necessary guarantee of communication"?
   你如何看待"倾听是沟通的前提和必要保证"？
3. What are key points of your opening statement?
   己方开场阐述的要点有哪些？
4. What are the three important factors of "asking"?
   "问"的三个重要因素是什么？
5. How do you see "if you answer positively all the questions, it is not necessarily the best way"?
   你如何看待"如果您正面回答所有问题，这不一定是最好的方法"？
6. In negotiation we need to "listen to his words and observe his actions". What does "action" refer to?
   在谈判中，我们要"听其言，观其行"。"行"指的是什么？
7. Among various communication skills, which can best reflect the distinguishing characteristic of negotiation?
   在各种沟通技巧中，哪种最能体现谈判的显著特征？
8. What is the importance of "persuasion skills"?
   "说服技巧"的重要性何在？

Answers for Reference　参考答案

1. Negotiation is completed by means of information exchange between the two sides of the negotiation. In the negotiation, information transmission and reception need to be completed by means of listening, narration, questioning, answering, watching, debating and persuasion among the negotiators. The negotiators must pay attention to the use of negotiation skills at any

time on the negotiation table, so as to accurately grasp the behaviors and thoughts of the other side.

谈判是借助谈判双方的信息交流来完成的，谈判中信息传递与接收需要通过谈判者之间的听、叙、问、答、看、辩及说服等方法来完成，谈判者在谈判桌上必须随时注意谈判技巧的运用，以便准确地把握对方的行为与思想。

2. Language communication is the most basic way for human beings to exchange information with each other, and listening is the most basic and important way to obtain the other's information, so listening is the premise and necessary guarantee of communication. Carnegie said: "If you want to be a good conversationalist, be a dedicated listener first." Franklin said: "The key to a successful conversation is to listen more and never pretend to understand." Dorothy Dix said: "The shortcut to fame is to lend your ears, not your tongue to everyone."

语言交流是人类互相交换信息的最基本方式，倾听则是获取对方信息的最基础和最重要的方式，所以倾听是沟通的前提和必要的保障。卡耐基说："如果你希望成为一个善于谈话的人，那就先做一个致力于倾听的人。"富兰克林说："与人交谈取得成功的重要秘诀就是多听，永远不要不懂装懂。"多罗西娅·迪克斯也说："成名的捷径就是把你的耳朵而不是舌头借给所有人。"

3. Key points of your opening statement are as follows.
己方开场阐述的要点如下。

① Start with a clear idea and clarify the theme to be solved in this negotiation, so as to focus the attention of both sides and unify the understanding of both sides.

② Show the benefits that your side should get through negotiation, especially the vital benefits to your side.

③ Show your basic standpoint.

④ The introduction should be principled, not specific, and as concise as possible.

⑤ The opening presentation should be expressed in a sincere and relaxed way, so that the other party can understand your intention and create a harmonious atmosphere for negotiation.

① 开宗明义，明确本次谈判所要解决的主题，以集中双方的注意力、统一双方的认识。

② 表明己方通过谈判应得到的利益，尤其是对己方至关重要的利益。

③ 表明己方的基本立场。

④ 开场阐述应该是原则性的，而不是具体的，尽可能简明扼要。

⑤ 开场阐述应以诚挚和轻松的方式来表达，让对方明白己方的意图与创造和谐的谈判气氛。

4. "Asking" generally includes three important factors: content, time and method, that is, what to ask, when to ask and how to ask.

"问"一般包含三个重要因素：内容、时间、方式，即，问什么、何时问、怎么问。

5. The answer in negotiation is a process of proving, explaining, refuting or promoting one's own point of view. Generally, you should answer the other's questions in a realistic and positive way. However, the questions are often variable, put forward after careful consideration and design by the other party, which may contain strategies or traps. If you answer all the questions in a positive way, they are not necessarily the best way to answer, so you must use certain skills to answer them.

谈判中的回答，是一个证明、解释、反驳或推销己方观点的过程。通常，应当针对对方的问题实事求是地正面作答，但是，由于提问往往变数很多，是对方深思熟虑、精心设计之后才提出的，可能含有谋略或陷阱，如果对所有的问题都正面回答，并不一定是最好的答复，所以答复也必须运用一定的技巧。

6. Negotiation is not only the exchange of language, but also the exchange of behavior, which is called "listening to his words and observing his actions". The "action" here refers to the silent language such as posture, movement, facial expression, etc. The information transmitted by the silent language can sometimes replace or even exceed the role played by the voice language, because the information transmitted by them is authentic.

谈判不仅是语言的交流，也是行为的交流，就是所谓"听其言观其行"。这里的"行"，指姿势、动作、面部表情等无声语言，通过无声语言所传递的信息，有时可以代替甚至超过有声语言所起的作用，因为它们所传递的信息真实可信。

7. "Debate" can best reflect the distinguishing characteristic of negotiation, and the bargaining in negotiation is concentrated on "debate".

"辩"最能体现谈判的特征，谈判中的讨价还价就集中体现在"辩"上。

8. Persuasion is a very important work, often throughout the negotiation. Sometimes even if your motivation is good and your point of view is correct, you can't persuade the other party, or even you may be refuted by the other party. If you want to persuade others, you should not only uphold good motivation and master the correct point of view, but also master subtle communication skills and persuasion skills.

说服是一项很重要的工作，常常贯穿于谈判的始终。有时候即使己方动机良好、观点正确，却不能说服对方，甚至还可能被对方驳倒。要想说服他人，不仅要秉持良好的动机、掌握正确的观点，还要掌握微妙的沟通技术、说服技巧。

Chapter 8　Etiquette of International Business Negotiation

第 8 章　国际商务谈判礼仪

In international business communication, the success or failure of business transactions often depends not only on the trading conditions such as product quality and price level, but also on the attitude towards customers, the requirements for oneself, and the mastery and application of international business etiquette. If you know the cultural customs of the other party, know the international business etiquette practices, use certain etiquette to regulate your own behavior, show pretty good external image and internal cultivation, perform self-confidence and proper speech and behavior, express friendship and goodwill to customers, win respect and appreciation, and reflect the level of civilization and social fashion of his own country and nation, it will certainly enhance the trust and friendship of both sides and promote the transaction.

国际商务交往中，企业交易的成败往往不仅取决于产品质量、价格水平等交易条件，还取决于对客户的态度、对自己的要求，取决于对国际商务礼仪的掌握和运用。如果了解对方的文化习俗，熟悉国际商务礼仪惯例，用一定的礼仪来规范自身的行为，表现出良好的外在形象和内在修养，言谈举止自信得体，向客户表达友好和善意，赢得尊重和欣赏，同时又反映出自己国家、民族的文明程度和社会风尚，必将增进双方的信任和友谊，促进交易达成。

Section 1　Dress Etiquette

第 1 节　服饰礼仪

Dress etiquette is the most basic etiquette in international business negotiation.

服饰礼仪是国际商务谈判中最基本的礼仪。

1. Dressing　着装

Negotiators should choose suitable clothes according to their own temperament and body characteristics. In terms of the style of clothing, although there are many styles of clothing for all nationalities in the world, men's suits and women's suits have become the generally recognized dress on the negotiation table.

Dark color is suitable for international business negotiation occasion. The monochrome clothing of black, dark blue, gray and dark brown can be considered to give the impression of preciseness, steadiness and maturity to the negotiation opponents.

The jacket, trousers and vest (if any) of men's suit shall be made of the same materials. When wearing, it is not allowed to put on sweaters and expose underwear, to roll up sleeves and turn over sleeves. It is required to wear ties or bow ties. Meanwhile, it is also required to wear leather shoes with coordinated color and style. It is not allowed to wear tourist shoes and sports shoes.

Women usually wear suits and skirts. In summer, they can also wear dresses or long (short) sleeve blouses with skirts or trousers. In other seasons, they can also wear sweater suits with windcoats or coats. Women's clothing shall not be exposed, transparent, ultra short or too long. Suspenders shall not be worn. Underwear shall not be exposed. When wearing skirts, the opening of socks shall not be exposed. Long tube silk stockings shall be worn, but mesh style shall not be worn. The color shall be appropriate and intact. The color and style of shoes and hats are harmonious. It's better not to wear sandals, especially slipper sandals without back belt.

谈判者应根据自身的气质、体型特点，选择适宜的着装。从服装的样式来讲，尽管世界各国各民族的服装样式繁多，但男士西服正装和女士西服套裙已成为谈判桌上普遍认可的着装。

国际商务谈判场合的着装颜色以深色调为宜，可考虑选择黑色、深蓝色、灰色、深褐色的单色服装，给予谈判对手严谨、稳重、成熟的印象。

男士西装的上衣、长裤、西装背心(如有)需用同种材质的面料，穿着时不可内套毛衣和外现内衣，不可卷袖和翻袖，应佩戴领带或领结，同时配穿颜色款式协调的皮鞋，不可穿旅游鞋和运动鞋。

女士着装一般以西装套裙为佳，夏季也可着连衣裙或长(短)袖衬衫配裙子或西裤，其他季节也可着毛衣套装外配风衣或大衣。女装不可暴露，不可透明，不可超短也不宜过长。不可穿着吊带装，内衣更不可外现。穿裙装时袜口不能露在外，应穿长筒丝袜，但不可穿网眼款式，颜色得体，无残破。鞋帽色泽款式协调。最好不穿凉鞋，特别是无后带的拖鞋式凉鞋。

2. Jewelry 首饰

When wearing jewelry in international business negotiations, women should pay attention to the following.

The style of jewelry should not be exaggerated, with less as the best, worn on the "finishing point".

The color of jewelry should be coordinated with the dress.

The wearing of jewelry is in line with the convention. For example, a ring is usually only worn on the corresponding finger of the left hand, married on the ring finger and unmarried on the forefinger.

Don't wear a rough one.

女士在国际商务谈判中佩戴首饰应注意以下事项。

首饰的款式不应夸张，以少为佳，画龙点睛。

首饰的色泽应与着装协调。

首饰的佩戴符合惯例，比如，戒指一般只戴一枚，戴在左手对应的手指，已婚戴在无名指，未婚戴在食指。

不戴做工粗糙的首饰。

3. Makeup 化妆

Ladies can moderately make up, but make-up should not be too thick, especially not to use strong fragrance cosmetics. Never look in the mirror and make up in front of people.

女士可适度化妆，但妆不宜过浓，尤其不可使用浓香型化妆品。切忌在众人面前照镜子和补妆。

Section 2　Meeting Etiquette

第 2 节　会见礼仪

The etiquette of the basic meeting activities of international business negotiations, such as welcome and seeing off, meeting, and talking, are as follows.

迎送、见面、交谈等国际商务谈判的基本会见活动的礼仪惯例如下。

1. Welcome and seeing off 迎送

(1) Determination of welcome standards 确定迎送规格

For visiting guests, comprehensive consideration and arrangement shall be made according to their identity and status, as well as the nature of the negotiation and the relationship between the two parties. There should not be too many ushers and escorts. Generally, the identity and status of the main ushers and escorts should not be far from the other side. It is appropriate to be counterpart and equal. If the parties can not appear for some reason, they can be replaced by the persons with equivalent positions or deputy positions, but they must explain to the other side. Sometimes, they can arrange the ushers and escorts in an unusual way based on the development of the relationship between the two sides or other needs.

对来访客人，要视其身份和地位以及谈判的性质和双方的关系等综合考虑安排。迎送人员不宜过多，通常主要迎送人的身份和地位要与对方的差距不大，对口、对等为宜。当事人因故不能出面，可由职位相当人士或副职代替，但须向对方作出解释。有时从发展双方关系或其他需要出发，可破格安排迎送。

(2) Mastery of arrival and departure time 掌握抵离时间

When greeting, you should wait before the arrival of the guests, and when seeing off, you should arrive before boarding flight (train, ship).

迎接时应在来客抵达之前等候，送行时应在客人登机(车、船)之前到达。

(3) Other considerations 注意其他事项

Assign special personnel to assist the guests in handling the entry and exit procedures, ticket business, luggage check-in and other procedures.

During the reception, leave the airport (station, wharf), ask the guest to get on the right side of the reception vehicle and enter the back of the vehicle to take a seat. The host gets on the left side of the vehicle, the interpreter takes the seat on the right side of the driver in the front row, the same as when returning.

When guests arrive at the hotel, don't arrange activities immediately and give them time to rest, bathe and change clothes.

指派专人协助客人办理出入境手续及票务、行李托运等手续。

接访时，离开机场(车站、码头)，请客人从接待车辆的右侧车门上车并于后排就座，主人从左侧车门上车，翻译坐前排司机右边的座位，送归时亦如此。

来客抵达入住酒店，一般不马上安排活动，给予客人休息、沐浴、更衣的时间。

2. Meeting 见面

(1) Introducing 介绍

Usually, the host party with a higher status or the host negotiator introduces the welcome personnel and negotiation members to the visitors first, and then the other party does. The general order of presentation is women first and high status first.

When making a formal introduction to the other party, the honorific name of the other party and the surname or full name of the other party shall be used. For example, the other party is Dr. John Knox, a general manager of a company from London, UK. You can introduce Li Pei, deputy manager of your export department, as follows: "Doctor Knox, Mr. managing director, please allow me to introduce deputy manager of our export department Li Pei to you."

通常由东道主一方身份、职位较高者或主谈人先将本方欢迎人员、谈判成员介绍给来客，之后对方再介绍。介绍的一般顺序是女士优先，身份、职位高的优先。

在向对方做正式介绍时，应使用对方的尊称和对方的姓或完整姓名。比如，对方是来自英国伦敦某公司的总经理 John Knox 博士，可以这样向对方介绍本方的出口部副经理李沛："Knox 博士，总经理先生，请允许我向您介绍我方出口部副经理李沛。"

(2) Greeting 致意

Handshake is a common greeting etiquette in the world. In some countries, bowing, kissing, hugging, and combining hands are also used to greet. If the two sides are far away, raise your right hand, smile and nod.

握手是国际上通用的见面致意礼节，有些国家还采用鞠躬、亲吻、拥抱、双手合十等方式致意。如果双方相距远，可举右手、微笑、点头致意。

(3) Business cards exchange 名片交换

① Business cards are generally designed in two languages, one is the native language, the other is English, usually printed on two sides.

② The business card is usually placed in a special business card box, which is then placed in a briefcase or other suitable location for easy access at any time.

③ The exchange of business cards is generally carried out at the first meeting. After the guests are introduced, they first hand over the business card. When handing over the business card, it is usually advisable to hand out the business card by two hands with the English side facing up and the native language side facing down.

④ To accept a business card, you should express gratitude, nod and smile, read it carefully, and put it in your own business card box or clip it onto the document. If you receive more business cards when you attend the meeting, you can spread them out on the table and match them with people, and put them away at the end of the meeting.

① 名片设计一般采用两种语言，一种是本国语言，另一种是英语，通常正反两面印制。

② 名片一般放在专门的名片盒内，名片盒再放入公文包内或其他合适的位置，以便随时取用。

③ 名片交换一般在初次见面时进行，客人被介绍之后先递名片。递名片时通常把英文的那面朝上，本国文字的那面朝下，双手递出为宜。

④ 接受名片应表示感谢，点头微笑，认真阅读，郑重放入自己的名片盒内或夹到文件上。如果参加会谈时接到的名片较多，可将名片在桌上摊开并将名片与人对号，会谈结束时再将名片收起放好。

(4) Conversation and behavior 谈话与举止

① What to talk about. Generally speaking, we do not talk about irrelevant topics, and the content does not involve personal privacy, absurdity, and obscenity.

② Talk distance. In formal negotiation, two sides are generally separated by the negotiation table to talk to each other. In general conversation, there is no fixed distance between the two parties. It's better to feel natural, comfortable and clearly.

③ Gestures in conversation. The movement should not be too large, the gesture should be civilized, and the range should be appropriate. Don't slap or pull the other party casually. Don't point your fingers at the other or take a pen, ruler and other things to point at the other. When the other party speaks, he should not look left and right, be absent-minded, or do casual actions such as looking at your watch, stretching, or playing with things.

① 谈话内容。一般不谈无关话题，内容不涉及个人隐私、荒诞离奇、黄色淫秽。

② 谈话距离。正式谈判一般隔开谈判桌，两厢对坐商谈。交谈距离没有具体规定，以双方感觉自然、自在和听得清为宜。

③ 谈话时的动作手势。动作不宜过大，手势文明，幅度合适。不随便拍打、拉扯对方，不用手指指向对方或拿笔、尺子等物指向对方。对方发言时不能左顾右盼、心不在焉，不应做看手表、伸懒腰、玩东西等漫不经心的动作。

Section 3 Banquet Etiquette

第3节 宴会礼仪

Banquet and going to banquet are two aspects of banquet, and we should also learn to master relevant etiquette.

宴请与赴宴是宴会的两个方面，也应学习掌握相关礼仪。

1. Banquet 宴请

(1) Banquet method 宴请方式

According to the importance of the transaction, cost, time and other factors, choose formal banquet, informal banquet, family banquet, work meal and other forms.

根据交易的重要程度、费用、时间等因素，选择正式宴会、便宴、家宴、工作餐和其他形式等。

(2) Name of invitation and invitee 邀请名义和对象

The name of the invitation depends on the reason.

It is mainly based on the identity of the host and the guest to determine whom is invited, the identity of the host and the guest should be equal.

因事由而定邀请名义。

主要依据主、客双方的身份，确定邀请对象，主、客的身份应对等。

(3) Invitation scope 邀请范围

According to the nature of the banquet, the way the other party entertains us, international practice, etc. determine the guest of honor and accompanying personnel.

按照宴请的性质、对方招待我方的做法、国际惯例等，确定主宾和陪同人员。

(4) Time and place of banquet 宴请的时间和地点

The two sides negotiate with each other to determine time and place of banquet. Customers usually follow the master.

双方商议确定宴会时间和地点，通常客随主便。

(5) Table and seat 桌次和座次

For a single room and single table banquet, the host and the guest of honor sit close to the interior and face the door of the room. Generally, the guest of honor is arranged to sit on the right side of the host's seat. Other people on the host side and other guests sit next to each other. The position determines the distance from the host's seat.

In case of multiple tables, the table number is determined by the distance from the main table.

单间单桌的宴请，主人和主宾坐在靠里边朝向房门的位置，一般安排主宾坐在主人的右手边，东道主方面的其他人和其他客人两两相邻而坐，职位的高低决定离主人的座位的远近。

多桌的情况下，以离主桌位置远近决定桌次高低。

(6) Dish selection 选菜

The main consideration is the taboos and preferences of the guest of honor and other guests. It is better to open a menu in advance and ask for the consent of the other party. The banquet should not be too luxurious.

主要考虑主宾和其他客人的禁忌与喜好，最好事先开立菜单，征求对方同意。宴请不宜追求过分豪华气派。

2. Going to banquet 赴宴

(1) Invited 应邀

If you are invited to attend, you should reply as soon as possible. After accepting the invitation, it should not be changed at will.

接到邀请，能否出席，应尽早答复。接受邀请后不宜随意改动。

(2) Time of attendance 出席时间

Being late, leaving early and staying too short are all disrespectful behaviors.

迟到、早退、逗留时间过短，都是失礼行为。

(3) Seated 入座

Sit at the table and seat arranged by the host.

按东道主安排的桌次、座次就座。

(4) Eating 进餐

When the host announces the start of banquet, the meal will begin. When eating, keep a proper distance between the body and the table, so as to facilitate the food and not affect the adjacent seats. Try to avoid burping, sneezing, yawning and so on. If you can't control, cover your mouth and nose with napkin.

主人招呼即可开始进餐。用餐时，身体与餐桌之间保持适当的距离，以方便取食物和不影响邻座为宜。尽量避免打嗝、打喷嚏、打哈欠等。如无法忍住，应用餐巾纸遮住口鼻。

(5) Drinking 饮酒

When the host and the guest propose a toast and make a speech, you should stop eating, talking, listening and paying attention to the host or the guest. You should drink in moderation and not force others to drink.

在主人和主宾敬酒、致辞时，应暂停进餐，停止交谈，注意倾听，并向主人或主宾行注目礼。自己饮酒要适量，不能勉强他人饮酒。

(6) Tea or coffee 喝茶或咖啡

When drinking tea or coffee, you should use your left hand to pick up the saucer or coffee plate, and use your right hand to pick up the cup. Do not scoop up tea or coffee to drink with the teaspoon or coffee spoon.

喝茶或喝咖啡时，要用左手端起茶碟或咖啡碟，右手端杯喝。不要将搅拌用的茶匙或咖啡匙把茶或咖啡舀起来喝。

(7) Talk 交谈

Pay attention to the talk with people at the same table, especially the left and right neighbors. You should introduce each other and talk briefly.

注意与同桌的人交谈，特别是左右邻座。应相互介绍认识，并做简略交谈。

Terminology　本章术语

1. etiquette 礼仪
2. dressing 着装
3. jewelry 首饰
4. makeup 化妆
5. welcome and seeing off 迎送
6. meeting 见面
7. banquet 宴请
8. going to banquet 赴宴
9. introducing 介绍
10. greeting 致意
11. business cards exchange 名片交换
12. invitation 邀请
13. attendance 出席

Exercises 本章练习

What is the importance of mastery and application of international business etiquette?
掌握和运用国际商务礼仪的重要性何在?

Answers for Reference 参考答案

In international business communication, the success or failure of business transactions often depends not only on the trading conditions such as product quality and price level, but also on the attitude towards customers, the requirements for oneself, and the mastery and application of international business etiquette. If you know the cultural customs of the other party, know the international business etiquette practices, use certain etiquette to regulate your own behavior, show pretty good external image and internal cultivation, perform self-confidence and proper speech and behavior, express friendship and goodwill to customers, win respect and appreciation, and reflect the level of civilization and social fashion of his own country and nation,it will certainly enhance the trust and friendship of both sides and promote the transaction.

在国际商务交往中,企业交易的成败往往不仅取决于产品质量、价格水平等交易条件,还取决于对客户的态度、对自己的要求,取决于对国际商务礼仪的掌握和运用。如果了解对方的文化习俗,熟悉国际商务礼仪惯例,用一定的礼仪来规范自身的行为,表现出良好的外在形象和内在修养,言谈举止自信得体,向客户表达友好和善意,赢得尊重和欣赏,同时又反映出自己国家、民族的文明程度和社会风尚,必将增进双方的信任和友谊,促进交易达成。

Chapter 9 Practical Questions, Issues and Analyses on International Business Negotiation

第9章 国际商务谈判实战问题及解析

Question 1. "How much is it?" and its'answer.

问题1. "这个多少钱?"以及它的答案。

At trade fair, quite a few buyers would like to ask this question "How much is it?". Rookie sellers usually answer briefly a figure, for example "USD20.00", without taking influencing factors such as quantity, quality, destination, delivery term, seasonal demands, fluctuations in exchange, payment mode, commission and so on into consideration.

An appropriate answer to the question of "How much is it?" would probably be "Thank you for your quotation. You know, although this is a a simple question, the answer to it is not rather simple. I would like to make use of a few minutes to ask you a few questions, and then a definite answer would be followed."

After you are cooperated and have got answers to your questions, you are able to give a definite and accurate quotation.

在交易会上,不少买家会问"这个多少钱?",新手卖家通常会简单回答一个数字,例如"20.00美元",而不考虑数量、质量、目的地、交货期、季节性需求、汇率波动、支付方式、佣金等影响因素。

对"这个多少钱?"的恰当回答也许可以这样:"谢谢您的询价。您知道虽然这是个简单的问题,但答案不那么简单。我想用几分钟的时间来问您几个问题,然后就会有一个明确的答案了。"

在你得到对方的配合并得到你问题的答案后,你就可以给对方一个明确而准确的报价。

Question 2. What do you think of "Quote it deserves"?

问题 2. 如何看待"报它应报之价格"？

This is a question about pricing.

Many Chinese producers would like to use the way of cost plus pricing, which is one of cost oriented pricing. They focus on if they can cover their own production cost and earn a percentage of profit at the quoted price, and think less about market, competition and other things.

For a veteran, pricing is also rather difficult, which needs long term learning and experience accumulation to be proficient at composition of price(cost, fees, profit, tax and so on), different influencing factors(partially described in above question 1), various ways of pricing(cost oriented pricing, demands oriented pricing, competition oriented pricing), goals(maximize current profit, keepa good relationship with the business counterpart, expand and consolidate market share, cope with competitors) and strategies of pricing of the enterprise (for a new product, for a group of products, for different areas, for different grades etc.), and then it becomes possible to quote it deserves.

这是一个关于定价的问题。

很多中国生产商都希望采用成本加成的定价方式，这是一种成本导向的定价方式。他们关注的是自己的生产成本是否能够覆盖，是否能以报价赚取一定比例的利润，而较少考虑市场、竞争等问题。

对于一个老手来说，定价也是相当困难的，需要长时间的学习和经验积累才能精通价格的构成(成本、费用、利润、税收等)、不同的影响因素(在上述问题1中有部分描述)、各种定价方式(成本导向定价、需求导向定价、竞争导向的定价)、定价目标(最大化当前利润，保持与业务对手的良好关系，扩大和巩固市场份额，应对竞争对手)和定价策略(对一个新产品，对一组产品，对不同地区，对不同产品等级等)，然后才有可能报它应报的价格。

Question 3. Why would Chinese exporters like to quote on CIF basis? Why would Chinese importers like to have quotations on FOB basis?

问题 3. 为什么中国出口商想按 CIF 报价？为什么中国进口商希望按 FOB 报价？

Under CIF Chinese exporters effect insurance and delivery, under FOB Chinese importers effect insurance and delivery.

In the past time, China was lack of foreign exchange, so Chinese importers and Chinese exporters on relevant above mentioned basis could contact Chinese insurance company and

Chinese shipping company to effect insurance and delivery by paying in RMB.

With the increase of China's reserve of foreign exchange, the saving of foreign exchange becomes less important, Chinese importers and Chinese exporters on relevant above mentioned basis take more consideration about the smoothness of cooperation with the familiar insurance company and shipping company.

CIF条件下中国出口商办理保险和运输，FOB条件下中国进口商办理保险和运输。

过去，中国缺外汇，中国进出口商会在上述基础上联系中国保险公司和中国海运公司，以人民币支付保险费和运费。

随着我国外汇储备的增加，节约外汇的重要性逐渐降低，我国进出口企业更多考虑的是在基于上述交易条件与熟悉的保险公司和航运公司打交道，合作顺畅。

Question 4. Why is it better, if possible, to make a specific inquiry rather than a general inquiry?

问题4. 如果可能的话，为什么做具体询盘比一般询盘更好？

The reason is very simple. Inquiry is usually a request made by buyer for the information on the supply of certain goods, which is an invitation to make offer. If inquiry is not specific, accordingly offer won't be made to meet buy's real request. If buyer does not want waste time to make seller ask what on earth you want to buy and accordingly you give answers over and again, you would better make your inquiry specific.

For example, if buyer makes inquiry like this: "Please quote your lowest price for men's shirts and state the earliest delivery date". Let's analyze buyer's request for the price of men's shirts and leave alone delivery. If you do not make seller know what materials, style, size, color etc. you exactly want, seller is certainly going to have to ask you and make sure of them, which obviously wastes time. As you know, price of cotton shirts is usually different from that of polyester shirts, and there is also difference between long sleeve shirts and short sleeve shirts.

原因很简单，询盘通常是买方对某些货物的供货信息提出的要求，是一种发盘邀请。如果询盘不具体，相应的发盘也不会满足买方的实际要求。如果买家不想浪费时间让卖家问你到底想买什么，而你相应一遍又一遍地给出答案，你最好把你的询盘具体化。

例如，如果买方这样询盘："请报男式衬衫的最低价格，并说明最早交货日期"。让我们分析一下买方对男式衬衫价格的要求。如果你不让卖方知道你想要什么材料、款式、尺寸、颜色等，卖方肯定要问你并弄清楚，这肯定浪费时间，因为你知道，棉衬衫的价格通常不同于涤纶衬衫的价格，长袖衬衫和短袖衬衫也有区别。

Question 5. How do you see "Hope for the best. Prepare for the worst"?

问题 5. 如何看待"报最好的希望，做最坏的打算"？

In terms of negotiation idea, Chinese negotiators have long taken "Harmony is the most precious, peacefulness is to be cherished." as guiding ideology since ancient times. Modern western negotiators and scholars go in for "Win-Win", and "Win-Lose"concept is being abandoned gradually. They strongly think counterpart also need to exist and develop. To some extent, the best on one side means the worst on the other side. Chinese and the western people coincide with each other on this point, so they usually hope for the best, prepare for the worst, and try to strike a happy medium though negotiation.

From the angle of preparation for negotiation, at the phase of preparation, although negotiators work out top goal, desirous goal, acceptable goal and bottom goal for future use, top goal is usually rather difficult to be realized in negotiation. Both sides of the negotiators may probably meet each other halfway, and the possibility of realizing the second or the third goal is bigger.

就谈判理念而言，中国谈判人员自古以来长期把"和为贵"作为指导思想。现代西方谈判者和学者们追求"双赢"，"我赢你输"(或"我输你赢")的观念正逐渐被摒弃。他们强烈认为对方也需要生存和发展。在某种程度上，一方最好意味着另一方最坏，中国人和西方人在这一点上是一致的，所以他们通常抱最好的希望、做最坏的打算，并试图通过谈判找到一个愉快的中间地带。

从谈判准备的角度来看，在谈判准备阶段，虽然谈判者制定出了最高目标、实际需求目标、可接受目标和最低目标以备随后使用，但最高目标通常在谈判中很难实现，双方可能会在谈判中相互妥协，实现第二或第三目标的可能性更大。

Question 6. What is the importance of getting prepared top target, desirable target, acceptable target and bottom line for not only price but also other terms of the deal in advance?

问题 6. 不仅针对价格，而且对其他交易条款，谈判前制定最高目标、实际需求目标、可接受目标和目标底线的重要性何在？

Although price is the core of a business negotiation, and quite a few of other terms and conditions of the deal could be measured by price to some extent, getting prepared top target, desirable target, acceptable target and bottom line for not only price but also other terms of the deal in advance is meaningful, which is favorable to make thorough preparation for the negotiation in details, brings much more flexibility to negotiator, and increases possibility of a concluding the business.

虽然价格是商务谈判的核心，交易的许多其他条款和条件在一定程度上可以用价格来衡量，但是事先制定好交易的最高目标、实际需求目标、可接受目标和底线，不仅对价格而且对交易的其他条款都是有意义的，这有利于对谈判在细节上进行充分的准备，给谈判人员带来更大的灵活性，增加成交的可能性。

Question 7. Why is it proper for the seller working out a price list on FOB basis rather than on other trade terms before international trade fair?

问题 7. 为什么卖方在国际贸易展会之前适宜以 FOB 术语而不是以其他贸易术语制定价格表？

Buyers from various countries or areas attend international trade fair, and they have different requirements for delivery term. It is unnecessary and impossible for the seller to anticipate all of needs and prepare price list on all of trade terms. It would be better for the seller working out a price list on FOB basis rather than on all of trade terms and geting the rate of freight of major ports as well as the rate of insurance premium prepared before international trade fair, and calculating flexibly according to different requirements at fair.

来自不同国家或地区的买方参加国际贸易展会，他们对装运条款有不同的要求，卖方没有必要也不可能预见到所有要求，并就所有贸易术语准备价格表。在国际贸易展览会之前，卖方最好在 FOB 基础上制定一份价格清单，而不是就所有贸易术语操作，并备妥主要港口的运费率和保险费率，在展会上，根据不同要求灵活地计算。

Question 8. How do you persuade your foreign counterpart to accept L/C?

问题 8. 如何说服你的外国生意伙伴接受信用证？

Having no experience, some negotiators bargain with counterparts on payment mode just only by emphasizing that L/C is usual practice of his company. Actually, L/C is not versatile and all powerful, which unavoidably has advantages and disadvantages. They need to command firmly all of advantages and disadvantages of L/C for both parties of importer and exporter and apply to negotiation correctly. If you are exporters, you would better analyze the advantages of L/C for the importer. If you are importers, you would better explain the advantages of L/C for the exporter.

有些谈判者没有经验，只强调信用证是公司的惯例，就付款方式与对方讨价还价。实际上信用证并不是万能的，它难免有利有弊，需要牢固掌握信用证对进出口双方的所有利和弊，并运用到谈判中。如果你是出口商，你最好为进口商分析一下信用证对他的好处，如果你是进口商，你最好为出口商解释一下信用证对他的好处。

Question 9. When exporters offer importer a period of time of credit, could exporters ask for a certain amount of interests? How do exporters draw bill for exchange?

问题 9. 当出口商向进口商提供一定的信用期(付款账期)时，出口商可以要求一定的利息吗？出口商如何签发汇票？

Yes. When exporters offer importer a period of time of credit, exporters could of course consult with importers and ask for a certain amount of interests and make it reflect on the draft.

An example of draft with the interestsis as follows.

可以。出口商当然可以跟进口商协商要求有关利息，并将其反映在汇票上。带息汇票的样本如下。

凭
Drawn under
信用证或购买证第　　　号　　　　　　　日　期　　年　　月　　日
L/C or A/P No.　　　　　　　　　　　　　　dated
按　　　　　息　　　　　付　　款
Payable with interest @　　　　% Per annum
号码　　　　　　汇票金额　　　　　　　中国　盐城　　年　　月　　日
No.　　　　　Exchange for　　　　　　Yancheng China·
见　票　　　　　　　　　　　　　　日　后(本汇票之副本未付)付
At　　　　　　　　Sight of this FIRST of Exchange(Second of Exchange being unpaid)
Pay to the order of　　　　　　　　　　　　　　　　　或其指定人
金　额
the sum of

此　致
　To

Question 10. What's the best concession?

问题 10. 什么是最好的让步?

Negotiation is an art, and also an art of concession. Appropriate and effective concession is favorable for successful conclusion of negotiation and promotion for the deal as well as harmony of relationship between both parties.

The best concession is that you are most willing to make, and your counterpart could feel deeply and understand it's absolutely not easy to do it.

谈判是一门艺术,而且是一种让步的艺术,适当有效的让步有利于顺利结束谈判和促进交易,有利于双方关系的和谐。

最好的让步是你心甘情愿做出的,并且你的对手能深刻地感受和明白做这件事绝对不容易。

Question 11. Is it appropriate to ask back the excess of concession?

问题 11. 是否应该收回超额让步?

Now that making concession in the negotiation has been regarded and taken as an art, it needs careful study. Anyway, different people have different views on it. Some scholars propose it is appropriate to ask back the excess of concession, but we hold totally different view. We think concession should be made seriously. Once excess of concession has been made, it is improper to ask back because it is related to the credit of the negotiator.

既然谈判中的让步已经被视为一门艺术,它就需要被认真研究。当然,不同的人对让步有不同的看法。有学者提出,可要回超额让步部分,但我们持完全不同的观点。我们认为应该认真对待让步。超额让步一旦做出,就不宜再要回,因为这关系到谈判者的信誉。

Question 12. Different methods of commission calculating and their applications in negotiation.

问题 12. 佣金计算的不同方法及其在谈判中的应用

(1) Based on CIF price including commission, multiplied by commission rate, to calculate commission amount.

以包括佣金在内的 CIF 价(即 CIF 含佣价)乘以佣金率,计算佣金额。

① Multiply commission rate by the contract amount directly to get commission amount.

An example is as follows.

Contract amount CIFC3% USD1000 per metric ton.

Commission amount=Contract amount USD1000 × Commission rate 3%=USD30

Actual income of the seller=USD1000-30=USD970

将佣金率直接乘以合同金额得到佣金额。

下面是一个例子。

合同金额 CIFC3%每公吨 1000 美元。

佣金额=合同金额 1000 美元×佣金率 3%=30 美元

卖方实际收入=1000-30 美元=970 美元

② The price proposed by the seller is CIF USD1000 and the buyer requires 3% as commission during the negotiation, the seller can quote the price including commission as follows in order to guarantee the actual net income of USD1000.

Price including commission = CIF net price USD1000 ÷ (1 – Commission rate 3%) = USD1030.93

Commission amount = Price including commission USD1030.93 × Commission rate 3% = USD30.93

卖方提出的价格为 CIF 1000 美元，买方在谈判过程中要求 3%的佣金，卖方可以报出含佣价，以保证实际净收入 1000 美元。

含佣价=CIF 净价 1000 美元÷(1-佣金率 3%)=1030.93 美元

佣金额=含佣价 1030.93 美元×佣金率 3%=30.93 美元

(2) Based on CIF net price, multiplied by commission rate, to calculate commission amount.

以 CIF 净价乘以佣金率计算佣金额。

An example is as follows.

Both parties conclude the transaction on CIFC3% basis at a price USD1000 per metric ton, at the same time, it is agreed that the commission shall be calculated on the basis of CIF net price.

CIFC3%=USD1000=CIF net + CIF net × 3%

CIF net=USD970.87= Actual income of the seller

Commission amount=USD970.87×3%=USD29.13

下面是一个例子。

双方按 CIFC3%成交，每吨 1000 美元，同时约定佣金按 CIF 净价计算。

CIFC3%=1000 美元=CIF 净价+ CIF 净价×3%

CIF 净价=970.87 美元=卖方实际收入

佣金额=970.87 美元×3%=29.13 美元

Above methods are all based on CIF, commission amount is calculated.

以上方法均以 CIF 价计算佣金额。

(3) We can also use CIF price minus freight, and insurance premium to calculate FOB value,and then multiply the commission rate to get commission amount.

我们也可以用 CIF 价减去运费和保险费计算出 FOB 价，然后乘以佣金率得到佣金额。

Question 13. Different ways of reducing or even avoiding the loss caused from appreciation or depreciation of currency and their applications in negotiation.

问题 13. 减少甚至避免汇率变动所造成损失的不同方法及其在谈判中的应用

The simplest way is, if possible, to settle the deal with local currency, or hard currency for export settlement and soft currency for import settlement.

Both parties may also negotiate the business and conclude the contract with a value keeping clause, making the rate of foreign exchange fixed.

Spot payment methods are applicabale.

Methods of exchange transaction, credit, investment and so on could also be taken into consideration.

最简单的办法是，如果可能的话，用本币结算，或出口结算用硬币，进口结算用软币。

买卖双方还可以协商达成订有保值条款的合同，把汇率固定下来。

可采用即期付款方式。

也可考虑外汇交易、信贷、投资等方式。

Question 14. Could exporters ask for the arrival time of L/C and designate notifying bank of L/C?

问题 14. 出口商能否要求信用证的到达时间并指定信用证通知银行？

Comparing with time of establishment of L/C, time of arrival of L/C is more meaningful for the beneficiary(exporter), and beneficiary would better ask for the arrival time of L/C and designate notifying bank in the contract in order that he or she is able to acquire L/C as quick as possible.

与信用证开立时间相比，信用证到达时间对受益人(出口商)更有意义，受益人最好在合同中要求信用证到达时间并指定通知银行，以便尽快获得信用证。

Question 15. What "I" is included in "CIF"?

问题 15. "CIF"中包含什么"I"？

"I"stands for insurance, and "CIF"means cost,insurance and freight.

Quite a few exporters without rich experience of negotiation make quotation on CIF basis with just only a figure,eg.CIF Nagoya USD60.00/DOZ, and they neglect to attach an explanation for"I"in quoted "CIF". What exact insurance coverage is included in quoted CIF?Does "I" in this "CIF" stand for WPA or FPA or All Risk?Is there an additional risk accompanied? "I" should be definite and clear.

"I"代表保险，"CIF"是指成本、保险和运费。

不少没有丰富谈判经验的出口商只报 CIF 价，如 CIF 名古屋 60.00 美元/DOZ，忽略了在所报的 CIF 中附上对 I 的解释，所报 CIF 中具体包括哪些保险险别？这个 CIF 中包含水渍险、平安险还是一切险？是否伴随着附加险？I 应该是明确的。

Question 16. How to balance principle and flexibility?

问题 16. 如何平衡原则和体现灵活性？

Negotiators should insist on principles and execute company's policies and regular practice, and also show some flexibilities. Let's analyze a case, which is a letter in reply to customer's requirement for payment by D/P.

"Although we have confidence in your integrity, our usual terms of payment by sight L/C remain unchanged in all cases with new clients. So, for the time being, we regret our inability to accept your D/P terms. Maybe after several smooth and satisfactory transactions, we can consider other flexible ways."

In this case the use of L/C for all new customers as company's policy, principle and regular practice are elaborated. It is certain and unchanged,anyway,flexibility is also reflected in the possibility of change to other payment mode when both parties get acquainted. The customer is clearly told that. This is helpful for both parties' mutual understanding.

谈判者应该坚持原则，执行公司的政策和惯例，也应表现出一定的灵活性。让我们分析一个案例，它是一封回复客户对付款交单要求的信。

"虽然我们对你方的诚信有信心，但我们通常的即期信用证付款方式在任何情况下对所有新客户都保持不变。所以，目前我们很遗憾不能接受你方的付款交单条件。也许经过几次顺利而令人满意的交易后，我们可以考虑其他灵活的方式。"

在这个案例中，回信说明了公司对所有新客户使用即期信用证的政策、原则和惯例。它是确定的和不变的，然而，也体现了灵活性，客户被清楚地告知，在当双方熟知之时可能改用其他支付模式，这样做，有助于双方相互理解。

Question 17. Negotiation on C.T.D. / M.T.D.

问题17. 关于联合运输单证/多式联运单证的谈判

Combined Transport document (C.T.D.) or Multimodal Transport Document(M.T.D.) is a document, covering at least two different modes of transport, which evidences the combined transport contract and indicates that the multimodal transport operator shall take over the goods and shall be responsible for delivering according to the clauses in the contract.

Combined Transport B/L(C.T.B/L), which covers at least ocean marine transport (or inland waterway transport) and at least other one mode of other transport, is one kind of Combined Transport Documents.

According to Rule 3 and Rule 4 of "Uniform Rules For a Combined Transport Document (ICC Publication No.298 1975)" and Article 5 and Article 6 of "United Nations Convention on International Multimodal Transport of Goods 1980" C.T.D.(or M.T.D.) could be issued negotiable or non-negotiable, which means C.T.D.(or M.T.D.) could be a document of title. Of course, it also could be not a document of title.

In negotiation, if effectiveness and function of C.T.D./M.T.D. are involved, for example, "Could C.T.D. act as a document of title?" Relevant negotiators should inquire the multimodal transport operators to make sure,then negotiate with the other party.

联合运输单证(C.T.D.)或多式联运单证(M.T.D.)是一种单证，至少涵盖两种不同的运输方式，表明联合运输合同成立，并表明多式联运经营人应当按照合同的约定接管货物并负责交付。

联运提单(C.T.B/L)是一种联合运输单证，至少包括海洋运输(或内河运输)和另外一种运输方式。

根据《联合运输单证统一规则》(国际商会第298号出版物，1975年)第3条和第4条以及《1980年联合国国际货物多式联运公约》第5条和第6条，C.T.D.(或M.T.D.)可以签发为可转让或不可转让单证，这意味着C.T.D.(或M.T.D.)可以是物权凭证，当然，也可以不是物权凭证。

在谈判中，如果涉及 C.T.D./M.T.D.的效力和职能，例如，"C.T.D.可以作为所有权凭证吗？"有关谈判人员应询问多式联运经营人，确认无误后，再跟对方谈判。

Question 18. Negotiation on sample charges and samples keeping.

问题 18. 关于样品费用和样品保管的谈判

Both parties of negotiators could consult with each other about whether charge for samples and the amount of charges.

If sales are by samples, they could be either according to the seller's sample or the buyer's sample.

If sales are by the buyer's sample, the seller may duplicate it to send the duplicate sample to the buyer for confirmation. After confirmation it becomes sales by the seller's sample. In order to avoid future disputes about samples and bulk cargo, both sides would better seal and keep relevant samples.

谈判双方可以就样品是否收费和收费金额进行协商。

如果是按样品销售，可以按卖方样品或买方样品。

如按买方样品销售，卖方可复制样品送买方确认，确认后即为按卖方样品销售。为避免日后有关样品和大货的纠纷，双方最好密封保存相关样品。

Question 19. Negotiation on the application of law and jurisdiction of international business contract.

问题 19. 关于国际商务合同的法律适用和管辖权的谈判

A contract is an agreement between two or among more competent parties in which an offer is made and accepted, and each party benefits. It is an agreement which sets forth binding obligations of the relevant parties.

In the fulfillment of the contract, it is hard to avoid disputes. In order to solve disputes, litigation may be used. Negotiators would better consult with each other to stipulate a clause of the application of law and jurisdiction in the contract, and make their willingness about the application of law and jurisdiction in the contract, it is because although it has been reflected in the legal regulations and legal practice all over the world that the most closest connect doctrine provides the basic guide in the choice-of-law legislation in the field of foreign contract, quite a few law courts generally take the principle of autonomy as prime principle in the law application and jurisdiction of international busineee contract.

合同是指两个或两个以上有能力的当事方之间的协议，在该协议中，发盘被提出并被接受，每一方都从中受益。它是一种协议，规定了有关当事方具有约束力的义务。

在履行合同过程中，难免会发生纠纷，为了解决纠纷，可以采用诉讼的方式，谈判人员最好相互协商，在合同中规定一条法律适用和管辖权的条款，使他们关于法律适用和管辖权的意愿体现在合同中，这是因为，尽管在世界各国的法律法规和法律实践中都有所反映，最密切联系原则是涉外合同立法选择的基本指导原则，但在国际商事合同的法律适用和管辖中相当一部分法院普遍以意思自治原则为首要原则。

Question 20. Negotiation on force majeure

问题20. 关于不可抗力的谈判

Force majeure means the frustration of the contract by the party in question results from natural or social forces including flood, earthquake, typhoon, fire, war, government decrees of prohibition and so on beyond the control of man. The party shall be free from liability for performance or be given an option of prolonging the performance of the contract owing to the above mentioned event or series of events.

There are different interpretations to the terms among countries in the world. Negotiators should not regard force majeure as a common sense in the world, but discuss it in details and come to an agreement about it stipulated in the contract, i.e. force majeure clause. The way of colligation, clarifying what terms of force majeure covers, is the best way to stipulate the force majeure clause.

不可抗力是指当事人因自然或社会因素，包括洪水、地震、台风、火灾、战争、政府禁令等超出人的控制而使合同受阻。由于上述事件或一系列事件，该方不承担履行责任或有权延长合同的履行。

世界各国对不可抗力的解释各不相同，谈判人员不应将不可抗力视为世界范围的共识，而应详细讨论，并在合同中就不可抗力达成一致，即不可抗力条款。综合式方法制订不可抗力条款，阐明不可抗力条款涵盖哪些内容，是规定不可抗力条款的最佳方式。

Question 21. Negotiation on more or less clause

问题21. 关于溢短装条款的谈判

Inexperienced negotiators care much more about more or less in quantity, and care less about more or less in amount. When payment mode is agreed and stipulated as L/C, this question of more or less clause becomes extremely important.

According to UCP 600, documentary L/C means any arrangement, however named or described, that is irrevocable and thereby constitutes a definite undertaking of the opening bank to honor a complying presentation of documents, briefly, it is a conditional written promise of payment from opening bank for the beneficiary on the condition of presentation of required documents. We may take L/C as a kind of value paper, and amount of it is fixed. If more or less clause is stipulated in L/C as "X% more or less is allowed in quantity", the amount of shipped quantity excess will not be covered and paid by L/C, only if more or less clause is stipulated in L/C as "more or less X% is allowed in quantity and amount", the amount of shipped quantity excess will be covered and paid by L/C.

经验不足的谈判者更关心数量的增减，而较少关心金额的增减，当付款方式被约定为信用证时，溢短装条款问题就显得尤为重要。

根据 UCP 600，跟单信用证是指开证行的任何不可撤销的兑付安排，无论其名称或描述如何，均构成开证行兑现合格单据的明确承诺，简而言之，这是开证行对受益人的以提交符合要求单据为条件的书面付款承诺。我们可以将信用证当作一种有价证券，其金额是固定的，如果信用证中溢短装条款规定"允许数量增或减 X%"，则多装的数量对应的金额将不会涵盖在信用证内、不会被兑付，只有在信用证中溢短装条款规定"允许数量和金额增或减 X%"的情况下，信用证才会覆盖并支付多装数量对应的货款。

Question 22. Negotiation on commercial inspection and legal inspection

问题 22. 关于普通商业检验和法定检验的谈判

Commercial inspection is inspection agreed upon by both parties of the buyer and the seller. Standards, methods, time and place of inspection could be consulted and agreed by both parties.

Legal inspection is mandatory inspection executed according to relevant laws by relevant authorities. Standards, methods and so on of inspection are decided by relevant laws.

Both sides of a negotiation of the deal should consider if the inspection of this deal involves relevant laws and regulations, and cooperate with relevant authorities to complete legal inspection.

普通商业检验是买卖双方约定的检验。检验的标准、方法、时间和地点可由双方协商一致。

法定检验是有关部门依法实施的强制性检验，检验的标准、方法等由有关法律规定。

交易谈判双方应考虑本次交易的检验是否涉及相关法律法规，并配合相关部门完成法律检查。

Question 23. Negotiation on proper packing

问题 23. 关于适当包装的谈判

Let's analyze the following letter which is from your business counte part.

Letter：

Our Order for 1000 doz. Gent's Shirts

We dispatched to you this order as per yesterday's cable：

"1000DOZ MENSSHIRTS HAIDABRAND MAYSHIPMENT DIRECT STEAMER PLSCONFIRM"

Particular care should be taken about the quality and the packing of the goods to be delivered in this first order. It is the usual practice here that 10 shirts are packed to a carton and 10 cartons to a strong seaworthy wooden case. There will be a flow of orders if this initial order proves to be satisfactory.

We are enclosing our Confirmation of Purchase in duplicate. Please sign one copy and return it to us for our records. As soon as we receive your confirmation, a letter of credit will be opened through Barclay's Bank of London.

We trust this order will be the first of a series of deals between us.

It is likely ponderous overkill for shirts outer packing, actually cartons as outer packing lined with shockproof corrugated cardboard and wrapped up with damp proof polythene sheets are as seaworthy as wooden cases and can stand rough handling, besides, cartons are less expensive and lighter to carry. Anyway, in negotiation if your counterpart insists on using wooden cases, you may also meet his demand and ask him to pay extra charges.

让我们分析一下下面这封来自你的商业伙伴的信。

信函：

我方 1000 打男式衬衫的订单

我们昨天电报向你方发出了订单："1000 打海达牌男式衬衫 五月份装直航船 请确认"。

应特别注意第一批货物的质量和包装。我们这里的惯例是 10 件衬衫装在一个纸箱里，10 个纸箱装在一个结实的适于海运的木箱里。如果初次订货的这个订单被证明是令人满意的，就会有一系列的订单跟进。

随函附上我方购货确认书一式两份。请在其中一份上签字确认并交回我们存档。一旦我们收到您的确认,我们将通过伦敦巴克莱银行开立信用证。

我们相信这一订单将是我们之间一系列交易中的第一笔。

对于衬衫,木箱很可能是一种沉重过度的外包装,实际上纸箱作为外包装,内衬防震瓦楞纸板,用防潮聚乙烯包裹,与木箱一样适合海运,经得起野蛮装卸,此外,纸箱更便宜,更轻便。但话又说回来,在谈判中,如果对方坚持使用木箱,你也可以满足他的要求,并要求他支付额外费用。

Question 24.Negotiation on the deal of delivery at frontier

问题 24.关于边境交货的交易谈判

The use of delivery term DAF is appropriate for the deal of delivery at frontier.To choose a specific place in border area acceptable by both parties is important, and this place should be convenient for both parties to deliver the cargo,the factor of customers supervision should also be considered.

装运术语 DAF 适用于边境交货,在边境地区选择一个双方都能接受的特定地点是很重要的,该地点应便于双方交货,还应考虑海关监管因素。

Question 25. Negotiation on fire risk

问题 25. 关于火险的谈判

Speaking of cargo transport insurance in international business, risk loss and insurance coverage is a triangular relationship. Risk is the cause of loss,loss is the result of risk, coverage is introduced and used to cover possible loss from risk. During the transit from departure to destination, if the cargo suffers loss caused by fire, and it has been covered in insurance policy/certificate, the insured could file a claim to ask the insurer to compensate. However, the cause of fire is complex and various, fire may be caused by thunder and lightning stroke(natural calamities), sudden high temperature change(general extraneous risk), negligence and carelessness of cabin crew or other persons(general extraneous risk), striking rocks and collision with floating ice(fortuitous accidents of the carrying ship), artificial arson(special extraneous risks), spontaneously combustion.

(inner cause)… Negotiators would better give much attention to all potential causes of fire, and consult with business counterpart to cover the cargo against fire risk with appropriate insurance coverages to reduce or even avoid losses. In most textbook, writers just define fire risk as fortuitous accident of carrying ship, which is obviously insufficient.

就国际贸易中的货物运输保险而言，风险、损失与保险是一种三角关系。风险是损失的原因，损失是风险的结果，保险被引入并用于承保风险可能造成的损失。在货物从出发地到目的地的运输过程中，如果货物遭受火灾造成损失，并且保险单/保险凭证已经承保，被保险人可以提出索赔，要求保险人赔偿。但是火灾原因是复杂多样的，火灾可能因雷击(自然灾害)、突然的高温变化(一般外来风险)、船员或其他人员的疏忽大意(一般外来风险)、触礁和与浮冰碰撞(运载船舶意外事故)、人为纵火(特殊附加险)、自燃(内在原因)……谈判人员最好注意所有潜在的火灾原因，并与生意伙伴协商，以适当的保险险别承保货物的火灾风险，以减少甚至避免损失。在大多数教科书中，作者只是将火灾风险定义为运载船舶的意外事故，这显然是不够的。

Question 26. Negotiation on trade business with inland transport

问题 26. 关于含内陆运输的贸易业务的谈判

Take and analyze an example of the business with inland transport as follows.

A Chinese exporter of coffee negotiates with an Italian importer about a deal, delivery from Kunming via Guangzhou to Genoa by land-marine, which includes inland transport from Kunming to Guangzhou by truck and ocean marine transport from Guangzhou to Genoa by steamship. This is a typical export business of inland areas.

A Chinese exporter in this case would better quote on CIP basis rather than on CIF basis. The reason is as follows.

(1) In terms of transport mode, CIP is more flexible than CIF, more suitable for the export business of inland areas. CIF applies only to ocean marine transport or inland waterway transport, but CIP is suitable for any mode of transport.

(2) In terms of risk division, under CIF, if the exporter delivers the goods to the carrier in Kunming, in other words, when the carrier takes over the goods in Kunming, the risk of the loss of or damage to the goods will be transferred from the exporter to the importer. However, under CIF, when the exporter delivers the goods on board the ship at Guangzhou port, the risk of the loss of or damage to the goods will be transferred from the exporter to the importer. Obviously, comparing with CIP, under CIF the exporter has to take a bigger risk and bear much more responsibilities.

(3) In terms of convenience of negotiation for payment, under CIP, the exporter is able to

get relevant transport document like combined transport document or combined bill of lading from the carrier in Kunming when he delivers the goods to the carrier, accordingly, he is able to negotiate payment in Kunming immediately. It is favorable for him to rotate his capital. However, under CIF when the goods arrive at Guangzhou port and are loaded on board the ship, the exporter is able to acquire bill of lading from the carrier. Obviously, it takes much more time for him to negotiate payment.

Anyway, above mentioned proposal and analysis are on the condition that a multimodal transport operator is available, the importer is willing to accept combined transport and it's document, otherwise, the exporter would better cover the goods for inland transport carefully and sufficiently with insurance.

举例说明并分析一个含内陆运输的贸易业务。

一家中国咖啡出口商与一家意大利进口商谈一笔交易，从昆明经广州陆海联运到热那亚，包括从昆明到广州的汽车运输和从广州到热那亚的海运，这是典型的内陆地区出口业务。

在这种情况下，中国出口商最好按 CIP 报价，而不是 CIF 报价，理由如下。

(1) 就运输方式而言，CIP 比 CIF 更灵活，更适合内陆地区的出口业务，CIF 仅适用于远洋运输或内陆水运，CIP 适用于任何运输方式。

(2) 就风险划分来说，在 CIP 条件下，如果出口商在昆明将货物交给承运人，也就是说，当承运人在昆明接管货物时，货物的灭失或损坏的风险将从出口商转移到进口商，但是，在 CIF 条件下，当出口商在广州港装货上船，货物灭失或损坏的风险才由出口商转移到进口商身上，显然，与 CIP 相比，CIF 下出口商要承担更大的风险，承担更多的责任。

(3) 就议付货款的便利性而言，在 CIP 条件下，出口商在昆明向承运人交货时，可以从承运人处取得联合运输单证或联运提单等相关运输单证，因此，他可以立即在昆明议付，对他周转资金有利，但是，在 CIF 条件下，当货物到达广州港并装船，出口商方可从承运人那里获得提单，显然，他需要更多的时间来议付货款。

无论如何，上述建议和分析都是在有多式联运经营人、进口商愿意接受联合运输及其单证的条件下提出的，否则，出口商最好谨慎而充分地为内陆运输的货物投保。

Question 27. Negotiation on documents presentation time under L/C and relevant operation

问题 27. 关于信用证交单时间及相关操作的谈判

Generally 15 days after delivery date within expiry are stipulated as documents presentation date in L/C. Sometimes it is shortened, eg. 10 days stipulated in the following example.

A Japanese buyer wants to import tied cotton cloth from a Chinese seller in Yunnan province, payment is by L/C, delivery is made from Kunming to Shanghai by truck and from Shanghai to Kobe by sea. It takes 2 days to arrive at Kobe port after the cargo is loaded on board at Shanghai port. Japanese buyer would like time of documents presentation as short as possible, he wants 5 days, at most not more than 10 days, otherwise it's unfavorable for him to take delivery promptly at destination port, he also has to pay extra storage fee. Obviously, the seller is unwilling to do so because time is too tight for him to get prepared all of necessary documents for negotiation in Kunming, the time of forwarding original of B/L from Shanghai to Kunming needs at leas a few days by courier service. There is a contradiction between both parties. They have to negotiate and find an ideal solution to satisfy both sides. Perhaps cargo telex release and payment negotiated by copy of bill of lading are applicable.

在信用证中，通常规定在交货期后15天内提交单据，有时会缩短，如下面例子中规定的10天。

日本买家欲从云南省的中国卖家处进口扎染棉布，付款方式为即期信用证，从昆明到上海由卡车装运，从上海到神户海运，货物在上海港装船后2天到达神户港。日本买家希望交单时间尽可能短，他希望5天，最多不超过10天，否则不利于他在目的港及时提货，还需要支付额外的仓储费。显然，卖方不愿意这样做，因为他在昆明准备所有必要的议付文件时间太紧了，从上海到昆明快递提单正本就需要至少几天的时间。双方之间存在矛盾，他们得通过谈判，找到一个理想的解决方案来满足双方。也许货物电放和通过提单副本议付货款是适用的。

Question 28. Negotiation on exclusive sales and sole agent

问题28. 关于包销和独家代理的谈判

Exclusive sales, also known as sole distribution, refers to the way in which an exporter grants the right of operation of a certain or a certain kind of goods to a certain foreign customer in a certain region and within a certain period of time through an exclusive sales agreement.

Sole agent, also known as exclusive agent, is an agent who acts on behalf of the principal in a designated area. The principal may not entrust another second agent in the designated area. Therefore, the exclusive agent is used in the export business, and the principal gives the agent the franchise to sell the designated goods in a specific area and within a certain period of time.

There are of course differences between these 2 modes of trade. The distinguishing one is that exclusive sales belong to selling, sole agent is a kind of agency.

The key point related to negotiation on exclusive sales and sole agent that we discuss here, is their similarity, which is exclusiveness.

Once an exclusive distributor/a sole agent is determined, in the region and within the period of time, another distributor/agent is impossible to join in. The exporter/principal's sales have to be dependent on the exclusive distributor/sole agent, so the exporter/principal should be cautious. Comprehensive consideration is necessary. Decision should not be made in a hurry, especially for those new customers.

包销，又称独家经销，是指出口商通过独家销售协议，在一定的地区和一定的时间内，将一个或者一类商品的经营权授予某个外国客户的方式。

独家代理，又称排他性代理，是指在指定区域内代表委托人行事的代理。委托人不得在指定区域委托第二代理人。因此，在出口业务中使用独家代理，委托人给予代理人在特定地区和一定时期内销售指定货物的特许权。

这两种贸易方式当然有区别，区别之一是，包销，出口商和外国包销商之间是销售关系；独家代理，委托人和外国代理人之间是一种委托代理关系。

关于包销和独家代理的谈判，我们在这里讨论的关键点是它们的相似性，这就是排他性。

一旦确定一个包销商/独家代理人，在该地区和一段时间内，另一个经销商/代理人无法再加入，出口商/委托人的销售必须依赖于包销商/独家代理。因此出口商/委托人应谨慎，需要综合考虑，不应急着做决定，尤其是对那些新客户。

Question 29. Negotiation on soft clause of L/C

问题29. 关于信用证软条款的谈判

The beneficiary can not control or do it, but the seemingly reasonable L/C clause is "soft clause", the opening bank shall have the initiative to release the payment liability unilaterally at any time. With soft clause, irrevocable L/C is actually revocable.

For example, L/C stipulates "inspection certificate signed by the applicant must be submitted for negotiation payment", this is a soft clause.

The exporter should learn and accumulate experience to be good at indentifying soft clause in negotiation, but not accommodate the importer to accept soft clause easily.

受益人不能控制或做不到，开证行有权随时单方面解除支付责任，但看似合理的信用证条款就是"软条款"。带软条款的不可撤销信用证实际上是可撤销的。

例如，信用证规定"由开证申请人签署的检验证书必须提交议付"，就是软条款。

出口商应学习和积累经验，善于识别谈判中的软条款，不要轻易迁就进口商，接受软条款。

Question 30. Negotiation on application of different versions of Incoterms and UCP for documentary credits

问题30. 关于不同版本的国际贸易术语解释通则和跟单信用证统一惯例的谈判

Sometimes negotiators use some professional terms directly in negotiation and ignore what versions of Incoterms and UCP for documentary credits they belong to. It is easy to bring misunderstanding and disputes in this way, and it is necessary to attach some words about versions.

有时谈判者在谈判中直接使用一些专业术语，而忽略了这些术语属于哪个版本的国际贸易术语解释通则和跟单信用证统一惯例，这样容易引起误解和争议，所以有必要附上几个字说明术语所属版本。

参 考 文 献

[1]刘园. 国际商务谈判(第四版)[M]. 北京：首都经济贸易大学出版社，2014.
[2]白远. 国际商务谈判理论、案例分析与实践(英文版·第四版)[M]. 北京：中国人民大学出版社，2015.
[3]窦然. 国际商务谈判(英文·第二版)[M]. 上海：复旦大学出版社，2015.
[4]刘园. 国际商务谈判(英文版·第二版)[M]. 北京：对外经济贸易大学出版社，2017.
[5]刘婷. 国际商务谈判(英文版)[M]. 北京：对外经济贸易大学出版社，2012.
[6]黄伟，钱莉. 国际商务谈判(英文版)[M]. 北京：冶金工业出版社，2012.
[7]肖云南. 国际商务谈判(英文版)[M]. 北京：清华大学出版社，北方交通大学出版社，2005.
[8]罗杰·费希尔，威廉·尤里，布鲁斯·巴顿. 谈判力[M]. 北京：中信出版社，2012.
[9]杰弗里·埃德蒙·柯里. 国际谈判——国际商务谈判的策划与运作[M]. 北京：经济科学出版社，2002.
[10]杰勒德·尼伦伯格，亨利·卡莱罗. 谈判的艺术[M]. 北京：新世界出版社，2012.
[11]Roger Fisher, William Ury. Getting to yes—negotiating an agreement without giving in[M]. UK：Random House, 2012.